Criminal Justice and Moral Issues

Robert F. Meier
University of Nebraska, Omaha

Gilbert Geis
University of California, Irvine

Roxbury Publishing Company
Los Angeles, California

Library of Congress Cataloging-in-Publication Data

Meier, Robert F. (Robert Frank), 1944–
Criminal justice and moral issues / By Robert F. Meier and Gilbert Geis.
     p. cm.
Includes bibliographical references.
ISBN 1-931719-62-4
1. Criminal justice, Administration of—Moral and ethical aspects. 2. Crime—
    Moral and ethical aspects. 3. Social control. 4. Decriminalization. 5. Law
    and ethics. 6. United States—Moral conditions. I. Geis, Gilbert. II. Title.

HV7419M43 2006
172' .2—dc22   2005005486
                                                                          CIP

CRIMINAL JUSTICE AND MORAL ISSUES

Publisher: Claude Teweles
Managing Editor: Dawn VanDercreek
Production Editor: Nina M. Hickey
Copy Editor: Virginia Hoffman
Proofreader: Christy Graunke
Typography: Pegasus Type, Inc.
Cover Artist: Marnie Kenney

ISBN 1-931719-62-4

ROXBURY PUBLISHING COMPANY
P.O. Box 491044
Los Angeles, California 90049-9044
Voice: (310) 473-3312 • Fax: (310) 473-4490
Email: roxbury@roxbury.net
Website: www.roxbury.net

For Katherine. I admire very much her high standards for friendship and I am so grateful she relaxed them for me. Thank you.

And for Dolores and in memory of Robley Geis.

Contents

Acknowledgments

We are grateful to a number of people who have helped us with advice and technical assistance. At the University of Nebraska at Omaha, thanks are due to June Turner, Geri Murphy, and Steve Culver for their organizational skills, and to Angela Patton for her technical assistance. The influence of Herman Goldstein and Frank Remington is much evident in this volume. Special thanks are also due to Bella Bowman for her research assistance, and to Bella, Margaret Mainelli, Janice Rech, and Brenda Todd who all supplied much needed and appreciated personal support.

At the University of California at Irvine, the library's interlibrary loan and document delivery service was particularly helpful, adding a further career-long debt to the goodwill and dogged competence of librarians. Pamela S. La Zar, Linda Michelle Weinberger, and Gerry Lopez led the library search team. Judy Omiya, Dianne Christenson, and Patti Edwards in the Department of Criminology, Law, and Society offered valuable assistance, and Corina Shell Oliver salvaged my soul with some magical maneuvers when a computer glitch overwhelmed me. Thanks are also due to Steve Reynard, Fred Caron, and Donald and Michelle Paolill.

We would also like to thank Claude Teweles for his good cheer and continued wisdom and to Nina M. Hickey, who amiably and carefully shepherded the manuscript into production. And, we would be remiss if we didn't include the reviewers who had some very good ideas about the direction and substance of the book. They include Richard A. Ball, Penn State–Fayette; Robert Boyer,

Luzerne County Community College; David J. Hirschel, University of Massachusetts–Lowell; Melodye Lehnerer, Southwest Missouri State University; Ann Lucas, San Jose State University; Bob Walsh, University of Houston–Downtown; and Anthony W. Zumpetta, West Chester University. ✦

Chapter 1

Morality, Harm, and Criminal Justice

The chapters in this book are concerned with significant, controversial, and perplexing issues—issues that have forced citizens and the criminal justice system to seek to reconcile judgments of harm with state intervention into our private lives. Our interest centers on six specific forms of behavior—prostitution, drug use, homosexuality, abortion, pornography, and gambling—against which moral codes in the United States historically supported criminal penalties. Today, some remain illegal, others are tolerated, ignored, or overlooked, and at least one—gambling—is often endorsed and encouraged.

We have chosen to examine ingredients of these behaviors for several reasons. First, they traditionally have been regarded as core issues in debates regarding the proper role of morality in the framing of criminal justice guidelines, and they most readily come to citizens' minds when they consider the general topic of morality and law. Besides, each of us generally has an opinion on, and perhaps a personal stake in, how these behaviors are to be regarded and dealt with.

Second, there is a long course of scholarship and debate about the six behaviors that offers historical perspective and insight regarding how they have been viewed in different times and in different places. Homosexuality between men and young boys was commonplace in early Greek society; in other places, if discovered, it carried a penalty of death. In the United States gambling has experienced a see-saw trajectory. Lotteries abounded in early American history; later they were condemned as morally reprehensible and corrupt and made illegal. Today, lotteries and a wide variety of other games of chance (and fewer of skill) are prominent in most American jurisdictions. Gambling rarely is addressed in moral terms at present, but rather is seen as a political, social, and psychological issue.

Third, each behavior illustrates a different dimension of the relationship between law and morality in regard to questions of social control and social harm. Abortion is presently legal everywhere in the United States during the first trimester of pregnancy, but competing forces make it uncertain to what extent that principle will be eroded in days ahead and whether it will survive a well-organized campaign to return to earlier arrangements or, at least, to allow each state to decide for itself what abortion approach shall prevail. The legal status of a fetus continues to be a fiercely debated issue.

The use of some drugs is illegal, but questions continue apace about the justice of outlawing only certain pharmaceutic products, such as marijuana and heroin, while allowing others, such as alcohol and cigarettes. Skeptics sometimes wonder why the most massive killer of all, the consumption of too much food, is not a higher priority than the enforcement of laws against illegal drugs.

Prostitution remains against the law in all states except Nevada, with the moral justification that fornication and adultery deserve to be controlled. But it is clear that a considerable amount of both fornication and adultery goes on without the involvement of prostitutes. Feminists offer the argument that legal prostitution would devalue all women and further reduce them to the status of commodities, whose sexuality is purchasable rather than freely offered. Stipulated side effects of prostitution—theft, disease, public disturbances—also are advanced as reasons to try to control legally what is seen as an immoral behavior.

Homosexual behavior in private has now come under the protection of the law, though a considerable portion of the public regards it as an immoral activity. There is no definitive conclusion regarding whether the behavior is a choice or a biological imperative. Political pressure more than scientific evidence led the American Psychiatric Association to drop homosexuality from its roster of mental diseases and disorders, a pivotal move in the campaign to remove it from the concern of the criminal law (Bayer 1981). Some say that a sexual orientation that cannot produce offspring defies divine will; others believe that no harm is associated with homosexual activity and that its practice should be the concern only of those who prefer to engage in it.

Moral and legal considerations also surround pornography and gambling. The former activity was responsible for a deep divide in the feminist movement that has never been fully repaired, as one group deplored pornography as a despicable blot on social life, promulgated almost exclusively by men and often depicting women as subordinate sexual objects. It was argued (though there were two sides to the argument) that pornography was a precursor to crimes against women, such as rape and other forms of sexual assault. On the other side, some feminists maintained that the campaign of their sisters against pornography was an unwarranted rejection of first amendment principles that protected free expression. Few had a kind word for pornography but the moral issue came down to a question of which value deserved the most support (Brownmiller 1999).

Gambling, the last of the behaviors considered, has lost almost all of the moral disapproval that once surrounded it, in large part because of church ventures into bingo games to raise ever-needed funds for religious activities. Nonetheless, gambling continues to be in disfavor with many sacred and secular commentators, not to mention economists and psychologists. Compulsive gambling is related to criminal activity by bettors who steal to secure funds for further wagering, and the activity clearly places an uneven economic burden on the poor who disproportionately replenish state budgets by investing in lottery tickets. On the other side, there is a vocal group of writers who find gambling a stimulating experience in what otherwise is often a dull existence, as well as an opportunity to entertain glorious fantasies of untold wealth to be achieved through the selection of winning combinations.

There are, of course, other behaviors that might reasonably be viewed as more important or more illustrative, raising equally significant concerns. We have attempted in this introductory chapter to at least suggest useful lessons from some of these other behaviors, such as laws against usury and statutes that require motorcyclists to wear helmets.

Those who favor criminalizing the behaviors we discuss in this book often insist that, most fundamentally, all societies need to enforce a common morality and that such behaviors fall outside the limits of what should be permitted by the criminal justice system. They further maintain that some of the behaviors inflict harm on those who engage in them, and that a decent society has the obligation to protect its less careful members from their own self-destructive impulses. James Q. Wilson points to what he sees as a malaise permeating contemporary American society. "Many Americans worry that the moral order that once held the nation together has come unraveled," he writes. "Despite freedom and prosperity—or worse, perhaps because of freedom and prosperity—a crucial part of the moral order, a sense of personal responsibility, has withered under the attack of personal self-indulgence" (Wilson 1997, 11). In a forceful argument for this position, Patrick Devlin, then a British high court judge, maintained that social harm will result if we fail to secure adherence to a general standard of morality, and that such harm threatens a society's survival:

> Societies disintegrate from within more frequently than they are broken up by external pressure. There is disintegration when no common morality is observed and history shows that the loosening of social bonds is often the first stage of disintegration, so that society is justified in taking the same steps to preserve a moral code as it does to preserve its governmental and other institutions. (Devlin 1965, 13; for a summary of Devlin's position, see Feinberg 1988, 133–155; for a rebuttal, see Hart 1968)

Much better known, because it was the source for the title of a highly regarded novel by Ernest Hemingway, is the seventeenth-century dictum of John Donne:

> No man is an island of itself; every man is a piece of the continent . . . a part of the main. . . . Any man's death diminishes me, because I am involved in mankind, and therefore never send to know for whom the bell tolls: it tolls for thee. (Donne 1624, No. 7)

Donne's position argues that the injury or death of any of us—the prostitute, the drug addict, whomever—diminishes us all.

Those who oppose outlawing the behaviors we discuss say that they do not represent a threat to the integrity of the society and that they should not be the business of the law. They point out that there are less coercive and less punitive tactics that can be employed to convince persons to remedy what are deemed to be untoward and hurtful actions. The successful campaign to reduce cigarette smoking has involved a barrage of instructive propaganda as well as rules that prohibit smoking in public and private spaces. Tax policies incessantly force up the price of cigarettes and insurance companies adjust premium rates based on whether the customer is a smoker or nonsmoker. Could not similar policies be applied to other activities that now are addressed by the criminal law?

Opponents to recourse to the criminal law for some of the behaviors that we will examine often call attention to analogous kinds of acts that are regarded with legal indifference. The use of outlawed narcotics, for instance, they consider to be no different, and perhaps even less serious a personal and social problem, than drinking alcoholic beverages.

The trend has distinctly favored those who have campaigned for the removal of some of the behaviors discussed in the following chapters from the criminal justice roster, though the moral status of several of them, particularly abortion, remains highly controversial. Lotteries, once forbidden, are now part of everyday life, with tickets on sale at convenience stores and other neighborhood sites. Homosexuality has been moved to the criminal justice closet.

However, dispute over the proper moral and legal standing of these behaviors does not abruptly end with the removal of some of them from the statute book. There exists an intense and continuous battle to reverse the U.S. Supreme Court's ruling permitting abortions, and a contrary effort to reinforce the legitimacy of that court opinion. Homosexuality for some people remains a carnal sin that must not be tolerated just because it is no longer defined as criminal. Current debate centers on the question of whether same-sex partners ought to be allowed to marry and enjoy the benefits that accompany that status. Often mentioned, because it has emotional clout, is the fact that if one member of a gay couple that has cohabited for a quarter of a century is hospitalized, the other may not be allowed to visit because he or she is not a member of the patient's family. After the Walt Disney Corporation extended health benefits to same-sex partners of its employees, delegates to the Southern Baptist convention, representing a membership of 16 million people, voted to boycott Disney Company stores and theme parks if they continued what was labeled an anti-Christian and anti-family action.

Controversy also abounds regarding the manner in which law and morality ought to regard narcotic use. Those favoring approaches that do not rely on criminal justice point out that the longstanding law enforcement tactics have proven to be a dismal failure and only encourage the underground traffic in drugs by raising the risks and therefore the price and the profit of the trade. On the other side, those opposing decriminalization maintain that matters would be even worse if the law were no longer able to at least nibble away at the margins of narcotics use and narcotics trafficking.

Disagreements about the behaviors we will look at are acted out in political debates, arguments before courts and legislatures, and in conversations among neighbors. This book is about these disagreements. Consider two questions: What kinds of problems can the law solve? What kinds of problems can the law create? The questions suggest that the law can do both, although most conceptions of legal justice emphasize the first consideration and overlook the second. Our premise is that the law can create as well as resolve problems and that often other patterns of social control may be better able to deal with such problems. Most people do not commit atrocious and malevolent acts because they are afraid of legal consequences but rather because such things offend their own values and/or would invite criticism and disrepute among persons whose good opinion they see as important to their self-esteem.

Crimes Without Victims?

The behaviors that we will discuss have sometimes been grouped under the title "crimes without victims" or "victimless crimes." The term first gained widespread currency in social science circles when it was employed as the title of a monograph by Edwin Schur (1965). For Schur, crimes without victims involved illegal acts for which there were no complaining witnesses. The prostitute and the customer transact their business like any other merchant and patron; so do drug users and drug sellers. Homosexual couples mutually agree to do what they do, just as heterosexual couples do. When abortions were illegal, a woman sought out a service that would meet her need, and unless there were complications she would not complain to the authorities about the transaction. And nobody need look at pornography or gamble unless they choose to.

In time, the term "victimless crime" lost favor within the social sciences, primarily because it was apparent that for all the denominated acts there were actual victims, even if they were remote from the criminal transaction. Drug use and prostitution imposed costs on the community that were a consequence of the fallout from the behavior: prostitutes paid no taxes, drug users often committed property offenses to obtain money to feed their habits (Wright and Decker 1994, 1997). Some persons insisted that the practitioners themselves were the victims of what was seen as their immoral self-indulgence. In regard to pornography, as we have noted, it was claimed that it encouraged outrages against women, redefining them as sex objects rather than as human beings.

Legal historians had earlier discussed somewhat parallel concerns under the heading of "public welfare offenses" (Sayre 1933) which made criminal such activities as selling intoxicating beverages, even though the seller did not know or suppose the liquor sold by him to be intoxicating. "It could hardly be doubted," the judge in one such case observed, "that it would constitute no defense to an indictment for obstructing a highway if the defendant could show that he mistook the boundaries of the way, and honestly supposed that he was placing the obstruction on his own land" (*Commonwealth v. Boynton* 1861, 160). Similarly, Mehitabel Mash was convicted of bigamy on the basis of the following facts. Her husband, Peter Mash, to whom she had been married for almost four years, went out one morning, saying that he would return for breakfast shortly. When he did not come back for three and a half years, his wife then married William Barrett. When she learned a month later that Mash was still alive, she immediately left Barrett. She was said to be a woman of "good character and virtuous conduct" and to have made extensive efforts to learn Mash's whereabouts. But the law of the time required a seven-year wait before it could be presumed that a missing spouse was deceased. Mehitabel Mash was convicted because it was deemed "essential to preserve the family and the good order of society," though the Massachusetts governor pardoned her before a sentence could be imposed (*Commonwealth v. Mash* 1844).

Bigamy has always been a difficult crime to defend on philosophical grounds. If two or more women prefer to marry one man, why should it be illegal? Similarly, if two or more men choose to be wed to one woman? Before the Mormon Church withdrew its approval for polygamous marriage, some Latter-Day Saint women in such arrangements claimed that the companionship of other wives, the sharing of chores, and the higher standard of living than they otherwise were likely to achieve (for polygamous husbands tended to be wealthy) were fine advantages. Other Mormon women complained vehemently, particularly about jealousies and favoritism (Young 1954).

"Sumptuary laws," which forbade people of lesser social standing to wear elegant clothing, were another predecessor to "victimless crimes." The term comes from the Latin *sumptuarius*, which means "expensive." The laws sought to restrict extravagance and self-adornment which were believed to detract from more attentive religious observance (McManus 1993; Hunt 1996; Goodrich 1998).

There are also offenses called "inchoate crimes," which tend to be vague, catch-all statutes designed to give police the power to arrest persons they suspect of something untoward or whom they merely consider to be cluttering the landscape in an unappetizing way. Loitering has been the quintessential inchoate crime; it was so vaguely defined that the U.S. Supreme Court, ruling on a Jacksonville, Florida, ordinance, found it unconstitutional (*Papachristou v. City of Jacksonville* 1972). The case involved two black men driving in a car with two white women. All four had clean records but nonetheless were arrested for vagrancy. The charge was "prowling by auto," supported by the allegation that the vehicle had stopped near a used car lot that had recently been robbed.

More recently, along the same lines, the United States Supreme Court in 1999 declared unconstitutional a Chicago ordinance that decreed that if a policeman reasonably believed a person to be a gang member and that person was "loitering" (defined as "remaining in one place with no apparent purpose") and disobeyed a warning to move along, he or she could be arrested. In the three years it was operative, the ordinance resulted in

42,000 arrests. A Supreme Court justice asked how it could satisfactorily be established that a person had "no apparent purpose."
The justices declared that the right of individuals to remain in
public places of their choice is a fundamental part of their liberty.
In dissent, Justice Antonin Scalia offered a scathing critique of the
majority view. "No one in his right mind," Scalia wrote, would
read the phrase "with no apparent purpose" to mean anything
other than "without any apparent lawful purpose." Scalia cut to
the core of the moral issue that underlies much of what we consider in this book: He thought the decision favored "gang members and associated loiterers over the beleaguered law-abiding
citizens" and claimed that the ordinance was "a perfectly reasonable measure," that it was only "a minor limitation upon the free
state of nature" and "a small price to pay for liberation of the
streets" (*City of Chicago v. Morales* 1999, 74).

Generally put, an inchoate crime involves an innocent act
combined with some malicious intent. Often the judgment comes
down to an assessment of the alleged perpetrator. Consider the
case of a would-be assassin who puts sugar in his intended victim's beverage, believing the white substance to be arsenic. There
is no confession and no proof of the lethal intent, but a jury may
well convict on evidence of the infamous character of the defendant, on the principle that bad people are likely to have had bad
intentions (Yankah 2004).

The term "victimless crimes" took on a polemical as well as an
analytical marking. Most commonly it was invoked to persuade
people that such offenses should not be outlawed, even if they are
believed to be morally despicable. In an effort to keep the playing
field level, the following chapters will offer viewpoints that cut
both ways so that the reader is better able to reach and support a
personal conclusion. We will also refer briefly to what might be
tagged as victims without crimes—harmful acts that are not criminally sanctioned. The concept encompasses a broad range of behaviors that create victims, acts which, if they were illegal, often
would be regarded as white-collar crimes. The claim is made that
corporations and the industrialists who run them are so powerful
that by means of campaign contributions and other forms of lev-
erage they are able to keep legislators from enacting laws that
might control some of their harmful behaviors. A domestic corporation, for instance, is perfectly free to relocate a manufacturing

plant outside the country, throwing thousands of employees out of work, so that it can secure cheaper labor and make greater profits.

Obviously, neither the infliction of harm nor Judeo-Christian or other religions' precepts dictate totally what will or will not be attended to by the criminal justice system. We pay little or no formal attention to some biblical positions. Cursing one's parents, for example, is a death penalty offense in the Old Testament, as it was in colonial times, though the penalty was never exacted. Adultery and fornication, denounced in religious edicts, are discussed today with gregarious exuberance on television talk shows, and though they carry penalties in some states, the laws against them are enforced very rarely, if at all. In early America, however, adultery, though consensual, was another capital crime, but the letter of the law was almost invariably tempered with mercy. The only occasion on which the penalty was invoked in New England was in 1643 in Massachusetts, when James Britton and 18-year-old Mary Latham were sent to the gallows (Winthrop 1996; Banner 2002, 6). The Puritans adopted the Old Testament rule that adultery could be committed only with a married woman; the marital status of the male partner did not matter. The underlying rationale involved the use of the criminal law to protect the male's bloodline (McManus 1993).

That these almost moribund statutory injunctions can be dusted off and employed as the basis of a court proceeding was demonstrated recently by a wave of prosecutions in Idaho against young boys who had impregnated unmarried teenage females. They were charged with fornication, defined in the Idaho Code §18-6603 as involving "any unmarried person who shall have sexual intercourse with an unmarried person of the opposite sex." A prosecuting attorney justified what he was doing with the explanation, "It's a sad thing for a child to only know his or her natural father as someone who had a good time with the mother in the back seat of a car." Typically, a convicted couple would receive a three-year probation term and be required to attend parenting classes, to complete high school, and not to use drugs, alcohol, or cigarettes. Civil rights activists have objected that the Idaho law is enforced only against teenagers, which they insist is discriminatory (Brooks 1996).

The Notion of Harm

The idea of harm is one of the key elements involved in understanding why certain behaviors are forbidden by law and subject to punishment by the state. Forbidden harms typically involve physical injury, death, or the loss of property that the owner has a legal right to possess. There also are some offenses, most notably treason, where the damage is regarded as falling upon the state, which is said to represent the best interests of all, or at least most, of its citizens.

The criminal law, taken as a whole, can be regarded as protecting against harm and, more arguably, enforcing moral guidelines. The harm need not be inflicted; it need only be seen as reasonably related to the act that is outlawed. Attempted rape may be charged against an arrested person even though the overt act involved no more than light touching of a woman's shoulder or a lewd remark (Chappell et al. 1971). Criminal law usually does not attend to more subtle kinds of harm, most notably those that create psychological damage. Also, there may not be any harm at all created by some acts that are outlawed, only the statistical probability that some harm might result. Driving under the influence of alcohol or drugs is a serious offense, even though most drivers in such a condition navigate their way to their destination uneventfully. The behavior is proscribed because, compared to other motorists, a higher percentage of intoxicated or drug-high drivers will not be in adequate control of their vehicles and may injure or kill other people. Also, arresting such drivers can serve as a warning to others to avoid driving when not in full control of their faculties.

Joel Feinberg, in the first of his four magisterial volumes on the relationship of morality and criminal law, divides the rationales that are advanced to support one or another restriction on unfettered liberty into the following categories:

It has been held (but not always by the same person) that it is always a good and relevant reason in support of penal legislation that (1) it is reasonably necessary to prevent hurt or offense (as opposed to injury or harm) to others (the *offense* principle); (2) it is reasonably necessary to prevent harm to the very person it prohibits from acting, as opposed to "others" (*legal paternalism*); (3) it is reasonably necessary to prevent inherently immoral behavior whether or not such conduct is harmful or offensive to anyone (*legal moralism*). (Feinberg 1984, 13)

The fourth principle, Feinberg observes, is somewhat distinct from the first three. It holds that a satisfactory reason for restricting a person's liberty is that it is reasonably necessary to prevent moral (as opposed to physical or economic) harm to the person himself or herself. This is a common ground for opposing pornography and it is labeled *moralistic paternalism.*

Morality and Criminal Law

Criminal law draws its dictates from the preferences of those in a position to determine its content. Beliefs about morality interact with beliefs about harm to determine a jurisdiction's criminal code. Moral precepts that ruled American colonial life were derived from biblical roots. Virtually every criminal statute in the Massachusetts Bay Colony appended a biblical reference to indicate its authority (Elliott 1952, 22). If behavior was not covered in the *Laws and Liberties*, issued in 1648, the operating principle was that it should be dealt with according to biblical doctrine. Typical was the colony's law against blasphemy, carrying a death penalty (which was never inflicted), which was drawn from a biblical injunction in Leviticus. The law read:

> If any person within this jurisdiction whether Christian or pagan, shall wittingly and willingly presume to blaspheme the holy name of God, Father, Son, or Holy Ghost, with direct, express, presumptuous, or high-handed blasphemies, either by denying the true God, or his creation, or government of the world; or shall curse God in like manner, or reproach the holy religion of God as if it were a political device to keep ignorant men in awe . . . they shall be put to death. (Cushing [1648]1978, 5)

In early Maryland, the law that was adopted from the 1629 Parliamentary enactment in England called for penalties against a person who was "a common swearer, blasphemer, or curser." The original penalty involved burning a hole in the wrongdoer's mouth for a first offense, branding a "B" on his forehead for the second, and death for the third. In 1723, the penalties in Maryland were considerably lessened. Records show a number of prosecutions, including one against Captain Thomas Bradnox, who was charged with having uttered at least "100 oaths" (Semmes 1936, 162). The disagreement on the legitimacy of blasphemy laws can be found in two nineteenth-century court decisions. "Christianity is part of the common law of Pennsylvania; and maliciously to vilify the Christian religion is an indictable offense," one appellate court declared (*Updegraph v. Commonwealth* 1824, 394), while another flatly disagreed: "It is settled that Christianity is not part of the common law of this country," a New Hampshire court proclaimed (*Hale v. Everett* 1868, 206; see also Brenner 2003). It was only in 1970 in *State v. West* that the 341-year-old Maryland law was declared unconstitutional because it violated the first amendment guarantee of free speech. The case involved a man charged with swearing at a police officer following his arrest. Fear of blasphemy charges and ideas of propriety had underlain the taboo nature of such English expressions as "bloody" (a corruption of By Our Lady) and "zounds" (a corruption of God's wounds).

Suicide and Attempted Suicide

A particularly telling intermingling of moral dictates and criminal law involved the outlawing in earlier times of the act of suicide in both the United States and England. Attitudes in earlier civilizations toward suicide were contradictory. The Athenians prohibited it, showing their disapproval by cutting off the hand of the person who had committed suicide and refusing to bury it with the body. In ancient Rome, the philosopher Seneca summarized what appears to have been the prevalent Stoic view on suicide: "As I choose the ship in which I will sail and the house I will inhabit, so I will choose the death by which I will leave life" (Lecky 1904, 220). Seneca propounded a view of suicide that is at times echoed today:

> Just as in a ship that springs a leak, you can always stop the first or the second fissure, but when many holes begin to open and let in water, the gaping hull cannot be saved, similarly, in an old man's body, there is a certain limit to which you can sustain and prop its weakness. But when it comes to resemble a decrepit building—when every joint begins to spread and while one is

being repaired another falls apart—then it is time for a man to look about him and consider how he might get out. (Seneca 1961, 30.2)

Seneca himself committed suicide by slitting his veins and then taking hemlock, the poison that had been used to kill Socrates. His wife, Paulina, chose to kill herself at the same time by the same method (Tacitus 1996).

Those who committed suicide in medieval times could not be buried in hallowed ground but instead were interred at a crossroads with a stake driven through their body, a tactic designed to prevent the tainted soul from escaping (Radzinowicz 1948–1953, I, 196–197). Obviously, the suicide could not be punished personally, but the state confiscated the offender's property, which gave the authorities considerable incentive to keep the criminal prohibition in place.

The Bible contains no clear injunction against suicide. During the Council of Arles in 452, the Catholic church adopted such a position, supporting it with the thesis that "whoever kills himself, thereby killing an innocent person, commits homicide." Suicide is seen in Catholic doctrine as thwarting God's will, given that it is a divine prerogative to determine when life shall end. Later, when the law against suicide was removed from the English and American statute books, there remained a prohibition against "attempted suicide." This law is employed to provide the state with the authority to take into custody persons believed to constitute a danger to themselves.

Physician-Assisted Suicide

Debates surrounding the morality of suicide focus at the present time on the question of doctor-assisted suicide. If sane people formally declare a desire to die, and if it can be demonstrated that they are in pain—perhaps terminally ill—and there seems to be no likelihood that their condition will improve, should they be allowed to enlist a doctor to allow them to leave this life? If so, how far should such a "right" extend? If a physician is given the right to assist in suicide, why should that right be withheld from those close to the person, such as a husband or wife, if they receive written permission which is witnessed by a notary or court official? But is it not possible that a person, forced to live and given succor, might change his or her mind about suicide? (For the opposing viewpoints of two doctors, see Angell 1997 and Foley 1997.)

Each year about 15 percent of American doctors receive one or more requests for help in suicide and they grant about one-quarter of such requests. In the past, most requests were from people with intractable pain from cancer and other diseases. Today, such pain can largely be controlled. What patients most fear now is the loss of control and dignity and the dependence and financial burden typically associated with the final stages of a fatal illness (Back et al. 1996). It is notable that 50 percent of the outlay of money for Medicare, the medical program for the elderly, goes to take care of persons in the last six months of their life (Hillyard and Dombrink 2001).

Persons opposed to physician-assisted suicide, a group that includes most American medical societies, say that it can be a "slippery slope" (Wright 2000), an entry point that will expand to allow physicians to kill persons suffering from transient bouts of depression and children who have disabilities (Lode 1999). It also might encourage some people to give up rather than to fight to construct what could be a happy and fulfilling continued existence. Besides, to save money, pressure might be exerted to eliminate some who are on a downward spiral but would prefer to remain alive as long as possible.

Today, only Oregon permits physician-assisted suicide; some 171 people used the program to leave life from 1997, when it began, until the beginning of 2005. The Oregon law came under attack by the federal government when former Attorney General John Ashcroft threatened, under the terms of the Controlled Substance Act, to revoke the license of any doctor who participated in physician-assisted suicide and any pharmacist who sold a doctor a drug used in bringing about the death. But the Oregon Supreme Court in a 2–1 decision ruled that Ashcroft's position was an unwarranted intrusion into the affairs of the state of Oregon. Judge Richard A. Tallman wrote: "To be perfectly clear, we take no position on the merits or the morality of physician assisted suicide. We express no opinion on whether the practice is inconsistent with the public interest or constitutes illegitimate medical care. The question is simply who gets to decide" (*Oregon v. Ashcroft* 2004, 1123). Under existing law, the judge declared, it was not the Attorney General's call but the will of the Oregon legislature that should prevail. There was irony in Ashcroft's position. When he was governor of Missouri he had successfully petitioned the U.S. Supreme Court to endorse a law that mandated that judges in the state must retire when they reach the age of 70. He had based his argument on the fact that a state can pass legislation that trumps the federal requirement that no mandatory retirement age can be established (*Gregory v. Ashcroft* 1991).

In a particularly interesting analysis of physician-assisted suicide, Tania Salem points out that the law has medicalized suicide and maintains that what almost always has been a private act has been turned into a medical event. Under the Oregon approach, persons contemplating suicide must "request public endorsement and legitimization" of their desire, Salem points out (1999, 33).

Usury

The practice of usury provides an example of the manner in which ancient morality was initially embedded in criminal law, but subsequently was removed from the statute books in the face of what proved to be the more compelling demands of industrialism. Usury refers to the lending of money at very high rates of interest. John Noonan Jr. has described the evolution of social and legal concern with usury from medieval to current times:

> How can we appreciate the intensity of intellectual interest in usury in the sixteenth and seventeenth centuries, when its nature and extent were as lively an issue, and as voluminously discussed by reflective observers of commerce, as the nature and cure of business cycles are today? How much less can we grasp the spirit of a yet earlier age whose most perspicacious moralists described usury as a great vice which corrupted cities and church alike and held all men of property in bondage? Usury today is a dead issue, and except by plainly equivocal use of the term, or save in the mouths of a few inveterate haters of the present order, it is not likely to stir to life. (Noonan 1957, 1)

The ideas of Aristotle were particularly significant in determining early policies regarding usury. "The term usury," he wrote, "which means the birth of money from money, is applied to the breeding of money because the offspring resembles the parent." Continuing, Aristotle wrote in *Politics* (Book I, chapter 10), "Wherefore of all modes of making money this is the most unnatural."

Sanctions against usury first were levied by church authorities against the clergy, based on the biblical text of Psalms 15:5, which declares that a person who, among other things, "takes no interest on a loan" may dwell on God's sacred hill. There also were the words of Christ: "Lend freely, hoping to gain nothing thereby" (Luke 6:35). The ban was extended to laypersons around 450 A.D. by Pope Leo the Great, who inveighed against the *turpe lucum*, or the shameful gain, of usury. The theological principle was translated into secular law when the capitularies of Charlemagne outlawed usury in the Holy Roman Empire in the ninth century, defining it as a financial act in which "more is asked than given."

Between 1050 and 1175, the crime of usury was extended to embrace credit sales, which today would include the interest charged on credit card debts. Dante, the renowned poet of the medieval period, in his *Divine Comedy* (canto VIII) relegated usurers to the outer edge of the seventh circle of Hell.

The Protestant leader John Calvin was the first major theologian to insist that money lending would be sinful only if it injured one's neighbor; otherwise, it was acceptable. Each person's conscience was to be the guide. Loans to poor people would clearly be wicked, whereas loans to the rich or to a business were no different than profits from a sale. "Biting usury," or usury that sucks the substance of another while the usurer runs no risk and charges above a certain limit were condemned by Calvin, whose ideas gradually found their way into criminal law (Jones 2004).

It is striking to note how the legal designation of what was to be considered usurious varied with economic conditions. In the Middle Ages, the average annual interest rate was about 47 percent a year, a figure not much higher than that prevalent for small commercial enterprises in the United States during the 1930s (Robinson and Nugent 1935).

Today in the United States, there is neither a total ban on usury nor unrestricted freedom. Most states impose some ceiling on interest rates. But on the theory that usury laws are designed to protect only individual borrowers, loans to corporations are usually excluded from interest limits. Earlier conceptions of the immorality and illegality of usury obviously have given way in our time to a very different point of view. On rare occasions an out-of-the-ordinary case of usury may surface. An example is *First Bank v. Tony's Tortilla Factory* (1994). The bank had covered 2,165 checks written by Tony's despite insufficient funds in their account. They charged a fee of $20 for each check, a total of almost $50,000. Tony's Tortilla Factory lawyers argued that the percentage exceeded what was allowed under Texas' usury law. An appellate court agreed with them, but the state Supreme Court declared that the amount levied was a fee, a service charge, to cover the bank's alleged expenses in the matter and therefore was not the excessive interest outlawed by statute.

Bad Samaritans

Suicide and usury laws indicate that the tie between biblical dictates and criminal law can be severed if secular concerns come to prevail. The "Bad Samaritan" condition illustrates that criminal law may pay no heed to matters of morality that most of us regard as vital elements of a decent society. "Bad Samaritanism" denotes the fact that American law in virtually every jurisdiction does not require a person to aid another human being, even when this can be accomplished with no risk to the rescuer. A bystander, for instance, has no legal obligation to intervene if a blind man walking without a cane is going to step off the edge of a cliff to his death.

American law traditionally takes the position that one should not be burdened with the responsibility of aiding others. The reigning legal principle was cold-bloodedly set forth by the chief justice of New Hampshire more than a century ago.

> Suppose A, standing by a railroad, sees a two-year-old baby on the track and a car approaching. He can easily rescue the child with entire safety to himself. And the instincts of humanity require him to do so. If he does not, he may perhaps justly be styled a ruthless savage and a moral monster, but he is not liable in damage for the child's injury or indictable under the statutes for its death. (*Buch v. Amory Manufacturing Co.* 1898, 809)

The legal doctrine goes a step further and indicates that a person compassionate or foolhardy enough to intervene becomes liable thereafter for the consequences; in the absence of such intervention, the person remains juridically unassailable. A few exceptions to this rule exist. If the bystander has made an initial effort to assist, then that effort must be carried through. The bystander must also help those with whom there is a preexisting relationship, such as a spouse or kin, as well as those with whom there is a contractual duty to provide help.

The laissez-faire approach to offering aid is based on the idea that a free citizen should have no obligation to keep the public order and uphold public well-being. Four states—Minnesota, Rhode Island, Vermont, and Wisconsin—have rejected this position and enacted statutes that demand intervention when reasonably feasible. A few others specify such an obligation in regard to physical or sexual abuse of children (Hayden 2000).

The absence of a legal requirement to aid was glaring in a Nevada case in which a 7-year-old girl was lured into a restroom by an 18-year-old and then raped and killed. The murderer received a sentence of life in prison, but his friend, who had watched the entire episode by peering over the top of the wall in an adjacent toilet stall, walked away free, since he had no legal duty to stop the behavior or to report it. Commenting on this case, Marcia Ziegler observes:

> Perhaps the best reason behind enforcing duty to assist laws is the reason no legal scholar wants to discuss—the issue of morality. . . . Courts are reluctant to impose a seemingly moralistic obligation on uninvolved actors. But the evolution of any law is ultimately tied to society's sense of right and wrong; it is spurred by a feeling of what one "should do." . . . The morality concern is what makes it such a contentious issue. (Ziegler 2000, 554)

In contrast to the United States, virtually all European countries have provisions in their criminal codes that bystanders must intervene under reasonable circumstances. Doctors may be criminally charged if they fail to stop at the scene of an accident, for instance. In France, when the body of Jean Seberg, a prominent American actress, was found in a car on a Paris street, it was determined that she had died of an overdose of alcohol and pills. But since Seberg could not drive without her glasses (which were found in her apartment), it was believed that her body, when there might have been a chance to save her life, had been moved to the car. Criminal charges were brought against those who had been with her in the apartment (Richards 1981).

Motorcycle Helmets

Moral and ideological disputes today surround the issue of riding a motorcycle without a helmet. Twenty-nine states make the wearing of a helmet mandatory, while twenty-five have limited requirements which may, for instance, exempt persons over a certain age from the necessity to wear a helmet. Colorado, Illinois, Iowa, and New Hampshire have not required a motorcyclist to wear a helmet though many riders and their passengers do so voluntarily. And in five states motorcyclists who choose not to wear helmets must carry insurance policies that cover at least $100,000 of possible medical expenses (Stolzenberg and D'Alessio 2003). Since 1997, faced with heavy lobbying from motorcyclists, five additional states have abandoned helmet requirements—Texas, Florida, Pennsylvania, Kentucky, and Arizona. In each, the rate of deaths among motorcyclists has increased notably since the abandonment of the law. In Texas, for instance, the two-year rate before 1997, when the law was repealed, was 8.5 deaths per 10,000 registered motorcycles; for the 2001–2003 period that rate had escalated to 29.5, according to figures recorded by the National Highway Traffic Safety Administration. Louisiana, which abandoned the helmet requirement in 1999, restored it in 2004 after the motorcycle death rate rose from 6.8 per 10,000 before repeal to 83.5 per 10,000 subsequent to repeal of the law (Lundegaard 2004).

Statistics show that motorcyclists are four times more likely to be injured than persons riding in a passenger car and are 21 times more likely to die in an accident. Besides, the number of motorcycle deaths and injuries has been increasing each year (Schuster 2004). About half of these deaths result from a crash with another vehicle, usually an automobile. In slightly less than half of the cases, the motorcyclist's blood alcohol content was more than the legal maximum, a far higher percentage than is true for automobile fatalities. It is estimated that about 30 percent of the deaths could have been prevented if a helmet had been worn (Council on Scientific Affairs 1994).

Opponents of the mandatory helmet laws insist that they penalize behavior that endangers only the persons engaged in it.

They say that the choice should be that of the motorcyclists; if they elect not to wear a helmet, that is nobody else's business. They also challenge the accuracy of statistical claims about the safety of helmets and maintain that helmets, especially full-face models, block vision and suppress normal sensations of wind and speed and thereby can give riders a false sense of invulnerability and lead to excessive risk-taking. They also insist that the more important place for helmets is in automobiles since car crashes inflict a higher percentage of head injuries than those resulting from motorcycle accidents (Teresi 1995).

Another part of the argument about motorcycle helmets is that all human existence is filled with risk and that we cannot handcuff every exercise of freedom in an attempt to eliminate or reduce risks. After all, few would endorse the proposition that we cut down the awful toll of highway deaths by banning automobiles, or even by putting mechanical governors on them that would restrict their speed to 45 miles an hour or less, though the savings in life and limb would be impressive.

In places where helmet wearing is mandatory for motorcyclists, the general supporting rationale is that the inconvenience to the rider is hardly so burdensome as to constitute an intolerable deprivation of personal liberty. It is noted that there has been an almost universal acceptance of the requirement for automobile riders to fasten their seat belts. As one eminent legal scholar argued: "Any new law is some restriction on liberty, but not all restrictions are threats to it" (Woozley 1983).

But like so many of the issues that we will discuss, there are complicating and challenging sidebars. Motorcycle helmets form one of the elements in discussions of the proper role of the government in interfering with religious practices. The following passage notes some of the issues:

> A Sikh feels that his religion forbids him from wearing a motorcycle helmet; but state law requires helmets. A Hindu widow interprets her religion as requiring her to throw herself on her husband's funeral pyre [and thereby to be burned to death]— but the state law forbids suicide. Should religious objectors get exceptions from paternalistic law, such as laws forbidding snake handling, and the drinking of strychnine, laws prohibiting the use of peyote [a narcotic employed in some Native American re-

ligious rituals], and laws requiring people to participate in the Social Security system? [Opposed by Amish religious principles]. On the one hand it is tempting to say that people should have the right to practice their religion if they are hurting no one but themselves; but on the other, the widow-burning example might lead many to think otherwise. (Fraser 2003, 185)

The author points out that under the federal Religious Freedom Restriction Act, objectors must be given exemptions from laws that inhibit their religious practices "unless the law is the least restrictive means of furthering a competing government interest" (42 U.S. Code 2000bb).

That last phrase allows a good deal of room for interpretation. In a specific case, four Sikhs asked to be permitted to ride motorcycles without helmets because the religiously required Rishi knot into which they bind their hair onto the crown of their head under their cloth turbans makes it impossible to put on a motorcycle helmet properly. A California court was not sympathetic to the Sikh's claim. The motorcycle law, it ruled, did not prevent a Sikh from wearing a Rishi knot and turban and therefore did not prevent him from practicing his religion. "Rather, it prohibited him from riding a motorcycle on public highways without a helmet" (*Buhl v. Hannigan* 1993, 1616).

Determining Moral Standards

Determining the moral issues the law should address and those it should ignore can be a difficult task, but there have been suggested standards against which the appropriateness of legal involvement may be measured. Many support the view that official action may legitimately be taken against a behavior if some substantial harm to others can be demonstrated to result from it. John Stuart Mill put forward the classic, much-quoted advocacy of this position:

The sole end for which mankind are warranted, individually or collectively, in interfering with the liberty of action of any of their number, is self-protection. The only purpose for which power can rightfully be exercised over any member of a civilized community, against his will, is to prevent harm to others.

His own good, either physical or moral, is not a warrant. (Mill
[1859]1892, 6)

The Mill statement, however, often is not precise enough
when an attempt is made to use it to evaluate specific issues of
public policy. The terms "self-protection" and "harm to others"
allow so many interpretations that honest people may disagree
when confronted with the same set of facts. Mill does not tell us
how serious the harm has to be and how directly it needs to be
tied to a given act before the act reasonably should be banned.
Would the harm be sufficient, for instance, if it could be shown
that homosexuality is associated with a decline in the population
that is a "significant" factor in an inadequate number of people
for economic growth and satisfactory military defense? Should
there be a law against allowing children under the age of twelve
to leave school and take work in factories if they have the consent
of their parents who feel dependent on the pay they will receive?

Joel Feinberg (1984, 1985, 1986, 1988) has made a highly regarded attempt to put detailed flesh on Mill's proposals. In four
volumes totaling 1,366 pages, Feinberg offers elaborate discussions and proposed resolutions of each element of Mill's statement. Suffice it to say, as a slight summary, that he comes down in
favor of consensual bigamy and believes that there should be no
restraints on usury.

It is against the background of such considerations that in subsequent chapters we examine prostitution, illegal drug use, homosexuality, abortion, pornography, and gambling. One useful
approach to determine what should be the proper attitude of
criminal law toward such actions was offered by Herbert Packer
(1968). The conditions that Packer believed should be present before criminal sanctions are invoked include: (1) the conduct must
be regarded by most people as socially threatening and must not
be approved by any significant segment of the society; (2) the conduct can be dealt with through even-handed and nondiscrimina-
tory law enforcement; (3) controlling the conduct through the
criminal process will not expose that process to severe qualitative
or quantitative strain; and (4) no reasonable alternatives to the
criminal sanction exist for dealing with the behavior. These criteria also are not the last word on the subject and there are those
who will take issue with them, but they can be useful for pinpoint-

ing some of the concerns that must be resolved in determining what ought to be done—and not done—about the forms of behavior that we will consider in the following pages.

There is, of course, no reason why others need to regard either the Mill, Feinberg, or Packer postulations as conclusive: One of the vital strengths of democratic morality is that each of us is entitled to formulate and seek to advance our own standards and reach our own conclusions, hopefully after a well-considered assessment of available information. The issues that we will discuss speak directly to some of the core aspects of the kind of society we now have and the one we seek to construct. It is the aim of this book to provide information and insights that will contribute meaningfully to that ongoing debate.

References

Angell, Marcia. 1997. "The Supreme Court and Physician-Assisted Suicide—The Ultimate Right." *New England Journal of Medicine* 336:50–53.

Back, Anthony L., Jeffrey I. Wallace, Helene E. Starks, and Robert A. Perlman. 1996. "Physician-Assisted Suicide and Euthanasia in Washington State: Patient Requests and Physician Responses." *Journal of the American Medical Association* 275:919–925.

Banner, Stuart. 2002. *The Death Penalty: An American History.* Cambridge, MA: Harvard University Press.

Bayer, Ronald. 1981. *Homosexuality and American Psychiatry: The Politics of Diagnosis.* New York: Basic Books.

Brenner, Susan W. 2003. "Complicit Publication: When Should the Dissemination of Ideas and Data Be Criminalized?" *Albany Law Journal of Science & Technology* 13:273–429.

Brooks, James. 1996. "Idaho County Finds Ways to Chastise Pregnant Teens: They Go to Court." *New York Times,* October 28:A26.

Brownmiller, Susan. 1999. *In Our Time: Memoir of a Revolution.* New York: Dial Press.

Buch v. Amory Manufacturing Co. 1898. 44 Atl. 809 (N.H.).

Buhl v. Hannigan. 1993. 16 Cal. App. 4th 1612.

Chappell, Duncan, Gilbert Geis, Stephen Schafer, and Larry Siegel. 1971. "Forcible Rape: A Comparative Study of Offenses Known to the Police in Boston and Los Angeles." 168–190 in James M. Henslin, ed., *Studies in the Sociology of Sex.* New York: Appleton-Century-Crofts.

City of Chicago v. Morales. 1999. 527 U.S. 41.

Commonwealth v. Boynton. 1861. 84 Mass. (2 Allen) 160.

Commonwealth v. Mash. 1844. 48 Mass. 472.

Council on Scientific Affairs. 1994. "Helmets and Preventing Motorcycle and Bicycle-Related Injuries." *Journal of the American Medical Association* 277:1535–1538.

Cushing, John D., ed. [1648]1978. *Laws and Liberties of Massachusetts, 1641–1691.* Wilmington, DE: M. Glazer.

Devlin, Patrick. 1965. *The Enforcement of Morals.* London: Oxford University Press.

Donne, John. 1624. *Devotions Upon Emergent Conditions and Several Steps in My Sickness.* London: Augustine Matthews.

Elliott, Mabel A. 1952. *Crime in Modern Society.* New York: Harper.

Feinberg, Joel. 1984. *Harm to Others.* New York: Oxford University Press.

———. 1985. *Offense to Others.* New York: Oxford University Press.

———. 1986. *Harm to Self.* New York: Oxford University Press.

———. 1988. *Harmless Wrongdoing.* New York: Oxford University Press.

First Bank v. Tony's Tortilla Factory. 1994. 877 S.W.2d 285 (Texas).

Foley, Kathleen M. 1997. "Competent Care for the Elderly Instead of Physician-Assisted Suicide." *New England Journal of Medicine* 336:54–55.

Fraser, Adam. 2003. "Protected From Their Own Beliefs: Religious Objectors and Paternalistic Law." *Brigham Young University Journal of Public Law* 18:185–226.

Goodrich, Peter. 1998. Book Review: "Signs Taken for Wonders: Community, Identity, and a History of Sumptuary Law." *Law and Social Inquiry* 23:707–725.

Gregory v. Ashcroft. 1991. 501 U.S. 452.

Hale v. Everett. 1868. 59 N.H. 9 (1868).

Hart, Herbert L. A. 1968. *Law, Liberty, and Morality.* Stanford, CA: Stanford University Press.

Hayden, Amanda. 2000. "Imposing Criminal and Civil Penalties for Failure to Help Another: Are 'Good Samaritan' Laws Good Ideas?" *New England International and Comparative Law Annual* 6:27–46.

Hillyard, Daniel, and John Dombrink. 2001. *Dying Rights: The Death With Dignity Movement.* New York: Routledge.

Hunt, Alan. 1996. *Signs Taken for Wonders: Community, Identity and a History of Sumptuary Law.* New York: St. Martin's.

Jones, David W. 2004. *Reforming the Morality of Usury: A Study of Differences That Separated the Protestant Reformers.* Dallas: University Press of America.

Lecky, William E. H. 1904. *History of European Morals From Augustus to Charlemagne.* 3rd ed. New York: Appleton.

Lode, Eric. 1999. "Slippery Slope Arguments and Legal Reasoning." *California Law Review* 87:1469–1544.

Lundegaard, Karen. 2004. "Touting Freedom, Bikers Take Aim at Helmet Laws." *Wall Street Journal*, December 1: A1, A6–A7.

McManus, Edgar J. 1993. *Law and Liberty in Early New England: Criminal Justice and Due Process, 1620–1692.* Amherst: University of Massachusetts Press.

Mill, John Stuart. [1859]1892. *On Liberty.* London: Longmans, Green.

Noonan, John J., Jr. 1957. *The Scholastic Analysis of Usury.* Cambridge, MA: Harvard University Press.

Oregon v. Ashcroft. 2004. 368 F.3d 1118.

Packer, Herbert. 1968. *The Limits of the Criminal Sanction.* Stanford, CA: Stanford University Press.

Papachristou v. City of Jacksonville. 1972. 405 U.S. 176.

Radzinowicz, Leon. 1948–1953. *A History of English Criminal Law.* London: Macmillan.

Richards, David. 1981. *Played Out: The Jean Seberg Story.* New York: Random House.

Robinson, Louis N., and Rolf Nugent. 1935. *Regulation of Small Loan Business.* New York: Russell Sage.

Salem, Tania. 1999. "Physician-Assisted Suicide." *Hastings Center Report* 20 (May):30–36.

Sayre, Francis B. 1933. "Public Welfare Offenses." *Columbia Law Review* 33:55–58.

Schur, Edwin H. 1965. *Crimes Without Victims: Deviant Behavior and Public Policy.* Englewood Cliffs, NJ: Prentice-Hall.

Schuster, John W. 2004. "Riding Without a Helmet: Liability, Social Efficiency, and the More Perfect Wisconsin Compromise to Motorcycle Helmet Liability." *Iowa Law Review* 89:1391–1418.

Semmes, Raphael. 1936. *Criminal Punishment in Early Maryland.* Baltimore: Johns Hopkins University Press.

Seneca, Lucius Annaeus. 1961. *Ad Lucilium Epistulae Morales.* Richard M. Gummere, trans. Cambridge, MA: Harvard University Press.

State v. West. 1970. 263 A.2d 602 (Maryland Court of Special Appeals).

Stolzenberg, Lisa, and Stewart J. D'Alessio. 2003. " 'Born to Kill': The Effect of the Repeal of Florida's Mandatory Motorcycle Helmet-Use Law on Serious Injury and Fatality Rates." *Evaluation Review* 27:131–150.

Tacitus, Gaius Cornelius. 1996. *The Annals of Imperial Rome.* Michael Grant, trans. New York: Penguin Books.

Teresi, Dick. 1995. "The Case for No Helmets." *New York Times,* June 15:15.

Updegraph v. Commonwealth. 1824. 11 Serg. & Rawle, 394 (Pennsylvania).

Wilson, James Q. 1997. *Moral Judgment: Does the Abuse Excuse Threaten Our Legal System?* New York: Basic Books.

Winthrop, John. 1996. *The Journal of John Winthrop, 1630–1649.* Richard S. Dunn, James Savage, and Laetitia Yeandle, eds. Cambridge, MA: Harvard University Press.

Woozley, Anthony D. 1983. "A Duty to Rescue: Some Thoughts on Criminal Liability." *Virginia Law Review* 69:1273–1300.

Wright, Richard T., and Scott H. Decker. 1994. *Burglars on the Job: Street Life and Residential Break-Ins.* Boston: Northeastern University Press.

———. 1997. *Armed Robbers in Action: Stickups and Street Culture.* Boston: Northeastern University Press.

Wright, Walter. 2000. "Historical Analogies: Slippery Slopes and the Question of Euthanasia." *Journal of Law, Medicine & Ethics* 28:176–193.

Yankah, Ekov N. 2004. "Good Guys and Bad Guys: Punishing Character, Equality and the Irrelevance of Moral Character to Criminal Punishment." *Cardozo Law Review* 25:1019–1067.

Young, Kimball. 1954. *Isn't One Wife Enough?* New York: Holt.

Ziegler, Marcia M. 2000. "Nonfeasance and the Duty to Assist: The American Steinfeld Syndrome." *Dickinson Law Review* 104:525–560. ✦

Chapter 2

Prostitution/Sex Work

Prostitution can be defined briefly as the performance of acts of nonmarital sex as a vocation. A more elaborate definition was proposed by Paul Gebhard (1969, 24): "A female prostitute is a person who for immediate cash payment will engage in sexual activity with any person (usually male), known or unknown to her, who meets her minimal requirements as to age, sobriety, cleanliness, race, and health." The term "sex worker" is gradually replacing "prostitute," primarily because "prostitute" in common usage has a broad negative connotation, such as in the phrase "he prostituted his true talent in order to please his parents."

It has been argued that sexual intercourse between a married couple, particularly in the days before the feminist impact on contemporary attitudes and behavior, was much like prostitution. According to this view, a woman typically refused sexual favors to a man until she was engaged or was married to him and assured of his financial support. Thus, sexual access was being exchanged for economic gains, as if it were a commodity to be bartered. Such a stance may stimulate debate, but it fails to acknowledge the very real difference between the commercial enterprise of prostitution and other social arrangements that are governed by different conditions and rules.

Prostitutes, of course, are found in either gender. But both historically and currently the spotlight tends to be on female prostitutes because, unlike male prostitutes, they are regarded as exemplars of gender subordination and exploitation, a matter that highlights important political and ideological issues. We also will concentrate on women and girl prostitutes because they far outnumber their male counterparts (for representative studies of male prostitution see Cates and Markley 1992; West and de Villers 1993).

The Biblical Heritage

The dominant view of prostitution among Americans, one reflected in the laws that condemn its practice, has its roots in biblical tradition. The Old Testament contains many warnings against the pagan harlot, whose wantonness was seen as threatening the Hebrew theocracy. It cautioned against the prostitute, saying that "her house is the way to hell, descending to the chambers of death" (Proverbs 7:27). Jewish fathers were forbidden to turn their daughters into prostitutes (Leviticus 19:29), and the women of Israel were forbidden to practice prostitution (Deuteronomy 23:17).

Early Christian writers were more inclined to regard prostitutes as a necessary, even vital, evil. Saint Augustine believed that although what the prostitute did was morally wrong, even worse evils would arise if she did not provide an outlet for male lust. Augustine ([386]1844–1864, 984) declared: "Suppress prostitution, and capricious lusts will overthrow society." Saint Thomas Aquinas ([1273]1947, II, 1232), the medieval theologian who with Saint Augustine represents "by far the most important source of western sexual ethics" (Primoratz 1993, 167), reiterated this position. The prostitute, Aquinas wrote in *Summa Theologica*, "is like the filth in the sea or the sewers in the palace. Take away the sewer and you will fill the palace with pollution and likewise with the filth in the sea. Take away prostitutes from the world and you will fill it with sodomy" (Aquinas 2a2ae, q. 10, art. 4). This attitude, more tolerant than that of the Old Testament, is partly derived from the story of Christ and Mary Magdalene. Magdalene, according to tradition, was a prostitute who was forgiven her errant ways by Jesus (Luke 7:36–50; cf. Rushing 1994).

Criminal Law and Prostitution

On the roster of major outlawed behaviors that have stirred debate about the proper role of morality in criminal law, only the legal prohibition of prostitution has resisted change in the United

States during recent decades. Gambling, once outlawed throughout the country with the exception of Nevada, now flourishes with the blessing of the law. There are state-run lotteries and gambling casinos throughout the country. Slot machines are found on many Indian reservations, sometimes bringing riches to once-impoverished tribes and changing dramatically their traditional way of life and values. Abortion, once a tawdry, cheapening, and dangerous experience that was carried out under threat of criminal prosecution, is now permitted during the initial period of pregnancy by mandate of the United States Supreme Court. Marijuana laws, formerly enforced with draconian fierceness, have largely disappeared for those who use the drug in recreational quantities, though sanctions against "heavier" drugs such as heroin and cocaine remain severe.

Homosexuality, previously outlawed in all American states, is now regarded with indifference by the criminal law, and some state legislatures and courts have been debating the sanctioning of homosexual marriages. Many business enterprises now allow same-sex partners to be covered by the medical insurance of a corporate employee.

Explaining the Law's Intransigence

Why have these other crimes tied to moral views had such diverse histories? And why has prostitution remained steadfastly beyond the legal pale? For one thing, prostitution continues to be illegal because it largely involves dispossessed and politically weak persons. There will be no prominent female authors or famous Hollywood actresses, as there were on the issue of abortion, who will announce that they once had been a practicing whore. Nor will there be middle-class and upper-class parents, such as those in the debate over marijuana who lobbied for decriminalization because of anxiety that their pot-smoking children would be arrested and burdened with a criminal record. Nor will there be any respectable citizens, such as those who advocated legalizing gambling because they were inconvenienced and worried about police interference when they sought to place an illegal bet on a number or a sports event.

Finally, there will be no parades of successful mainstream people fighting for the legalization of prostitution as they did for gay rights. Prostitutes may proclaim that their way of life is a choice and not a sickness, as gays have done, and they may even mount the equivalent of Gay Lib public consciousness-raising events. But American lawmakers remain unimpressed. They appreciate that prostitutes lack political power and probably rarely vote.

Consequently, although the law has bent dramatically in regard to other kinds of congruent crimes, it has been unyielding regarding prostitution. Sex for pay continues to be interdicted. Its practitioners—most often, but not always, those who receive the money and not those who provide it—continue to be harassed, arrested, convicted, fined, tested for venereal infections and HIV, and sometimes sentenced to brief jail terms.

Prostitution and Sexual Liberation

For a time, it seemed that prostitution would devolve into a nonissue. The introduction of birth control pills, the feminist drive for equality, and the pronounced loosening of sexual taboos combined to create considerably greater opportunities for consensual sexual activity prior to and outside of marriage. Prostitution, it was presumed, would be priced out of existence because of the declining necessity to resort to pay-for-sex outlets. At least three major factors worked against such a development. First and probably foremost, the appearance of AIDS, a lethal immune system disorder, dramatically checked the growing number of casual sexual encounters.

Second, prostitution continues to survive because it offers a marketplace exchange of money for the unemotional provision of sexual gratification with no strings attached. Today, women, particularly those who are well educated and informed, demand sexual satisfaction from a partner as their right—a demand that some men may not always be willing (or able) to satisfy (McCormick 1994).

Prostitutes do not need to be wooed, flattered, or entertained, either romantically or sexually. Prostitutes will not complain the next morning that they were callously used or that their personal integrity was abused. As an example of customer satisfaction, one study indicates that almost half of the streetwalkers' clients in a New Jersey city engaged in sex with a prostitute more than once a month (Freund, Leonard, and Lee 1989). Though prostitutes do not provide romance or love, these males contend, neither will they make any claim to continue a relationship nor interpret their sexual conduct as anything other than a business transaction.

This point was emphasized in the pioneering study of male sexual behavior by Alfred Kinsey and his colleagues. "At all social levels men go to prostitutes because it is simpler to secure a sexual partner commercially than it is to secure a sexual partner by courting a girl." Kinsey and his colleagues also observed that intercourse with a prostitute is likely to be a good deal less expensive than intercourse resulting from courtship, which could involve (in Kinsey's oddly detailed inventory) "flowers, candy, 'coke dates,' dinner engagements, parties, evening entertainments, moving pictures, theaters, night clubs, dances, picnics, weekend house parties, car rides, longer trips, and all sorts of other expensive entertainment" before the male "might or might not be able to obtain the intercourse he wanted" (Kinsey, Pomeroy, and Martin 1948, 608). Sexual etiquette has changed considerably since Kinsey's time, but the underlying accuracy of his chauvinistic position is probably true for at least some significant portion of today's sexual interactions.

Third, prostitutes offer a service that is not otherwise readily available to persons who find themselves beyond the pale of sexual appeal. Those too old, unattractive, or shy, or those who are unable to easily find a consenting sexual partner, can turn to prostitutes as a simple solution to their problem. Prostitutes will also perform sexual acts (e.g., fellatio) that might otherwise be unavailable to some single or married males.

The Cast in the Performance of Prostitution

Prostitution involves people and institutions that play a number of different roles in the enterprise. At its core are the men and women who provide direct sexual stimulation to customers in return for money. Within this group, there is a considerable distinction between types of prostitutes. Streetwalkers, who have the lowest standing, make up between 10 and 20 percent of the cadre of prostitutes, and account for about 90 percent of the women arrested for prostitution. At the bottom of the streetwalking status ladder are women addicted to crack cocaine or heroin, who trade sex for drugs or for money to purchase drugs. Forty percent of the sex workers in this category reported violence from clients within the past year—25 percent were beaten, 13 percent raped, and 14 percent threatened with weapons (Surratt et al. 2004).

Then there are prostitutes who work in massage parlors and call girls, who are considered the more elite practitioners. They have taken to the Internet, cellular phones, and the camouflage of "escort services." The yellow pages of New York City's telephone book has 30 pages of listings for escort services, typically the code words for prostitution. There are fewer than half as many pages devoted to psychologists, plumbers, or real estate brokers. Debra Satz (1995, 68) provides a vignette of the cadre of call girls:

> Many call girls drift into prostitution after "run of the mill pro-miscuity." . . . Some are young college graduates, who upon graduation earn money by prostitution, while searching for other jobs. Call girls can earn between $30,000 and $100,000 an-nually. These women have control over the entire amount they earn as well as an unusual degree of independence, far greater than in most other forms of work. They can also decide who they wish to have sex with and when they wish to do so. There is little resemblance between their lives and that of the streetwalker.

A New York woman who runs an escort service told an inter-viewer that she keeps her operation small and manageable, em-ploying eight women. Her income, she said, is about $20,000 a week, tax free. She relies on a roster of 2,200 steady customers, most from suburban New Jersey, whose backgrounds she checks out carefully. Most sexual encounters take place in hotel rooms. The women, who sign a 10-page contract setting out their duties, specialize in what their employer calls "the girlfriend experi-ence," a slow-paced, affection-filled encounter that closely resem-bles a date. It usually includes flower petals on the pillow and a great deal of cuddling. Customers pay $300 an hour, two-thirds of which goes to the prostitute. Overnight stays cost $3,200 for 24 hours. Local women are rarely employed: typically, they fly in to Manhattan from Florida, California, and Canada for five-day stints (Jacobs 2004).

From interviews with working prostitutes, Wardell Pomeroy (1965, 184) documented that 40 percent remained in the business because of "the interesting people they meet." One call girl told him: "I have an eighth grade education and nearly every day I meet doctors, lawyers, bankers, and actors who I never would meet if I wasn't in the life." Her point was brought home in scandalous fashion when a $200-a-night call girl told a tabloid newspaper in 1996 about her assignations with a top advisor to President Clinton. Her client encouraged her to eavesdrop on his telephone conversations with Clinton.

In addition to the prostitutes, there are others who derive income from some part of the prostitution network. There are pimps who promote a prostitute's work and take most of her earnings. Pimps, who often run a stable of prostitutes, typically offer protection, romance, and security. Then there are the cab drivers, bellhops, hotel desk men and elevator operators, bartenders, and others whose jobs put them in a position to attract customers for a prostitute in return for a percentage of the woman's earnings (Reichert and Frey 1985). Those who rent premises for the purposes of prostitution also depend on the business for at least a portion of their livelihood. Finally, there are the customers of prostitutes—the "johns."

Urban Enforcement: Los Angeles

Like most metropolitan areas, Los Angeles has pockets of prostitution that cater to a particular clientele. The area around Disneyland is notorious for streetwalkers who make contacts with visiting foreigners. In some Los Angeles ghetto areas, prostitutes provide sex services for men who come to the United States to work, often illegally, but are unable to bring their wives or female partners from their own country. In addition, Los Angeles is believed to have the second highest rate of male homosexual prostitution in the country, trailing only San Francisco.

As the center of the motion picture industry, Hollywood provides a natural venue for prostitution and for the scandals that can accompany it. Two such episodes are illustrative. One involved a brief sexual encounter between a sex worker and a British film star, the other a young woman who ran a call girl service for motion picture and business moguls.

The BMW Caper

Hugh Grant, a well-known actor, was propelled into a different kind of limelight when he was apprehended by the police at 1:30 A.M. while parked in his open-top BMW on a Hollywood residential street, where he was the recipient of oral sex from a 23-year-old prostitute. The prostitute, an unmarried mother of three children with the working name of Divine Marie Brown, said that she had talked Grant into wearing a condom after he agreed to pay her $60 for oral sex. Had he been willing to pay another $40, Brown said, they could have gone to a hotel room and avoided arrest.

For Brown, the result was instant celebrity and a barrage of television appearances. She was hired to do a lingerie advertisement for Brazilian television, in which she warned wives and girlfriends that if they did not purchase racy undergarments, their men might end up seeking out someone like her ("Divine Brown's Unpromising Career" 1995). Her newfound—albeit short-lived—fame got Brown a leading role in an adult film, *Taking for Granted*, and allegedly earned her more than half a million dollars from show business deals. Several years later, claiming that a pimp had stolen all her money, she was arrested in Las Vegas for belligerently soliciting a customer in a gambling casino.

In court, both Brown and Grant were charged with lewd conduct and pleaded no contest. Brown was fined $1,350 and sentenced to jail for 180 days for having violated a probation order on a similar charge. Grant was given a $1,180 fine and a sentence of two years' probation.

William Buckley, a prominent columnist on the right side of the political spectrum, drew a lesson from the Grant-Brown episode that goes to the heart of the complicated effort to distinguish prostitution from other kinds of sexual behavior. Writing under the title of "Thou Shalt Not . . . What?" Buckley (1995, 71) noted, "Fornication is okay in a hotel, in front of a movie camera, but not in a car, certainly not in a car in Los Angeles."

The Hollywood Madam

Heidi Lynne Fleiss was in her late twenties when she was arrested for operating a call girl service. At age 13, Fleiss had 20 babysitters in her employ. She dropped out of school when she was 16 and established a liaison with a much older playboy-financier who gave her a Rolls-Royce for her twenty-first birthday. In 1990, backed by a television director and pornography filmmaker, Fleiss went into the call girl business. She refers to her operation as nothing more than a sensible adjunct to many other Hollywood enterprises and reports that she was paid $40,000 a night by a customer to do little more than play Scheherazade, the Sultan's wife in *Arabian Nights.*

On her income tax returns, Fleiss maintained that her earnings were generated by "personal counseling." SONY officials paid her thousands of dollars for one such session for executives of an overseas branch; SONY's tax report listed the outlay as a "development deal" (Shah 1993). Government agents estimated that Fleiss earned several hundred thousand dollars and reported only $33,000 of it on her tax return.

At Fleiss' trial, a business executive testified that he sent his private jet to pick up some of Fleiss' call girls. One of the women who worked for Fleiss told the court that she flew to Paris, Athens, and Las Vegas to have sex with clients (Boyer 1995, B4). After a state court guilty verdict was overturned, Fleiss was convicted in federal court of eight counts of conspiracy, income tax evasion, and laundering money, and received a 37-month prison sentence. She also was ordered to participate in a substance-abuse program and to perform 300 hours of community service.

For some, Fleiss' situation aroused passions that have persistently remained prominent in the feminist debate over prostitution. In an op-ed piece, attorneys Gloria Allred and Lisa Bloom (1994, B7) asked rhetorically: "Why is it immoral to be paid for an act that is perfectly legal if done for free?" They proceeded to offer an answer to their own question:

> The lines that our society has drawn in the name of morality have become absurd. A woman may agree to sexual acts with men she doesn't love as long as she does not directly charge them for sex. She may legally pose nude for money, genitalia displayed for photographers. She may dance nude, as provocatively as the customer likes, for money. She may engage in sexual acts for money with men she does not know or like in erotic films, magazines or before a live audience. She may sell her voice for "phone sex" with strange men. She may give a

naked man an erotic massage. She may marry a man she does not love and have sex in return for his financial support for the rest of her married life. Yet the sale of direct sexual acts remains illegal.

For some, the logic of the foregoing statement leaves something to be desired. They insist that Allred and Bloom's argument would not be best resolved by adding prostitution to the list of those behaviors now exempt from legal consequences, but rather by criminalizing most of the other specified acts.

Licensed Brothels: Nevada

In the United States, only Nevada legally allows prostitution. That development was the result of a 1971 state law in Nevada that outlawed prostitution in all counties with a population of more than 250,000 persons. The courts interpreted the statute to indicate that counties with fewer than that number of people could permit brothels to operate within their boundaries (*Nye County v. Plankinton* 1978).

Prostitution is now legally permissible in 14 of Nevada's 17 counties (though only 11 actually have it). There are 28 licensed brothels in the state, down from a high of 35 in the 1980s. Clark County, where Las Vegas is located, outlaws prostitution, as do Reno, Lake Tahoe, Loughlin, and Carson City. Nonetheless, many prostitutes are readily available in these cities for those who want to include them in their vacation package (Frey, Reichert, and Russell 1981).

Prostitutes working in the legal Nevada brothels are usually fingerprinted and required to carry identification cards. They also must undergo weekly medical examinations for gonorrhea and chlamydia and monthly syphilis and HIV tests. State law requires that houses of prostitution cannot be located on a principal business street or within 400 yards of a schoolhouse or church. Typically, prostitutes work in a complex of trailers on sites that are euphemistically called "ranches" (Albert 2001). The brothel takes half of their earnings, and as independent contractors they have no medical or other benefits (Bingham 1998).

It would seem that Americans are not certain whether they loathe prostitution or are intrigued by it—or both. Consider, for instance, the great success enjoyed by actresses who portray prostitutes in films—from the first Oscar in 1928 given for best actress to Janet Gaynor for *Street Angel*. In 1995, three of the five nominees for Academy Awards had portrayed hookers: Elizabeth Shue in *Leaving Las Vegas*, Sharon Stone in *Casino*, and Mira Sorvino in *Mighty Aphrodite*. Interpreting this phenomenon, film critic Molly Haskell (1974) believes that it represents what she calls "hooker chic."

The Wolfenden Report and Kerb Crawling

One of the most significant developments regarding the law of prostitution in the Anglo-American world was spurred in Great Britain by the 1957 report of the Committee on Homosexual Offences and Prostitution, known as the Wolfenden Report after the committee chair (Great Britain 1957; for an update, see Brooks-Gordon and Gelsthorpe 2002). Two committee recommendations received almost immediate parliamentary approval—that public solicitation by prostitutes be dealt with more severely and that those living on the earnings of prostitutes be criminally punished. The Wolfenden Committee, however, did not favor any change in the British policy that prostitution itself should not constitute a criminal offense. On this point, it observed:

> [W]e are not attempting to abolish prostitution or to make prostitution in itself illegal. We do not think that the law ought to try to do so; nor do we think that if it tried it could by itself succeed. What the law can and should do is to ensure that the streets of London and our big provincial cities should be freed from what is offensive or injurious and made tolerable for the ordinary citizen who lives in them or passes through them. (Great Britain 1957, 95)

Committee members granted that there might be something to the view that "the mere presence of prostitutes carrying on their trade was no more, and no less, a matter for police intervention than the presence of street photographers or toysellers" (Great Britain 1957, 128). But they were not taken with the argument sufficiently to endorse it. On the question of whether to punish the customers of prostitutes, committee members rendered what many regard as a rather chauvinistic conclusion. The report noted: "The simple fact is that prostitutes do parade themselves more habitually and openly than their prospective customers" (Great Britain 1957, 87).

The committee also reviewed a form of solicitation called "kerb crawling." Kerb crawlers are motorists who drive slowly, overtake women pedestrians and stop beside them with the intention of inviting them into their automobile for sexual purposes (Brooks-Gordon and Gelsthorpe 2003; Brooks-Gordon 2005). The committee granted that such behavior might offend women who are mistaken for prostitutes, but it concluded that the difficulties of legal proof are so burdensome that it did not appear reasonable to make kerb crawling a criminal offense.

When the Wolfenden recommendations were translated into law, Parliament attempted to overcome the danger of the inadvertent harassment of respectable women and to encourage the novice prostitute to mend her ways by requiring two warnings before a woman could be arrested for soliciting in public. The result was a rapid increase in the mobility of prostitutes from one site or city to another, but no apparent decline in their activity. Also, having exempted kerb crawlers from punishment, Parliament watched the increased use of automobiles as roving whorehouses. Taxi drivers and others were chauffeuring prostitutes and soliciting business from likely male pedestrians.

Kerb crawling was later outlawed and increasingly tougher penalties were decreed for soliciting women from or near a motor vehicle or on foot. In a study of 518 men arrested for kerb crawling, Belinda Brooks-Gordon and Loraine Gelsthorpe (2002) found several common responses: admission, admission to cruising but not to kerb crawling, and denial and excuses. The "cruisers" indicated that they were canvassing the area out of curiosity, that this was a form of entertainment for them.

Typically, men apprehended demonstrated a series of reactions, beginning with bemusement, then excuse-making, afterwards indignation and confrontation, and, finally, a pleading phase, in which the attempt was to avoid further proceedings or to be treated leniently. Reliance was often placed on claims of physical or psychological distress to explain their behavior or denial of any intention to do something illegal.

The most recent campaign against prostitution in London has focused upon sexually explicit advertising cards placed by prostitutes in telephone booths in the central city. The presence of the cards is said to discourage some people from using the booths and to encourage schoolchildren to collect and trade them. From 10 to 100 cards can usually be found in any one booth. In eight weeks the phone company removed 1.1 million of the advertisements. An ordinance now allows the police to issue a cease and desist order to advertisers. If the practice continues, phone service to the advertised number can be cut off. Skeptics presume that prostitutes will develop other tactics to attract customers. "They don't call it the world's oldest profession for nothing," said one (Ibrahim 1996, 4).

Feminism and Prostitution

The women's movement that flourished for a time in the early years of the twentieth century took a strong position against prostitution (Musheno and Seeley 1986). Jane Addams (1912), one of the movement's leaders, maintained that curtailing prostitution, particularly in public places, would considerably reduce any allure that might attract perspective recruits to the business. Her reasoning is similar to the argument today that the lifestyle of drug dealers in the slums—their expensive automobiles, elegant clothes, and desirable female companions—encourages youngsters there to emulate them.

The more recent powerful revival of the feminist movement, part of the social revolution that swept America in the 1960s, initially placed prostitution at the head of its roster of the major criminal behaviors that needed to be addressed. But feminist attention to prostitution took a lesser role because of an inability to convince streetwalkers and other women "in the life" that they ought to give up what they were doing and adopt a safer and more respectable lifestyle. As one prostitute put it, "A woman has the right to sell her sexual services just as much as she has a right to sell her brains to a law firm" (Jenness 1990, 405; 1993). Another said, "Radical feminism . . . sees all pros [prostitutes] as exploited sex slaves. I think this has left people confused, especially other feminists and the political left" (Overs 1994, 119).

After a while, the women's movement switched its criminal justice focus to rape (and later also to child and spousal abuse), though every once in a while issues regarding prostitution resurface, only to be abandoned because they produce an acrimonious internal splintering within feminist circles. The feminist debate on prostitution pits two conflicting interpretations against each other. The question is whether prostitution is an ugly and intolerable consequence of the power of men over women and the sexual exploitation of women, or whether it is a commercial enterprise like so many others that is engaged in by a seller who possesses a commodity that has a market value.

The schism within the women's movement on prostitution is said to be deep (Jolin 1994, 69). One arm of the feminist movement repudiates the idea that women freely choose prostitution, that prostitution is a valid job, and that it can be carried on in a humane manner. Prostitution, they insist, is based on male domination, the treatment of women as commodities, and enforced sexual access and sexual abuse. It is said to violate women's dignity and to represent a crime against women by men (Weitzer 1991).

Those who take this position regard prostitution as the product of a patriarchal society in which females are defined from an early age as sex objects. Child sexual abuse, incest, and similar female victimizations are said to lie at the core of entry into prostitution (Freeman 1989–1990). This position equates prostitution with slavery and points out that few words can evoke such contempt and loathing as the word "whore" or its equivalent in any language (Reanda 1991, 203). Often quoted is Simone de Beauvoir's (1953, 569) observation in *The Second Sex* that "prostitution sums up all the forms of feminine slavery at once."

Debra Satz (1995) argues that contemporary prostitution introduces and contributes to the perception of women as socially inferior to men. Her position raises questions about any social occurrence in which members of one gender do something that cannot be done, or at least not done as well, by members of the other gender. Athletic events, such as track meets, almost invariably show the men outshining the women. Should such events be eliminated because they make women appear to be inferior?

On the other side are feminists who believe that the problem is that their sisters-in-arms focus only on what they see as male sexual domination of women and that they fail to campaign for policies that would allow prostitutes to enjoy a more satisfying way of life. Laura Reanda (1991, 203) has berated some women—

"antiporn feminists and other moralists"—for not attending to the financial impoverishment of working and underclass women. "Eliminate this mammoth motivating force and much prostitution would disappear," she believes. Those left doing sex work would be "on the game" because they liked it; in this regard, "true sexual determination (a basic feminist demand) should include a woman's right to sell sex—if she wants to."

A woman in the world of prostitution has made the same point: "Antiporn feminists have patronizingly told strippers and prostitutes that we should raise our consciousness and develop self-esteem (by working as toilet cleaners and factory hands). No thanks, sisters" (Roberts 1994, 45). The viewpoint being criticized has been called the "brainwash theory" which, according to Gayle Rubin, "explains erotic diversity by assuming that some sexual acts are so disgusting that no one would willingly perform them. Therefore, the reasoning goes, anyone who does so must have been forced or fooled" (Rubin 1984, 306). Others go to the furthest extreme, like Camille Paglia (1994, 58–59) who insists that the prostitute is the "ultimate liberated woman, who lives on the edge and whose sexuality belongs to no one."

Legalizing Prostitution: Yeas and Nays

Some people believe that prostitution ought to be made legal, with no regulation whatsoever regarding how it is carried on, except for already existing laws about public decency (e.g., sex in public places) and similar matters. Others believe that it should be decriminalized but that practitioners ought to be licensed and subject to periodic tests to determine if they are free of venereal infections and HIV. Margaret Jane Radin (1996, xi), who holds this latter view, maintains that decriminalization is the most effective way to deal with the issue of "commodification," a process by which something, such as sexual services, comes to be viewed as merchandise. Radin (1996, 145) argues that "we should not subject poor women to the degradation and danger of the black market nor force them into other methods of earning money that seem to them less desirable than selling their bodies." At the same time, she believes that brokerage (pimping) and worker training (recruitment to prostitution) should be outlawed.

Prostitution, Venereal Disease, and AIDS

For a long period of time, until the appearance of the AIDS virus, considerable discussion centered around other diseases that prostitutes might transmit, most notably syphilis and gonorrhea. Given so high a level of intercourse for many prostitutes with so diverse a clientele, it was regarded as inevitable that many of them would sooner or later contract a venereal infection and pass the illness on to other customers who, in turn, would pass it on to other females with whom they subsequently had sexual contact.

At issue is the rate at which such outcomes occur under different arrangements for prostitution. Today, faced with the threat of AIDS, many prostitutes and many of their customers are particularly insistent about the use of condoms in any kind of sexual act. For the sex workers, their livelihood (not to mention their life) depends on not contracting disabling diseases. On the other hand, those prostitutes who use drugs, particularly crack cocaine, often have been reported to neglect taking precautions to avoid being infected with the HIV virus, the precursor of AIDS.

Prostitutes are reported to contract AIDS more through contaminated needles used in intravenous drug taking than from customers. In a study of 72 prostitutes, David Bellis (1990) found that those who used drugs did little to protect themselves or their customers from AIDS by relying on sterile needles or requiring the use of condoms. "Yeah, I'm concerned [about AIDS]," one woman said, "until I stick the needle in. When I'm hurting, dope's the only thing on my mind" (Bellis 1990, 30).

In a sophisticated study of the 350 licensed prostitutes in Nevada, where latex condom usage was made mandatory by law in 1988, Carole Campbell (1991) found that not one prostitute had ever tested HIV positive in the mandatory monthly procedure, though 13 applicants for brothel positions had done so. Campbell contrasts the Nevada rate with that in a number of other cities, including Colorado Springs (3.8 percent HIV positive), Los Angeles (3.7 percent), San Francisco (9.9 percent), and Miami (26.6 percent). Following up on Campbell's work, Alexa Albert and her colleagues (1995) noted that by the end of 1993, after 20,000 tests, there still had not been a single positive HIV result for a licensed Nevada prostitute. The same study reported that its review of 353 acts of sexual intercourse over nine days by Nevada prostitutes found no condom breakage, though there was slipping in about one out of twenty-five usages during intercourse and about the same rate during withdrawal (Albert et al. 1995; Remez 1996).

For all heterosexual intercourse, including that with prostitutes, there is a much lower risk for men than for women that the act will result in an HIV infection, and the risk of HIV is much lower for oral sex than genital intercourse (Lyman et al. 1986). Oral sex is believed to be the most common choice for the clients of prostitutes.

For prostitutes, their greatest danger of AIDS has been found to occur not from their work but from their sexual relations with high-risk, nonpaying persons with whom they have formed a romantic attachment and with whom they do not insist on the use of condoms (Campbell 1991). As an Australian prostitute noted, "I can't use a condom with my boyfriend. What'll he think—that I'm gonna charge him next?" (Waddell 1996, 81). Streetwalking prostitutes also often will not carry condoms on their person for fear that the police will use them as evidence that they are plying their trade (Davidson 1998, 65).

Other Impacts of Prostitution

Alfred Kinsey and his associates, in their monumental study of human sexual behavior, expressed surprise at the amount of attention concentrated on prostitution when it is measured by the importance that it shows numerically as a sexual outlet:

> The world's literature contains hundred of volumes whose authors have attempted to assay the social significance of prostitution. For an activity which contributes no more than this does to the sexual outlet of the male population, it is amazing that it should have been given such widespread consideration. Some of the attention undoubtedly has been inspired by erotic interest; but a major part . . . has centered around the question of the social significance of prostitution. The extent of the attention which the subject still receives in this country today is all out of proportion to its significance in the lives of most males. (Kinsey et al. 1948, 605)

The Kinsey quotation is itself rather puzzling, seeming to imply that the extent rather than the nature of behavior should be the criterion by which its importance may be reasonably measured. More people are killed by a variety of means—including traffic accidents—and many more die of avoidable lethal conditions, such as inadequate medical care, than are murdered each year in the United States. Nonetheless, murder is considered, and reasonably so, to be a very important issue. The reason that prostitution compels interest and concern, despite its relative unimportance in any numerical sense, is that it challenges values, raises basic moral questions, and involves the lives of human beings like the rest of us who may be injured or kept from harm by the view the law takes about their behavior.

Nevertheless, the extent to which men frequent prostitutes is not great and there is some evidence that it is declining. In a national survey of adult sexual behavior, it was reported that only about 16 percent of men ever paid for sex and that the proportion of men whose first sexual intercourse was with a prostitute declined from 7 percent of those who came of age in the 1950s to 1.5 percent of the men who came of age in the late 1980s and early 1990s (Michael et al. 1994, 62, 95).

Prostitutes, Pimps, and the Public

To adjudicate arguments regarding the proper legal and moral status that prostitution should have, it is necessary to examine four major participants in the activity: the prostitutes, their customers, pimps, and the larger society.

The Prostitute/Sex Worker

Research studies indicate that in contemporary times in the United States prostitution almost always is an occupation entered into voluntarily. Prostitution offers a considerable range of vocational advantages, including flexible work hours, contact with diverse kinds of people, a heightened sense of activity, and the opportunity to make substantial sums of money and pay no taxes. Such consequences do not accrue to all prostitutes, nor perhaps even to very many. For streetwalkers, prostitution can be a particularly dirty and dangerous enterprise. There can be beatings, nasty copulations, and little financial reward (Dalla 2002; Sanders 2005). The loss of self-esteem that often results from the practice of prostitution is, of course, a consequence of broader social attitudes, which themselves are at least partly a consequence of sanctions against such behavior. It seems likely that removing the legal ban against prostitution might raise the self-esteem of its practitioners because they would be employed in a legitimate occupation.

Unfortunately, no large-scale studies exist concerning the outcomes of the lives of prostitutes. This enormous gap in important knowledge was observed by Walter Reckless in a pioneering study of vice in Chicago. "What happens to girls who have once practiced prostitution?" asked Reckless (1933, 57). "No investigations so far made offer information upon which to base a positive statement." More than three-quarters of a century after Reckless' work, his point about the lack of information regarding the later lives of prostitutes remains true.

Part of the barrier hindering comprehensive longitudinal studies of prostitutes is that they are particularly difficult to locate years later. If they married, they may have taken their husband's family name. In addition, prostitutes often use aliases instead of their real names when they work. Besides, of course, former prostitutes in other roles would not be too willing to have an interviewer show up at their front door, questionnaire in hand. So we remain uninformed about a matter of great significance that could be resolved by diligent, tactful research.

Charles Winick and Paul Kinsie (1971) have reported a notably high suicide rate among prostitutes, with 75 percent of a sample of call girls said to have attempted to kill themselves. They also claimed that 15 percent of all persons who attempt suicide and are brought to public hospitals are prostitutes. This claim needs further substantiation but, if accurate, it suggests a high degree of alienation and unhappiness. Many fictional portraits depict prostitutes as golden-hearted damsels who, because of their innumerable contacts with men and a learned ability to cater to male desires, ultimately marry well above their original social position and settle down comfortably in suburbia. Others see them ending up prematurely as neglected corpses, lying anonymously on city morgue tables and buried in paupers' graves.

It seems likely, though uncertain, that no longer defining prostitution as a crime would lead to an increase in the number of its practitioners, unless it is true that the law is so peripheral that it has no impact on the participation in prostitution. Some would take the position that a possible increase in sex workers is nobody's business but that of the workers themselves. After all, they might declare, writing cigarette advertisements hardly seems more ennobling than catering sexually for profit to a lonely, perhaps physically disabled customer.

Customers/Johns

It could be argued that the abatement of prostitution by whatever means would encourage chastity and sexual abstinence among those who now consort with prostitutes. Another view is that the absence of prostitutes for sexual activity would lead men who frequent them to other means of releasing sexual energies. Outlets could be masturbation, more intense courtship or seduction patterns, sex by force, or behavior that psychiatrists label as inhibitions and sublimations, often involving the transfer of sexual energies into nonsexual pursuits, such as the drive for power or acts of aggression—or collecting stamps.

Much discussion has centered around the possibility that the absence of prostitution would lead men to seek sexual satisfaction by force. Acts of forcible rape and prostitution may indeed share some characteristics. Both are illicit, both can include brutality, and both often seem to involve the humiliation of the female. In neither behavior is the woman viewed as a person requiring sexual satisfaction nor is she likely to achieve such satisfaction. In neither are demands for sophisticated sexual performance placed upon the male. Indeed, studies of rape report that to a very large degree the offender is impotent during the commission of the crime (Burgess and Holstrom 1974).

Customers of prostitutes—the johns—have been the recent focus in San Francisco of a program that seeks to reduce their recourse to sex-for-pay. Instead of being convicted of the misdemeanor violation of soliciting a prostitute and paying a fine or doing community service, men are offered the option of taking a class to learn about the health and social implications of the sex trade. Those who complete the class do not have their criminal offense placed on record. Prostitutes, though they are also eligible for the training, rarely elect that option (Monto 2000). As one told a district attorney, "Honey, being in that class for six hours is money."

The participants are exposed to a slide show illustrating the effects of sexually transmitted diseases, and they hear lectures from, among others, a health care worker who quit prostitution seven years ago. She relates the danger, disease, degradation, and sometimes death that follow in the wake of prostitution. "How can anyone say it is a victimless crime?" she asks scornfully. One man, interviewed after his participation in the class, summarized what he had learned: "Going to a prostitute is cheaper financially, but not emotionally. I'm going to be working on finding a real girlfriend" (Ybarra 1996).

There has been an increase in efforts to arrest johns, usually by means of police operations that employ women officers as decoys (Nolan 2001). Some johns learn that the most effective way to identify an undercover policewoman who solicits them while they are driving by is to ask the woman to get into their car. If she is a police officer, she usually is under orders not to do so because if the john drives away he can thwart the other law enforcement officers who typically stand by to make sure that no harm comes to the female cop (Dodge, Starr-Gimeno, and Williams 2005).

The usual argument in favor of decoy tactics is that "it takes two to tango," that the male is as guilty as the female and deserves the same fate (Lefler 1999). Some jurisdictions impound the cars of men who solicit streetwalkers (Hubacher 1998). It is not clear whether this is an ideological position or a sensible method for controlling or decreasing the level of prostitution. The possibility of ideology trumping cost-benefit analyses arises when the issue of abortion is broached. Would those who desire stepped-up action against the male customers of prostitutes have also encouraged the arrest of women who underwent abortions during the time that abortion was illegal in the United States, or would they advocate a focus solely on abortionists?

On some occasions, irritated citizens mount campaigns against prostitution in their neighborhood. In New Haven, Connecticut, when the police closed the downtown red-light district, prostitutes relocated in the Edgewood Park area. One resident, disgusted at seeing solicitations for sex outside his window as he ate breakfast, organized a campaign to humiliate the customers. The group drove through Edgewood Park snapping photographs of johns, prodded the police to make arrests, and displayed posters with the name and address of the man they designated as "John of the Week" (Freedman 2000, 252).

An unusual approach to prostitution exists in Sweden, where in 1999 the sexual engagement of johns with prostitutes was outlawed, though prostitution itself remained legal. The rationale for the legislation was that prostitutes should be allowed the freedom to engage in whatever reasonable activity they chose, but that prostitution represented the result of the oppression of women by men; therefore, it was the men who should be arrested. In support of the measure, the government said that "although prostitution as such is not a wanted occurrence in society, it is not reasonable to criminalize the one who, at least in most cases, is the weaker party and is used by others to satisfy their own sexual urges" (Svanström 2004, 235).

Pimps

The belief that prostitutes, streetwalkers in particular, are often exploited by pimps is one of the major items on the roster of arguments raised against the abandonment of attempts to use the law to control or at least reduce the practice of prostitution. Public attitudes toward prostitutes seem to have become increasingly tolerant, although those toward pimps remain relentlessly hostile.

The relationship between pimps and prostitutes usually represents a mutual exchange in which both parties provide and secure things important to them. To the outsider, however, the prostitute clearly seems to be giving a good deal more than she gets. There also are pimp-prostitute relationships involving underage girls in which the acts of prostitution are coerced and the females are treated as chattel. Particularly susceptible to pimp persuasion are runaways, without adequate food, clothing, and shelter. For such relationships, Neal Katyal (1993) has urged that authorities should apply the Thirteenth Amendment which prohibits slavery in order to punish the pimps and others who coerce women into prostitution.

That a pimp lives on the work of women, often several women, is by definition his condition. Some argue that to the extent that an adult female chooses of her own volition to affiliate with a pimp, the liaison should be regarded as similar to any other formed freely by two persons who have reached the age of consent. Others disagree, contending that some women need to be protected from the unpleasant and dangerous consequences of actions that they may believe are voluntary but that actually are the product of their inferior status and, in some cases, the consequence of earlier sexual abuse within their families or elsewhere.

Pimps, like sex workers, subdivide into categories. At the top are the "macks." Most pimps are "players," the main cadre in what they call "the game." On the bottom rung are "tennis shoe pimps," who often are hooked on drugs and have only one woman working for them. As Celia Williamson and Terry Cluse-Tolar (2002, 1080) point out: "A pimp's chance of gaining a woman's attention is by looking good, smelling good, flashing his possessions, and presenting himself as someone who can counter boredom with both adventure and excitement." A pimp explained his recruitment tactic to the researchers:

> She may come here with . . . nothing. Dirty, strung out. Some of them don't even have a social security card, or state ID, nothing. I ask 'em if they want something better, you know, you can make some money. I'll set you up right. Let you have a few things in your life. You wanta have nice clothes, some good jewelry, be able to have your own place, maybe a little car to drive around in? (Williamson and Cluse-Tolar 2002, 1080)

Impact of Prostitution on Society

Illegal prostitution exists in large measure as a function of the efforts of our society and its citizens to regulate sexual behavior, so that in a sense the crime of prostitution is created by attempts to prohibit it. That paradox can perhaps be best understood by imagining a society in which sexual relationships are readily obtainable by all who seek them, in whatever form. Such a society is not likely to exist any more than one in which all persons can secure whatever it is that they desire. Prostitution serves to provide something that is not otherwise available, as Kingsley Davis has indicated:

The attempt to control sexual expression, to tie it to social requirements, especially the attempt to tie it to the durable relation
of marriage and the rearing of children, or to attach men to a celi-
bate order, or to base sexual expression on love, creates the opportunity for prostitution. It is analogous to the black market,
which is the illegal but inevitable response to an attempt to control the economy. The craving for sexual variety, for perverse
gratification, for novel and provocative surroundings, for ready
and cheap release, for intercourse free from entangling cares and
civilized pretense—all can be demanded from the woman
whose interest lies solely in the price. The sole limitation on the
man's satisfactions is in this instance, not morality or convention, but his ability to pay. (1966, 360)

The impact of legal or illegal prostitution on the moral fiber of
the nation under any of the diverse kinds of arrangements suggested is one of those questions that we cannot pretend to have
adequate answers for. We can only observe that moral fibers contain a large number of strands, and that the encouragement of hy-
pocrisy by outlawing a trade that is nonetheless covertly allowed
to continue may be just as, or more, damaging to a social system
than the tolerance of lawful prostitution. So too, encouragement
of a philosophy of live-and-let-live may or may not be a contribu-
tion to democratic vitality.

Among the major reasons for supporting legalized prostitution is that it could be more readily controlled and, for that matter,
taxed. Prostitutes, like barbers, attorneys, bus drivers, or doctors,
could be licensed after required training sessions to keep up with
the latest understanding of the basic aspects of their work, and
there could be penalties imposed for violation of specified
regulations.

On the other side is the argument that uncontrolled prostitution would result in a heavy increase in public annoyance on the
streets and residential disturbances in neighborhoods in which
prostitutes ply their trade. The question of the limits that should
be imposed on public behavior poses knotty questions. People are
allowed to beg from passersby, even though it may frighten some
and annoy many. But they are not allowed to walk about un-
clothed on public thoroughfares. If their work were to be made
legal, should prostitutes nonetheless be prevented from ap-

proaching potential customers or from publicly advertising their wares in less than subtle ways? Similar questions arise in regard to houses where prostitutes carry out assignations. If efforts are made to ban them from certain neighborhoods, it is a safe prediction that they will end up among the poor and powerless, a situation that hardly seems just. The resolution of this issue, like that of begging and other public nuisances, seems far from simple.

That prostitution encourages derivative kinds of criminal activity can hardly be denied by its defenders, though they may point out by analogy that allowing kissing does not necessarily encourage illegitimate births. One might suggest that crimes derived from prostitution, such as theft from a customer, should be prosecuted vigorously.

Conclusion

If we have done our job reasonably well, the contents of this chapter should make it clear that there is no simple answer to the moral issues that pertain to prostitution. We have seen that there is considerable diversity in the forms of sex work, and a moral position regarding some aspects may not carry the day in regard to others. We can seek help by recourse to Herbert Packer's decision-making criteria that we presented in the preceding chapter, but this is not likely to provide an unambiguous outcome. Packer observes, for instance, that for it to be outlawed the conduct must be viewed by most people as socially threatening and must not be approved by any significant segment of the society. How does one determine how "significant" those who hold a particular view are? And what exactly does "socially threatening" mean?

The arguments below are those most commonly raised for and against having prostitution outlawed. Individuals will differ on what weight they might accord any one of those arguments and how they will total them up. For some, one particular item alone may be conclusive. Remember too that we have dealt only with prostitution in the United States and, passingly, in the United Kingdom and Sweden. Considerable concern exists today about the trafficking of women, particularly in Asia and Africa, and the prostitution of very young girls, most notably in Thailand. Different moral conclusions might bear on these practices more than on the domestic arrangements that have been discussed in this chapter.

We have amalgamated a number of sources to summarize the most common points made in favor of loosening legal reins on prostitution and those favoring continuing or tightening present practices. The pro-decriminalization list is largely drawn from a United Nations (1959) compilation and from arguments advanced by Nickie Roberts (1994), an Englishwoman who tells how as a youth she was coerced into sexual intercourse by a police officer who threatened to arrest her for living off the earnings of a prostitute. Her "crime" was that, as a runaway, she had been supplied with food by prostitutes. The arguments against decriminalization are an amalgam of the United Nations report and ideas set forth by John Decker (1979, 20).

For Legalizing Prostitution

1. The current laws breed corruption. Making prostitution a crime often encourages clandestine operations and control by underworld organizations.
2. The laws turn the government into the trade's biggest pimp through fines which the women have to earn by further prostitution.
3. The laws institutionalize and reinforce the whore stigma, which encourages rape and violence against prostitutes and also against other women thought to behave like them.
4. The laws are a denial of a prostitute's basic civil and human rights. They make it illegal for women to work together for safety's sake (two or more women constitute a brothel under some state laws), effectively forcing women into the streets, where they must work alone and at great personal risk.
5. Much of the taxpayers' money is wasted on prosecuting and imprisoning prostitutes. This would be better spent on improving women's lives, providing housing, health care, child care, and education.
6. Illegal prostitution often leads to police behavior that is detrimental to the common good.

7. Outlawing prostitution represents an unwarranted invasion into the private lives of persons engaging in a voluntary activity.

Against Decriminalizing Prostitution

1. It is the responsibility of the government to regulate public morals in the interest of the public good; hence, to make prostitution a punishable offense.
2. The abolition of the legal ban against prostitution will merely replace controlled prostitution by more flagrant prostitution.
3. It would be difficult to enforce regulatory provisions against prostitution, when prostitution itself is not considered a punishable offense.
4. Women and girls on the borderline will be encouraged to take up prostitution by the mere fact that it is legal.
5. The absence of laws against prostitution will be interpreted by the public as the government's support of commercialized vice as a "necessary evil."
6. Humanistic concerns for the prostitute, the prostitute's family, her children, and her customers favor outlawing prostitution.
7. Criminalizing prostitution will inhibit the commission of other crimes associated with its practice.
8. To outlaw prostitution is to reduce the presence of a public nuisance.
9. Keeping prostitution illegal is no more intrusive than to seek to protect people from self-inflicted torments and deprivations, and much the same as efforts to protect them from eating adulterated food or buying flammable pajamas.
10. Psychotherapy, medical attention, job training, educational experiences, and child support are some of the services that ought to be provided to prostitutes to move them from "the life" into "life."

That there may be a greater number of arguments on one side or the other is of no importance in resolving the debate. It is the persuasive power and the logic of the arguments, backed by enlightening research, that should prevail.

References

Addams, Jane. 1912. *A New Conscience and an Ancient Evil.* New York: Macmillan.

Albert, Alexa E. 2001. *Brothel: Mustang Ranch and Its Women.* New York: Random House.

Albert, Alexa E., David L. Warner, Robert A. Hatcher, and James Trussell. 1995. "Condom Use Among Female Commercial Sex Workers in Nevada's Legal Brothels." *American Journal of Public Health* 85:1514–1520.

Allred, Gloria, and Lisa Bloom. 1994. "Perspective on Prostitution: Prosecution or Persecution?" *Los Angeles Times,* December 6:B7.

Aquinas, Thomas. [1273]1947. *Summa Theologica.* New York: Benziger Brothers.

Augustine of Hippo. [386]1844–1864. "De Ordine." 977–1020 in Jacques-Paul Migne, ed., *Patrologiae Cursus Completus,* Series Latina. Paris: P. Geuther.

Bellis, David J. 1990. "Fear of AIDS and Risk Reduction Among Heroin-Addicted Female Street Prostitutes: Personal Interviews With 72 Southern California Subjects." *Journal of Alcohol and Drug Education* 35:26–37.

Bingham, Micloe. 1998. "Nevada Sex Trade: A Gamble for the Workers." *Yale Journal of Law and Feminism* 10:69–99.

Boyer, Edward J. 1995. "Official Business: Former Clients Testify as Heidi Fleiss Trial Begins." *Los Angeles Times* June 30:B4.

Brooks-Gordon, Belinda. 2005. *Police, Prostitutes, and Their Clients.* Cullompton, Devon, UK: Willans.

Brooks-Gordon, Belinda, and Loraine R. Gelsthorpe. 2002. "The Hiring and Selling of Bodies." 193–210 in Andrea Bainham, Shelley Day Sclater, and Martin Richards, eds., *Body Law and Laws.* Oxford: Hart.

———. 2003. "What Men Say When Apprehended for Kerb-Crawling." *Psychology, Crime and Law* 9:145–172.

Buckley, William. 1995. "Thou Shalt Not . . . What?" *National Review,* July 31:71.

Burgess, Ann W., and Lynda Lytle Holstrom. 1974. *Rape: Victims of Crisis.* Bowie, MD: Brady.

Campbell, Carole A. 1991. "Prostitution, AIDS, and Preventive Health Behavior." *Social Science and Medicine* 32:1367–1378.

Cates, Jim A., and Jeffrey Markley. 1992. "Demographic, Clinical, and Personality Variables Associated With Male Prostitution by Choice." *Adolescence* 27:695–714.

Dalla, Rochelle L. 2002. "Night Moves: A Qualitative Investigation of Street-Level Sex Work." *Psychology of Women Quarterly* 26:63–73.

Davidson, Julia O'Connell. 1998. *Prostitution, Power, and Freedom.* Ann Arbor: University of Michigan Press.

Davis, Kingsley. 1966. "Sexual Behavior." 354–372 in Robert K. Merton and Robert Nisbet, eds., *Contemporary Social Problems,* 2nd ed. New York: Harcourt, Brace, and World.

de Beauvoir, Simone. 1953. *The Second Sex.* Howard M. Parshley, trans. New York: Knopf.

Decker, John F. 1979. *Prostitution: Regulation and Control.* Littleton, CO: Fred B. Rothman.

"Divine Brown's Unpromising Career." 1995. *Tampa Tribune,* August 12:14.

Dodge, Mary, Donna Starr-Gimeno, and Thomas Williams. 2005. "Puttin' on the Sting: Women Police Officers' Perspective on Reverse Prostitution Assignments." *International Journal of Police Science & Management* 7(2):71–85.

Freedman, Samuel D. 2000. *Jews vs. Jews: The Struggle for the Soul of American Jewry.* New York: Simon & Schuster.

Freeman, Jody. 1989–1990. "The Feminist Debate Over Prostitution Reform: Prostitutes' Rights Groups, Radical Feminists, and the Impossibility of Consent." *Berkeley Women's Law Journal* 5:75–109.

Freund, Matthew, Terri Leonard, and Nancy Lee. 1989. "Sexual Behavior of Resident Street Prostitutes With Their Clients in Camden, New Jersey." *Journal of Sex Research* 26:460–478.

Frey, James H., Loren Reichert, and Kenneth Y. Russell. 1981. "Prostitution, Business and Police: The Maintenance of an Illegal Economy." *Police Journal* 54:239–249.

Gebhard, Paul H. 1969. "Misconceptions About Female Prostitutes." *Medical Aspects of Human Sexuality* 8 (March):24, 28–30.

Great Britain. 1957. *Committee on Homosexual Offences and Prostitution,* Report (Command 282). London: Her Majesty's Stationery Office.

Haskell, Molly. 1974. *From Reverence to Rape: The Treatment of Women in the Movies.* New York: Holt, Rinehart, and Winston.

Hubacher, Art. 1998. "Every Picture Tells a Story: Is Kansas City's 'John TV' Constitutional?" *Kansas Law Review* 46:551–591.

Ibrahim, Youssef M. 1996. "In Kiosks of London, Card Games Get Dirty." *New York Times,* August 17:4.

Jacobs, Andrew. 2004. "Call Girls, Updated." *New York Times,* October 12:A21.

James, Jennifer. 1977. "Prostitutes and Prostitution." 368–428 in Edward Sagarin and Fred Montanino, eds., *Deviants: Voluntary Actors in a Hostile World.* Morristown, NJ: General Learning Press.

Jenness, Valerie. 1990. "From Sex as Sin to Sex as Work." *Social Problems* 37:403–410.

———. 1993. *Making it Work: The Prostitutes' Rights Movement in Perspective.* New York: Aldine de Gruyter.

Jolin, Annette. 1994. "On the Backs of Working Prostitutes: Feminist Theory and Prostitution Policy." *Crime and Delinquency* 40:69–83.

Katyal, Neal K. 1993. "Men Who Own Women: A Thirteenth Amendment Critique of Forced Prostitution." *Yale Law Journal* 103:791–826.

Kinsey, Alfred, Wardell B. Pomeroy, and Clyde E. Martin. 1948. *Sexual Behavior in the Human Male.* Philadelphia: Saunders.

Lefler, Julia. 1999. "Shining the Spotlight on Johns: Moving Toward Equal Treatment of Male Customers of Female Prostitutes." *Hastings Women's Law Journal* 10:11–35.

Lyman, David, Warren Winkelstein Jr., Michael Ascher, and Jay A. Levy. 1986. "Minimal Risk of Transmission of AIDS-Associated Retrovirus Infection by Oral-Genital Contact." *Journal of the American Medical Association* 255:1703.

McCormick, Naomi B. 1994. *Sexual Salvation: Affirming Women's Sexual Rights and Pleasures.* Westport, CT: Praeger.

Michael, Robert T., John Gagnon, Edward O. Laumann, and Gina Kolata. 1994. *Sex in America: A Definitive Survey.* Boston: Little, Brown.

Monto, Martin A. 2000. "Why Men Seek Out Prostitutes." 67–83 in Ronald Weitzer, ed., *Sex for Sale: Prostitution, Pornography, and the Sex Industry.* New York: Routledge.

Musheno, Michael, and Kathryn Seeley. 1986. "Prostitution, Policy and the Women's Movement: Historical Analysis of Feminist Thought and Organization." *Contemporary Crises* 10:237–255.

Nolan, Thomas W. 2001. "Galateas in Blue: Women Police as Decoy Sex Workers." *Criminal Justice Ethics* 20(Winter/Spring):63–67.

Nye County v. Plankinton. 1978. 587 P.2d 421 (Nevada).

Overs, Cheryl. 1994. "Sex Work, HIV and the State." *Feminist Review* 48:110–121.

Paglia, Camille. 1994. *Vamps & Tramps.* New York: Vintage Books.

Pomeroy, Wardell B. 1965. "Some Aspects of Prostitution." *Journal of Sex Research* 1:177–187.

Primoratz, Igor. 1993. "What's Wrong With Prostitution?" *Philosophy* 68:159–182.

Radin, Margaret Jane. 1996. *Contested Commodities.* Cambridge: Harvard University Press.

Reanda, Laura. 1991. "Prostitution as a Human Rights Question: Problems and Prospects of United Nations Action." *Human Rights Quarterly* 13:202–228.

Reckless, Walter C. 1933. *Vice in Chicago.* Chicago: University of Chicago Press.

Reichert, Loren, and James H. Frey. 1985. "The Organization of Bell Desk Prostitution." *Sociology and Social Research* 69:516–526.

Remez, Lisa. 1996. "Nevada's Licensed Sex Workers Achieve Minimal Condom Breakage Rates." *Family Planning Perspectives* 28:35.

Roberts, Nickie. 1994. "The Game's Up." *New Statesman & Society* 7 (July 16):44–45.

Rubin, Gayle. 1984. "Thinking Sex: Notes for a Radical Theory of the Politics of Sexuality." 267–319 in Carole S. Vance, ed., *Pleasures and Danger: Exploring Female Sexuality.* Boston: Routledge and Kegan Paul.

Rushing, Sandra M. 1994. *The Magdalene Legacy: Exploring the Wounded Icon of Sexuality.* Westport, CT: Berin & Garvey.

Sanders, Teela. 2005. *Sex Work: A Risky Business.* Cullompton, Devon, UK: Willan.

Satz, Debra. 1995. "Markets in Women's Sexual Labor." *Ethics* 106:63–85.

Shah, Diane K. 1993. "The Hardest Working Girl in Show Business." *Esquire* 120 (November):66–73.

Surratt, Hilary L., James A. Inciardi, Steven P. Kurtz, and Marion C. Kiley. 2004. "Sex Work and Drug Use in a Subculture of Violence." *Crime and Delinquency* 50:43–59.

Svanström, Yvonne. 2004. "Criminalising the John—a Swedish Gender Model?" 225–242 in Joyce Outshoorn, ed., *The Politics of Prostitution: Women's Movements, Democratic States and the Construction of Sex Commerce.* Cambridge: Cambridge University Press.

United Nations. 1959. *Study on Traffic in Persons and Prostitution.* New York: United Nations.

Waddell, Charles. 1996. "HIV and the Social World of Female Commercial Sex Workers." *Medical Anthropological Quarterly* 10:75–82.

Weitzer, Ronald. 1991. "Prostitutes' Rights in the United States: The Failure of a Movement." *Sociological Quarterly* 32:23–41.

West, Donald J., and Buz de Villers. 1993. *Male Prostitution*. New York: Haworth.

Williamson, Celia, and Terry Cluse-Tolar. 2002. "Pimp-Controlled Prostitution: Still an Integral Part of Street Life." *Violence Against Women* 8:1074–1092.

Winick, Charles, and Paul M. Kinsie. 1971. *The Lively Commerce: Prostitution in the United States*. Chicago: Quadrangle.

Ybarra, Michael J. 1996. "A Graphic Lesson for Patrons in Fight Against Prostitution." *New York Times*, May 11:12. ✦

Chapter 3

Drugs

Angel Raich had a list of ailments a mile long. The list involved serious conditions which confined her to a wheelchair. All that changed after Ms. Raich's physician prescribed marijuana to relieve some of her discomfort. As a result, she was able to escape her wheelchair and the pain was lessened considerably. But a step up in Drug Enforcement Administration (DEA) activity resulted in raids of the homes and gardens of many in the California medical marijuana community. The community filed a lawsuit in 2002 charging U.S. Attorney General John Ashcroft and DEA Administrator Karen Tandy with violating the constitutional rights of patients.

A hearing before a United States district judge found in favor of Ashcroft and Tandy, although there appeared to be merit in the plaintiff's (Raich and others) case. So they decided to take their case to the United States Ninth Circuit Court of Appeals in San Francisco. In December 2003 the court ruled in favor of the plaintiffs, finding that the federal government's actions against them were unconstitutional. Then the government appealed, pushing the case to the U.S. Supreme Court, which heard the case on November 29, 2004.

Why all this consternation and legal activity? It relates to the deep ambivalence most Americans feel about drugs. Drugs are sometimes good things that save lives. But drugs are sometimes bad things that destroy lives. Even more ironic, we could be talking about the same drug doing each of these things, reflecting how frequently or under what circumstances the drug is used.

Throughout the country, community, law enforcement, and political leaders have for decades been questioning the current policy on drugs. Newspaper editorials, television commentaries, network news specials—one of them made by venerated former CBS news anchor Walter Cronkite—have examined the national drug policy and found it to be wanting. Opinion has spanned the political continuum, with liberals protesting over violations of individual privacy and conservatives complaining that the policy was simply ineffective.

Few issues have been more controversial than drugs, partly because many Americans are ambivalent about their usage. On the one hand, most Americans engage in drug taking on a daily basis, some several times a day. Most of the substances are legal, such as headache and cold remedies; others are illegal, such as marijuana and cocaine. Some of the legal substances are regulated by law, such as alcohol and tobacco, but are easily obtained by adults. On the other hand, most people have a fear of drugs. Many believe them to be artificial and unnatural. Others dislike the effects of many of these drugs, including the health hazards associated with alcohol and tobacco, as well as the link between alcohol and violence. Furthermore, some of the drugs cause an unwanted condition of physical dependency, or addiction. If all this were not enough, drug taking is also seen by some as immoral behavior that reflects the character, or lack thereof, of the users.

So, drugs are both good and bad, depending on which drugs, who is taking them, the conditions under which they are taken, and a host of other more personal reasons. We want it both ways, which, of course, is the essence of ambivalence.

Since the 1800s, Americans have asked legal authorities not only to resolve this ambivalence but to solve the problem of drug taking. Legislatures have employed a policy of legal repression to control, prevent, and restrict the manufacture, sale, and use of certain drugs. American policy is at odds with that in many other countries, and observers are now wondering not only whether our present approach is inappropriate but whether it can ever work. To understand the dimensions of this policy, we need to understand the scope of the drug "problem," how this problem is conceived or defined, and what alternatives are available to address it. We will begin here with a seemingly simple question: What is a drug?

What Is a Drug?

To say that drug taking is an everyday experience for many Americans fails to give meaning and scope to the importance of drugs in the United States. The word "drug" is used in a number of different contexts, and the meaning often changes with the speaker. To some, drugs are substances that cause addiction; to others, they are healing chemicals when prescribed by a medical specialist; to others, they are recreational substances to be used only in social situations; to others, they are sources of high income and substantial prestige; and to still others, they are nothing more than perfectly legal foods, such as coffee, cola drinks, and cigarettes. Who is right? They all are.

Erich Goode (2005, 23–24) says that a drug is anything we think of as or call a drug. This simple statement reflects the current confusion regarding drugs. What is a drug? A chemical? Something that alters one's mood, alters one's body, or creates a habit? Drugs are not just chemicals; everything is made up of chemicals. Drugs may alter one's moods, but there are plenty of things that alter our moods that are not commonly perceived of as drugs, such as the effect a woman wearing a perfume has on some men, or the way a man walking in a certain way affects some women. In the same respect, drugs may alter one's body, but then so does a disease, fatty foods, or a bullet in the heart. Some drugs can be habit-forming, but so can everything from a popular television show to a particular breakfast cereal to a favorite chair. Likewise, some drugs can be addicting, but not everything that is addicting is a drug; a husband and wife in a codependent relationship can be just as addicted to each other. The properties that are said to belong to drugs clearly belong to countless other things, some of which are more emotional than chemical. Consequently, the overall confusion regarding the nature of drugs and the meaning of the word "addiction" makes the very notion of "drugs" a broad subject impregnated with many different meanings.

So, while there are chemical properties to drugs, they also have social and perceptual properties. But if drugs are simply things we define as drugs, the important question becomes why some things are called drugs while others are not. We commonly consider heroin a drug but often fail to give that same label to nicotine, even though both produce physical dependency with prolonged use. We usually consider marijuana to be a drug but do not always apply the same label to cola soft drinks, even though both are used recreationally and share a number of common properties. In some respects, the definition of "drug" is not nearly as important as its connotation. The social connotation of a term refers to how it is used in society, thus its context and meaning beyond the word's formal definition. The term "drug" contains two morally opposing connotations, each of which relates to how the drug is used: (1) a substance used in medicine, under controlled circumstances, to help people with a medical problem; or (2) a substance used illegally, under clandestine circumstances, with the effect of harm either to the user and/or to others. The former connotation refers to a "normal" circumstance; the latter implies deviant drug use.

These connotations—one socially approved, the other disapproved—can be used for the very same drug, depending on the circumstances. Opiates are "good" if used under medically approved circumstances to help relieve pain in a patient. However, they are "bad" if used illegally outside a medical context and/or for physical self-gratification. To make matters even more confusing, the same individual can use drugs legally at one time and illegally at another. The medical profession has a high number of addicts compared to other professions. Medical professionals can administer a legal drug appropriately at one time, such as to a patient, and administer that same legal drug inappropriately at another time, such as to themselves to get high.

The connotations for some drugs are so powerful that they are considered deviant regardless of the medical context. Heroin, for example, is an extremely powerful painkiller that has not been approved for medical use in the United States despite the fact that it is more effective than morphine, its medical cousin. Even morphine is treated suspiciously by the Drug Enforcement Administration, which might reduce the medically proven drug to be used less by physicians who fear possible prosecution (*Omaha World-Herald*, January 16, 2005).

Contemporary concern over drugs is widespread and has often reached the level of public hysteria. The present "War on Drugs" has failed to take into account two points having to do with the overall context in which drug taking is found. First, public concern over drugs is extremely faddish. For instance, some drugs are considered to be "in" at certain times; at other times they are "out." That is, public concern about drugs focuses for a short time on a particular drug and then moves on to another, independent of any characteristic of the drug or the result of the public attention.

In the 1960s, marijuana was of great concern. In the 1970s, there was much national discussion about methaqualone or "Quaaludes" and "Angel Dust." Heroin is always in vogue in drug discussions, but it appeared to be an epidemic in the 1970s. Through the mid-1980s, cocaine and heroin were the most talked about drugs. In the 1990s, it was crack cocaine, but there is some evidence that heroin is again surfacing as a drug of choice among many users. In each instance, the law has been perceived as not only the preferred method of intervention but the most effective as well—that is, as long as the penalties are high enough.

Second, drug-taking behavior in general is so much a part of the behavioral patterns of people in the United States that it is inconceivable that all segments of the American public will abstain from all drug use. Legal drug use is so common that it is virtually unrecognized as drug use at all. Many people do not consider coffee, cigarettes, or soft drinks as drugs or substances containing drugs.

Drug taking is learned initially by most people in the context of using legally available drugs. Taking such drugs is the first time most of us experience the association between chemical substances and desired end results, such as reducing headaches, increasing bowel regularity, suppressing appetite, clearing stuffed noses, or getting better sleep at night. This connection is crucial because some of the desired end results involve certain moods that can be produced only by certain drugs, some of which are illegal.

Most of our concern with drugs has been focused on relatively few substances, most of which are against the law to use. These substances, including marijuana, heroin, cocaine, and methamphetamines, share two important characteristics: (1) we have defined them as a "problem," and (2) we believe the law is the best means to solve this problem. Both of these characteristics have been questioned, especially in recent years, and one source of that doubt is the role of all drugs in our daily lives and the ways in which illegal drugs are used.

Patterns of Drug Use

There are 50 million people in the United States who regularly smoke tobacco, and there are 5 million others who are addicted to other drugs (National Research Council 2004, 1). Drugs can heal but drugs can also kill. When most people think of the expression "cause of death," they think of the specific cause, such as heart attack or cancer. However, one can ask what caused the heart to fail or the cancer to develop. Answering the latter question gives different kinds of answers. For example, a group of researchers, using data supplied by the Centers for Disease Control and Prevention, found that when risk factors are linked with specific causes of death, a different picture emerges (Mokdad et al. 2004). Smoking was the leading cause of death, followed by poor diet and physical inactivity, alcohol consumption, motor vehicle accidents, firearms, and illicit drugs.

The influence of drugs on the everyday life of perhaps most Americans is often unrecognized. Many Americans wake up in the morning with one drug on their mind: coffee (in effect, caffeine). At work, they may feel the need for a mid-morning drug (aspirin) as pressures build, then another drug (alcohol) at lunch. A mid-afternoon break may involve a cigarette (nicotine) and a cola (more caffeine). Then cocktails (alcohol) before supper, with wine (more alcohol) perhaps during the meal. Then an after-dinner drink, followed by another cigarette (how many drugs is that for the day?). In the evening and at night, some people need pills to stay awake; others want pills to sleep. At different times during the day, we might have consumed a prescription medicine for an illness or taken some over-the-counter cold remedy to relieve congestion. The next day, the cycle starts all over again.

Drugs are connected to several features of American life (especially television commercials) that promote their use. First, as previously suggested, there is a close connection in the minds of most people between drugs and physical well-being. For example, we come to learn that various physical discomforts can be alleviated with drugs. So if you have a headache, take aspirin.

Upset stomach? Take Alka-Seltzer. Menstrual cramps? Athlete's foot? Pains of any kind? The solution to all these problems is the same: drugs.

Second, the use of a drug like alcohol is often associated with certain social and life events and just as often dissociated with any discussion of drugs, particularly among laypeople. Even the oft-used phrase "drugs and alcohol" suggests that alcohol is not a drug. Yet alcohol is a widely recognized drug, one that is frequently used in the United States. Although most people do not drink heavily, some people consume large amounts of alcohol with considerable regularity—as clearly evidenced by countless Alcoholics Anonymous meetings across the country. For many, though certainly not everyone, drinking is closely associated with particular social or religious occasions. The following are among those occasions that commonly involve alcohol consumption:

- Birthdays
- New Year's Eve celebration
- Parties
- Celebrating a job or promotion
- Getting fired or demoted
- Birth of a baby
- Wake or funeral
- Sporting events
- Dates
- Religious ceremonies
- Graduations
- Weddings
- Meals
- Hospitalization
- Recovery
- Meetings with friends
- "Night-caps"
- Saturday nights

There are as many occasions for drinking as there are for greeting cards. And of course, some people don't need any occasion at all to drink.

Third, drug taking is also closely associated with the attainment of desired moods or psychological well-being. If we happen to have a mood that we do not like, we can alter it with drugs.

Sometimes, we can generate a new mood (e.g., euphoria) or alter an existing one (e.g., depression) with the same drug. It is the mood-altering property of some drugs that has both attracted and repelled many potential users, thus adding to the ambivalence many people experience about drugs. An example of this ambivalence is reflected in a *Time* magazine cover story a few years before cocaine grabbed national headlines. The cover illustrated a martini glass filled with white powder with the caption, "Cocaine: A Drug with Status—and Menace." In the story, cocaine was described as "no more harmful than equally moderate doses of alcohol and marijuana, and infinitely less so than heroin" (Baum 1996, 142).

People are touched by drugs in virtually all areas and walks of life. Illegal drug use, formerly concentrated on the coastlines of the United States, has become a growing problem in the Midwest as well, particularly with respect to methamphetamine. In addition to spreading throughout the Midwest, crystal meth has found its way onto many American Indian reservations. The Navajo Nation, the country's largest Indian reservation, where 180,000 people live, has been flooded with a particularly pure form of crystal meth called "glass" or just "G." For as little as $20, three or four people can get an all-day high. Already suffering from intransigent poverty, alcoholism, and a 43 percent unemployment rate, tribal leaders were slow to respond, but now are planning to criminalize the drug to make prosecutions easier (Murr 2004).

Illegal Drug Use: Marijuana

Marijuana is the most widely used illicit drug in the United States, based on the percentage of the population that is known to use the drug. The manufacture, sale, and use of marijuana is a crime in the United States, although some jurisdictions have reduced the penalty for possession of a small amount of marijuana to a misdemeanor. At the other extreme, some states have historically had very severe penalties associated with the possession of marijuana, including life imprisonment. Some other countries, such as the Netherlands, make marijuana illegal but tolerate its sale.

Marijuana use patterns in the United States show that it is confined mainly to persons in their twenties and younger (Goode 2005). Much of this use is irregular, and there are many people who have tried the drug once and not repeated the experience. Experimentation and continued use among people over 35 is rare but not unheard of. Marijuana use is found in all social classes, but it may be higher in the lower class than in other socioeconomic groups. This situation may reflect differences in the choice of drugs by social class. At the present time, about a quarter of the total American population has used marijuana at least once.

There is continued concern over the use of marijuana among younger people, especially adolescents. The National Institute on Drug Abuse (NIDA) sponsors an annual survey of roughly 50,000 high school students about their self-reported drug use. These surveys—often referred to as the "Monitoring the Future Study"—report that although marijuana use has declined, a sizable proportion of high school students indicated they had used the drug at least once. In the late 1970s, more than 60 percent of all high school seniors reported they had used marijuana, but by 1994, the figure was less than one-third. The data suggest that the percentage of those who have used continues to decline. One of the reasons for this overall reduction in marijuana usage is that high school seniors have been more likely in recent years to perceive greater risk—physical, medical, or legal—in smoking marijuana than during the years of peak usage.

The most recent survey has reported a decrease both in the prevalence and daily use of marijuana; use rates today are substantially below the peak years in the late 1970s (Johnston et al. 2004). Use declined to record lows in the early 1990s, then increased by the mid-1990s. It has been decreasing since that time. This decline is not apparently related to availability since between 83 and 90 percent of each year's high school senior class has reported they could get some marijuana easily or very easily (Johnston et al. 2004, 10).

Also in decline is the percentage of students who perceive significant risk to using marijuana. As a result, it does not appear that changes in the legal penalties account for fluctuations in use among young people, but instead changes in nonlegal or social control approaches, such as the national "Just Say No to Drugs" campaign. To the extent that young people perceive health risks and/or strong social disapproval with the use of drugs, they are less likely to resort to them. Rates of disapproval of occasional marijuana use among twelfth-graders began to drop around 1992; at about the same time, rates of occasional marijuana use among these students began to increase (see also Bennett et al. 1996, 155).

The use of marijuana is essentially a group activity, lending itself to occasions that promote friendships and participation in a social setting. Marijuana is usually smoked in intimate, or primary, groups as part of a pattern of their social relations. Marijuana use contributes to long-term social relations, to a certain degree of value consensus within a group, to a convergence of values as a result of progressive group involvement, and to the maintenance of a group's cohesive nature, among other things (see Goode 2005, 242–246). These are similar to the benefits that alcohol sometimes offers to middle-class groups that use it as a "social lubricant" at a party. The group nature of marijuana use is also sometimes necessary because interpersonal contacts are needed in order to get a supply of marijuana, to learn the special technique of smoking to gain maximum effect, and to furnish psychological support for continuing to engage in an illicit activity.

Illegal Drug Use: Heroin

Patterns in the use of heroin, a narcotic, are slightly different from those of marijuana for a number of reasons, including the physical consequences of prolonged heroin use, the usual method in which the drug is used, and that law enforcement has made the criminal-law control of narcotic drug use a higher priority over the years than the social control of non-narcotic drugs.

People have used heroin for thousands of years, but patterns of heroin use have changed over time. In the nineteenth century about two-thirds of the users were women, and addiction in the medical profession was widely acknowledged (Morgan 1981). The average age of addicts was then between 40 and 50, and some investigators believed that addiction was a problem of middle age, as most addicts took up the habit after the age of 30 (Lindesmith and Gagnon 1964, 164–165).

The United States may lead all countries in the number of heroin addicts, although such estimates are always extremely speculative. Heroin use expanded in the United States during the middle of the twentieth century. The first documented widespread use in large cities was reported after 1945 (Hunt and Chambers 1976, 53). It remained at low levels through the 1950s, then increased rapidly during the 1960s (see the review in Clinard and Meier 2004, chapter 9). Levels of use seemed to reach a peak in most cities during 1968 and 1969. By 1971, all large cities—those over one million in population—had experienced their peak, although use in smaller cities continued to increase during the 1970s. Patterns throughout the 1980s suggested that the levels of addiction present in the late 1970s appeared to level off, with estimates of the number of heroin addicts in the early 1980s being close to those believed to exist in the late 1970s (Trebach 1982; 1987). Although heroin addiction was not a growing problem in the 1990s (Reuter 1995), there are still as many addicts today as there were two or three decades ago. And although the number of addicts may not be increasing, heroin appears to have become popular among young celebrities, especially in the music industry. The deaths of such musicians as Kurt Cobain and Shannon Hoon and the overdose of members of Hoon's band, "Blind Melon," all suggest that heroin may be gaining adherents once again.

Not all heroin users are addicts. Some estimates suggest there may be about 500,000 heroin addicts (persons who use heroin every day) with an additional 3.5 million "chippers" (occasional users) in this country (Trebach 1982, 3–4). Others (Goode 2005, 21) put the figure of addicts at closer to one million. The existence of so many occasional heroin users suggests that the addiction process is not simply a result of the physical properties of heroin; other factors are involved. Addiction takes place over time and appears to be facilitated by the intravenous method of administering the drug. There are disagreements on the exact causes of addiction, but there is no mistaking the difficulty of overcoming the addiction once it occurs. Rates of relapse are very high with most forms of heroin-addiction treatment.

Heroin use among persons under 20 years of age is not common. The National Institute on Drug Abuse (NIDA) national survey of high school youth typically finds that very few students report ever having tried heroin. Recent estimates place the figure at 2 percent or less depending on the grade of the student

(Johnston et al. 2004, 25). Figures of reported heroin use among young adults are also very low—1 percent or less.

Addiction to opiates is now heavily concentrated among young, urban, lower-class males from large cities, particularly among blacks and Puerto Ricans. The high heroin addiction rate among blacks is partly a product of the concentration of heroin distribution traffic in many black urban areas. This facilitates the development of a street-addict subculture. The proportion of all addicts who are black is perhaps 30 percent, with the highest concentration in the northeastern part of the United States (Chambers and Harter 1987).

The linking of the disease AIDS to the use of contaminated needles has generated substantial fear among heroin addicts. The extent of AIDS among addict populations is not known but may be very high. We do know that the percentage of addicts who have AIDS in Europe has been increasing in recent years, prompting such countries as Switzerland to set up areas in cities where addicts can obtain sterilized needles free from legal intervention. The Centers for Disease Control and Prevention estimates that most of the new AIDS cases in the United States will occur among those sharing dirty needles, not among homosexuals.

Programs of clean-needle exchange are controversial. Critics charge that such practices may encourage illegal drug use and that there is some deterrent effect from the possibility of AIDS. Supporters of such programs claim that addiction exists largely independent of AIDS and that even prolonged use of heroin does not result in major health problems, unlike the use of many other drugs. As a result, these supporters suggest that addicts have more to fear from AIDS than from their drugs; and of course, AIDS can be spread to nonaddicts.

Along with the concern over AIDS, some have worried about the impact of changes in the economics of heroin. An increase in the world supply of heroin in the 1990s has had the effect of lowering the price of the drug in many markets, including the United States. This price reduction has rendered the drug more available to a larger number of potential users than in previous decades. The purity of heroin also increased about this time, permitting users to smoke or snort the drug rather than inject it. There is no evidence, however, that the number of addicts has increased as a result of these changes in the heroin economy. In fact, there is reason to believe that it is neither economics nor criminal law that prevents most people from using heroin; rather, it is the distinct possibility and fear of addiction.

Illegal Drug Use: Cocaine

Although cocaine was first isolated in the late 1800s, there was relatively little cocaine use in the United States until the 1970s and 1980s. Long regarded as a "desirable drug" because of its euphoric effect, the dominant pattern of cocaine use was sporadic and infrequent. The main reason for its infrequent use at that time was its short supply in the United States. As a result, its cost was very high, thereby limiting its availability to people of high income. The supply of cocaine is related to the way in which the drug is obtained and processed. Cocaine is derived from coca leaves that are best grown in the high mountain jungles of Colombia and Peru. The leaves must be harvested and treated chemically to release the cocaine. Inciardi (1986, 73–74) describes the processing:

> At [secret, nearby] jungle refineries, the leaves are sold for $8 to $12 a kilo [2.2 pounds]. The leaves are then pulverized, soaked in alcohol mixed with benzol . . . and shaken. The alcohol-benzol mixture is then drained, sulfuric acid is added, and the solution is shaken again. Next, a precipitate is formed when sodium carbonate is added to the solution. When this is washed with kerosene and chilled, crystals of crude cocaine are left behind. These crystals are known as coca paste. The cocaine content of the leaves is relatively low—0.5 percent to 1.0 percent by weight as opposed to the paste, which has a cocaine concentration ranging up to 90 percent but more commonly only about 40 percent.
>
> Once processed, the cocaine is taken to port cities in South America, then to supply points in the United States. High-speed boats and aircraft are used to smuggle the drug into the country, and a sophisticated system of distribution delivers the drug to users. At each point of the manufacturing and distribution process, the cocaine is diluted with, among other things, baking soda, caffeine, and powdered laxatives. Eventually, it has an average purity of 12 percent and sells on the street for about $100 per gram. With this process, 500 kilograms of coca leaves worth

about $4,000 to the grower results in eight kilos of street cocaine worth about $500,000.

The supply of cocaine changed in the 1980s. Improved roads in the coca-growing regions in Colombia permitted the use of large trucks to bring out more leaves from the high mountain jungles. As a result, there was much more exported cocaine than ever before. This increased availability served to introduce many new users to the drug and, in turn, produced new use patterns. Some forms of the drug are now cheaply obtained. As a result, cocaine is found among all segments of the population and in all areas of the United States.

By 1985, a new form of cocaine, called "crack" (or crack cocaine), was introduced into many urban areas. It is called crack presumably because of the crackling sound it makes when smoked. The substance is manufactured by soaking cocaine hydrochloride and baking soda in water and then applying heat. This results in relatively small crystals about the size of peas. Crack had been available prior to the mid-1980s, but it became popular when it was offered as an alternative to cocaine.

There are a number of reasons for the popularity of crack (Inciardi, Lockwood, and Pottieger 1993, 7). First, it can be smoked rather than snorted, thus more rapidly absorbed into the body. It thereby offers a very quick "high." Second, crack is cheaper than cocaine. A gram of cocaine for snorting might cost $60 or more depending on its purity, but the same gram can be transformed into anywhere from five to thirty crack rocks. For the user, individual rocks can be purchased for as little as $2, depending on the size. This has helped spread the drug to the young and to poor people. Third, crack is easily hidden and transportable, which facilitates illicit transactions.

Powder cocaine, long seen as the "champagne" of drugs, produces a relatively short euphoric experience, which is a main reason why some people use multiple doses, often up to 10 doses per day (Cox et al. 1983). The user is said to suffer no ill side effects, such as hangover, physical addiction, lung cancer, risk from dirty syringes, or burned-out brain cells (Inciardi 1986, 78). The cocaine euphoria is immediate and almost universally regarded as pleasurable. Because it seemed to have few negative side effects, cocaine developed a reputation as being an "ideal" drug. In 1974, one of President Jimmy Carter's assistants claimed that "cocaine . . . is probably the most benign of illicit drugs" (Walters 1996).

There may be as many as 3 million cocaine users in the United States, most of whom are occasional users. The annual Monitoring the Future survey of drug use found that the proportion of high school seniors who had used cocaine had reached a peak of about 12 percent in 1985 and had declined since that time until the early-1990s when use increased slightly. Use has been declining gradually since then (Johnston et al. 2004, 17). By 1995, only 6 percent of high school seniors had ever tried cocaine and only 1 percent had used it during the previous month (Johnston et al. 2004). The figures are even smaller for the use of crack cocaine. Judging from what people are spending on illegal drugs, a subject to be discussed shortly, it appears that cocaine use—and the use of other illegal drugs—may be declining in the United States. A Rand Corporation study, drawing from several sources, reported a general decrease in the use of illicit drugs in the United States since the mid-1980s (Reuter 1995). The most likely explanation for this reduction is not law enforcement efforts, but is probably related more to increased social disapproval and the perceived health hazards, including the fear of diseases such as AIDS.

It is also the case that illegal drugs are expensive and the cost exerts its own preventative effect. However, the price of cocaine has declined from an average cost of $423 per gram in 1980 to $211 per gram in 2000 (Goode 2005, 283). And, while the cost has declined, the purity of cocaine has increased by perhaps as much as 70 percent.

How Much Do Illegal Drugs Cost?

America's users spend a great deal of money on their illegal drugs, as their illegal status helps keep prices high. When any commodity is illegal, there likely will be no competing manufacturers, as well as no competitive system of distribution and sales. Everything must move underground. Supplying drug users is a risky proposition. The price goes up to compensate for the risks.

It is obviously difficult to determine how much users of illegal drugs spend, but some estimates have been offered. A study by Abt Associates, Inc., released in 2001 reported that the amounts are very high (Office of National Drug Control Policy 2004). In 2000, for example, it was estimated that Americans spent $61.3 billion on the following drugs: $33 billion on cocaine, $10 billion on heroin, $10.5 billion on marijuana, $5.4 billion on methamphetamine, and $2.4 billion on other illegal drugs and illicitly sold legal drugs. These estimates do not include "income in kind" payments. Other forms of exchange also create value. Dealers often keep drugs for personal use, users sometimes help dealers in exchange for payment in drugs, and some users perform sex for drugs, particularly for crack cocaine. When these additional values are added to cash payments, the total spent on illegal drugs increases by an estimated $10 billion or more.

By any measure, these costs are staggering. Such figures are even higher when one considers that they are part of the underground economy where no overhead is assessed and no taxes are paid. They also do not include the costs of making drugs illegal, the main expenditure being the cost of drug enforcement.

The Relationship Between Crime and Drugs

People arrested for crimes frequently test positive for recent drug use (Bureau of Justice Statistics 1995). Data collected from male arrestees in 1992 in 24 cities showed that the percentage of those testing positive for drugs ranged from 42 percent to 79 percent, and for females the range was from 38 percent to 85 percent. Such figures are generally consistent with estimates obtained from the annual survey of victims in the National Crime Victimization Survey. According to the 2002 survey, over 40 percent of the victims were unable to determine whether the offender had used drugs, but in those crimes where victims believed they could make a determination, nearly 40 percent reported that the offender was under the influence of alcohol and/or drugs at the time of the crime.

Such figures point strongly to a relationship between drugs and crime, but they are not helpful in determining exactly what the nature of that relationship might be. We know that drugs are related to crime in different ways. Some crimes are defined in terms of drugs (e.g., the manufacture of illegal substances), the effects of some drugs that may be related to the commission of crimes (e.g., alcohol-based assaults), or to the lifestyle of certain drug users (e.g., committing a crime to obtain money to buy an illegal drug).

Drug-Defined Crimes

There are a number of current laws that prohibit the manufacture, sale, and consumption of particular drugs, such as heroin. In addition to illicit drugs, there are other drugs whose consumption and manufacture are merely controlled, such as alcohol and prescription medicines. Narcotics, for example, are drugs that can lead to physical dependency or addiction and are controlled and limited to medical use. The concept of "addiction" usually entails the development of tolerance, or the need for greater amounts of the drug to induce the same effect. The nonmedical use of most narcotics (other than nicotine and caffeine) is illegal in the United States. Other drugs, such as Darvon, are illegal for general use but they may be prescribed by a physician for medical purposes.

Narcotics are not the only legally prohibited drugs. Other drugs, such as hallucinogens—a category that includes marijuana, hashish, and LSD—are also illegal even though they are not narcotics. Hallucinogens are mood-altering drugs and although there are some medical uses for them, such as the treatment of certain eye disorders, their manufacture and sale are presently illegal. Stimulants (e.g., amphetamines) are closely regulated by law, and some are used for medical purposes. Still other drugs are legal, such as alcoholic beverages, but their sale or use is limited in terms of age (those over 21 years old), times (Sunday sales are not permitted in some jurisdictions), and places (e.g., taverns, but not in a moving vehicle).

The Federal Bureau of Investigation (2004, 269) recorded 1.7 million arrests in 2003 for drug violations. About two-thirds of the arrests were for possession rather than manufacture or sale, and most of the possession arrests were for marijuana. In fact, nearly half of all drug arrests were for possession of marijuana.

Drug-Related Crimes

Drug-related crimes are those in which a drug's effect contributes to the commission of a crime. Alcohol, for example, is related to certain violent crimes, including assault and murder. In his classic study of homicide, Wolfgang (1958) found that alcohol was involved in about two-thirds of the homicides he investigated. In nearly 40 percent of the cases, both the offender and the victim had been drinking. Alcohol is also a factor in many instances of domestic violence and assaults. Oliver (1994, 15–16) summarizes the results of a number of studies that link alcohol and drugs with violent conduct, including homicide, assault, and robbery. It is clear that the use of alcohol and certain drugs facilitates the commission of other crimes.

The effects of drugs may also be related to crime in another sense. Some crimes are motivated by the need of the offender to obtain money to support continued drug use. Heroin addicts, for example, require substantial sums of money to purchase their drug, but the typical heroin addict is unable to raise the sums needed for a number of compelling reasons (see Stephens 1991). First, because heroin is illegal, the price is high; dealers are willing to risk arrest and imprisonment, but the rewards must be significant. This drives the price up. Second, most addicts do not have the kind of legitimate occupations that will generate enough income for their drugs. They do not have high levels of education or sophisticated job skills. Third, the lifestyle of the addict revolves around taking, enjoying, tolerating, or withdrawing from drugs. As a result, most addicts have neither the money, abilities, nor time to cope with their addiction without resorting to crime. Stealing (and, for some women, prostitution) requires little long-term commitment and if successful, provides an immediate return with which to obtain their drug.

Drug-Using Crimes

Many drug-users are recreational or occasional users of drugs, but others exist in a lifestyle that centers around drugs. Some criminologists have long observed that one of the most undesirable consequences of drug laws is that they drive drug users underground and into contact with more serious criminals. Because of their participation in a drug-using subculture, they are exposed to further criminal opportunities. Some of these opportunities will be important in providing money to purchase more drugs.

The distinction between "drug user" and "drug distributor" is often blurred. Although the terms "kingpin" and "pusher" suggest that those who manufacture or distribute illegal drugs are different from those who use them, this distinction is difficult to maintain on the streets. Many heroin addicts will also distribute the drug to other users in exchange for a personal supply of the drug, and most marijuana smokers appear to be both users and dealers with their friends.

Current Drug Policies and How We Got There

The overall policy in the United States with respect to drugs is one of legal repression. That is, the United States relies primarily on the criminal law to control the supply of many drugs and to bring drug users together with treatment programs to reduce demand. The criminal law is at the core of the basic policy regarding drugs, although many of the goals of this policy cannot be achieved through the law.

Current drug policy reflects the repressive actions taken in earlier years. Drug efforts during the Reagan and George H. Bush presidencies were sporadic but concentrated generally on interdiction. The use of military personnel, primarily the Coast Guard, and a reliance on the DEA constituted the main weapons against drugs, although treatment was not neglected completely. First Lady Nancy Reagan, for example, was instrumental in facilitating a series of drug-treatment programs utilizing space in local hospitals. These so-called "care units" were short-term programs of usually one month or less. When President Bush took office in 1988, he continued the theme, begun in the Reagan years, of "Just Say No!" to drugs.

The Office of National Drug Control Policy (ONDCP) strategy under President Clinton maintained a focus on reducing both supply and demands for illicit drugs; about two-thirds of the budget for the plan dealt with reducing supply, about one-third with increasing treatment and preventative efforts. There was particular attention to methamphetamines, an addictive stimulant whose use has been increasing in some parts of the country, especially rural areas. The plan called for mandatory minimum sentences for the sale of methamphetamines, sentences equivalent to those presently imposed for crack cocaine.

The Clinton ONDCP policy was a product of a particular political time and climate, though the policies of previous administrations were very similar. The Bush and Reagan presidencies, for example, also laid heavy emphasis on the use of law enforcement and military personnel to interdict drugs from coming into the United States. President Clinton attempted to balance a bit more than did Bush and Reagan the extent to which the focus should be on reducing demand for drugs rather than attempting only to reduce the supply. But the difference was a matter of degree.

The ONDCP under President George W. Bush states that the overarching goal for the current drug control strategy is the reduction of the number of drug users in the United States (Office of National Drug Control Policy 2004). The strategy outlines various major goals that are categorized and demands reduction in part by stopping use before it begins, the treatment of existing drug users, and disrupting the market of drugs by attacking the economic basis of drug trafficking. Although not all the specific objectives within each of these broad categories would entail the use of law enforcement (e.g., expansion of treatment facilities for addicts), the law is the primary weapon in drug control strategy. As such, the current drug policy essentially continues the policies of the last several decades with only slight changes.

Most drug violations and arrests occur at the state, not the federal, level. Has state interest in drug use declined? No, in fact, laws dealing with drug trafficking and use have become more harsh over time. Ask Ronald Allen Harmelin. He was arrested in Michigan for possession of 672 grams of cocaine, convicted, and sentenced to life imprisonment without the possibility of parole (Friedman 2004, 116). The U.S. Supreme Court in 1991 rejected Harmelin's appeal that the sentence was cruel and unusual punishment. Since Michigan has no death penalty, killing an entire family and owning a pound of cocaine can be treated as equal crimes in that state.

Not only have punishments for drug crimes become harsher over time, there have been attempts to reduce the discretion of judges in these cases. Many of the drug laws prescribe mandatory sentences, while some prohibit probation and parole.

Drugs, Race, and Ethnicity

American awareness of drug taking, and the subsequent rise in a legal response to this behavior, began in the 1800s, at a time when many patent medicines contained what would later be considered illegal drugs, particularly opiate derivatives (Inciardi 1986, chapter 1). These drugs, as well as raw opium, were widely used in the nineteenth century in the United States, particularly by women who took them for "female disorders." At that time, many of the drugs could be easily and legally purchased. Two important drugs are derived from opium—morphine, a potent drug that was isolated initially in 1804, and heroin, which is about three times more powerful than morphine, first isolated in 1898. In fact, heroin was originally manufactured by pharmaceutical chemists to be sold over drugstore counters as a cough remedy. Cocaine was first isolated in the late 1850s, but it did not become popular in the United States until the 1880s, when it was proclaimed a wonder drug and sold in wine products as a stimulant (Morgan 1981, 16).

Even the intravenous ingestion of morphine was not uncommon at the time. The 1897 edition of the Sears Roebuck catalog, for example, contained hypodermic kits that included a syringe, two needles, two vials, and a carrying case. The cost: $1.50. Extra needles were available for 25 cents or $2.75 per dozen (Inciardi 1986, 5–6).

As shocking as this may seem by today's antidrug standards, it was not this kind of drug taking that was of major public concern. That concern was later motivated not by the drugs themselves but by the kinds of people who used them. Some of the initial laws against drugs were directed at particular groups of opiate users, such as the Chinese and Mexicans. Patterns of opiate use were quite different around the turn of the century than they are in present-day cities.

One of the earliest laws on opiates was passed in 1875 in the city of San Francisco. It prohibited the smoking of opium in then-popular opium dens (Brecher 1972). The law was fueled by the public fear that Chinese men were luring white women into these dens for sexual purposes. Few Americans understood that opium dens occupied roughly the same position in Chinese culture as that of the saloon in white American culture. Although there were some opium addicts, most Chinese used opium infrequently and mainly on social occasions.

This first law displayed a number of characteristics that would be found in many of its successors: It prohibited the use of a particular drug associated with a particular group, without apparent regard to the physiological properties of the drug. In other words, it was not the physical effects of the opium or opiate derivatives that concerned lawmakers, but—in this case—the use of the drug by the Chinese.

The racial nature of the law was reflected in a number of its ingredients. The law ignored opium and other products made from opium that were used by whites in over-the-counter substances and in different forms (i.e., liquid, powder, or pill form). Instead, it focused on the smoking of opium in specially designated areas (i.e., opium dens). In other words, one could consume opium, but not by smoking and not in dens.

Federal drug legislation followed this city ordinance in 1888. As with the San Francisco law, the federal legislation attempted to restrict opium trading and smoking. As with the city ordinance, the federal law did not prohibit the use of opium itself, only how it was consumed; it did not prohibit the sale and use of opium in the form that was used by most whites and it did not restrict the actions of whites engaged in the opium trade.

There was apparently little concern with drug addiction in the late 1800s, at least no more than with drunkenness. But social awareness of addiction increased in the first quarter of the twentieth century. That concern eventually generated legislation, such as the Pure Food and Drug Act of 1906 and the Harrison Narcotics Act of 1914. The intent of the Pure Food and Drug Act was to regulate the manufacture of patent medicines and over-the-counter drugs that contained heroin and cocaine. The intent was to centralize the control of drugs in the medical profession which would issue prescriptions for the drugs only for "legitimate medical use" (Friedman 2004, 102) But the effect of the law was to make such substances illegal. The Harrison Act was initially a revenue measure designed to make drug transactions a matter of public record so that taxes could be paid on them. But it became a major piece of legislation that defined narcotic drug taking as illegal (which included cocaine as a narcotic, although it is not a narcotic) and defined as criminals all those who took those drugs.

One might think that the intent of the legislation was to control addiction, but it was not merely the fear of addiction that fueled this legislation. Samuel Gompers, president of the American Federation of Labor from 1886 to 1924, used racist imagery to accelerate drug legislation. Herbert Hill writes:

> Gompers conjures up a terrible picture of how the Chinese entice little white boys and girls into becoming "opium fiends." Condemned to spend their days in the back of laundry rooms, these tiny lost souls would yield up their virgin bodies to their maniacal yellow captors. "What other crimes were committed in those dark fetid places," Gompers writes, "when these little innocent victims of the Chinamen's wiles were under the influence of the drug, are almost too horrible to imagine. . . . There are hundreds, aye, thousands, of our American girls and boys who have acquired this deathly habit and are doomed, hopelessly doomed, beyond the shadow of redemption." (1973, 51)

Subsequent legislation broadened the definition of illegal drugs to include marijuana and hashish. Because it does not dissolve in water, marijuana cannot be injected; it must be taken orally by smoking and eating, and its effects are variable and slow. As a result, research on the medical use of marijuana never materialized to the degree of research on opiate drugs and cocaine. Even today, although there is reason to believe that marijuana might be useful in some limited medical situations, it does not have the cloak of medical legitimization worn by many other drugs. Noteworthy, though, was the passage of referendums in 1996 in both Arizona and California to allow marijuana use on a doctor's order to ease pain, such as that associated with cancer. Early in 1997, Attorney General Janet Reno announced that federal agents would withdraw drug-prescribing privileges and perhaps criminally prosecute physicians who "pushed" marijuana for their patients on the basis of the new California and Arizona statutes. Reno maintained that the referendums represented illegal intrusion by the states into a matter controlled by federal law.

As with other drugs that were subsequently made illegal, marijuana use was associated initially with marginal social groups. Large-scale use around the turn of the century was reported among migrant workers in the American Southwest. Eventually, as marijuana users migrated to urban areas, its use spread to other urban immigrant groups, such as African Americans. Some occupational groups were closely associated with marijuana; jazz musicians, for example, reportedly had especially high rates of marijuana use through the 1920s and 1930s. Spurred by the vigorous campaign of Harry Anslinger, commissioner of the Treasury Department's Bureau of Narcotics, marijuana legislation was not long in coming. The use of marijuana outside the mainstream of white, middle-class society, and the lobbying efforts of the Bureau of Narcotics resulted in the Marijuana Tax Act of 1937.

The racist motivation of this early legislation is unmistakable, as is the fear generated by certain drugs. Throughout the twentieth century, it has been the characteristics of users, not those of the drugs, that have been the better predictors of drug laws.

The Prohibition Experience

During the first part of this century, the United States experienced a major effort to control drugs by the use of criminal law. The first, and most important, was the enactment of the Eighteenth Amendment to the Constitution, popularly known as "Prohibition." It prohibited the production, sale, and distribution of alcohol for purposes of consumption and remained in effect from 1920 to 1933. Prohibition resulted from the efforts of groups of citizens who became moral crusaders seeking to persuade others of the sins of alcohol consumption and the need to enact the law to solve the problem. Public drinking, often done in taverns and largely concentrated among lower-class citizens, was the immediate target for temperance groups. These groups believed strongly that alcohol consumption was bad for both people and their behavior. Drinking was also condemned as a reflection of the absence of moral values.

Motivated less by racial than by class and moral differences, prohibition was controversial at the time and has remained so today. It is claimed by some that Prohibition was a failure, that it was unable to stop the consumption of alcoholic beverages, and that in various ways it made drinking problems worse. Others claim that Prohibition, while not successful in every respect, did accomplish much to reduce problems associated with heavy drinking.

Regardless of one's position on the consequences of Prohibition, our interest lies in the use of the law to solve drug problems, including those related to alcohol, marijuana, heroin, and cocaine. There are a number of arguments that have been raised against a legal solution to drug and alcohol problems. The major ones are summarized here with respect to Prohibition, but most of them are applicable as well to the legal prohibition of other drugs and, in fact, other so-called "vices." These arguments, adapted from McWilliams (1993, 70–79), are listed as follows:

1. *Prohibition created disrespect for law.* Prohibition was immediately unpopular among many different types of individuals, particularly those involved in the manufacture, distribution, sale, and consumption of alcoholic beverages, who found obvious and self-interested fault with the legislation. But so too did many others, including those who did not drink frequently or heavily. Their objections reflected a different position on the use of alcohol. Those who did not believe that drinking was wrong, and those who violated the law because of that belief, may have extended their negative feelings about Prohibition toward other laws as well. As a result, many otherwise law-abiding citizens broke the law.

2. *Prohibition eroded respect for organized religion.* The Prohibition movement was essentially a middle-class Protestant movement. Bolstered by biblical pronouncements regarding the misuse of alcohol, as well as a faith in the ability of Protestantism to create a better world, Prohibitionists justified their actions not only in terms of reducing a social problem (i.e., alcoholism), but also on the basis of high moral principle (Timberlake 1963, chapter 1). Prohibitionists made much of the terrible toll drinking took upon the drinker's family and employer. What they might have underestimated was the number of people who drank alcoholic beverages without the kind of costs in-

curred by such heavy drinkers as alcoholics. And as Prohibition failed, it undercut organized religion, which was considered responsible for its unsuccessful policy.

3. *Prohibition greatly expanded the power of organized crime.* Organized criminal syndicates existed in the United States prior to Prohibition, but their activities were confined to local areas and their operations limited. With the advent of Prohibition, these syndicates expanded their horizons and increased their power by meeting the demands of those segments of the public eager to drink. Some syndicates, such as those in Chicago, became very wealthy and their leaders extremely powerful, not only in matters of organized crime but in politics as well.

4. *Prohibition corrupted the criminal justice system.* Police, judges, and correctional personnel were contaminated by organized crime's exploitation of Prohibition and the money earned from it. Criminal justice officials were often bribed to look the other way in regard to bootleggers and others involved in the illegal alcohol trade. In some instances, the high profits that syndicates generated underwrote a long-lasting relationship with criminal justice officials that would extend well beyond the period of Prohibition.

5. *Prohibition overburdened the criminal justice system.* The caseload of criminal justice systems in many jurisdictions escalated as a result of Prohibition. Although this is almost inevitably true for any newly outlawed behavior, the volume of alcohol cases was extremely high during the 1920s, particularly in the larger cities. And as criminal justice officials attempted to deal with the increase in cases of bootlegging, illegal distribution, and illegal sales, these alcohol-related cases kept officials from dealing with other, more serious crimes.

6. *People were harmed financially, emotionally, and morally by Prohibition.* In 1919, those legitimately involved in alcohol production, distribution, and sales were put out of work. It happened quickly, although not without warning, as many jurisdictions had already enacted "local options" that prohibited saloons and alcohol by the drink. Nevertheless, the tsunami of Prohibition sometimes drowned

those in the restaurant, sporting, and entertainment industries. It took several decades for these industries to rebound after Prohibition, in large part because the end of Prohibition coincided with the beginning of the Great Depression.

7. ***Prohibition caused physical harm.*** It is often overlooked that Prohibition in fact physically harmed some people. With only illegally manufactured distilled spirits to drink, there were those who consumed beverages that were poorly made. Some of the people who made illegal alcohol, often in their bathtubs and under less than sanitary and scientifically controlled circumstances, manufactured it incorrectly, putting together concoctions that were deadly. Consumers had no way of knowing the quality of the alcoholic beverages they were consuming.

8. ***Prohibition changed the drinking habits of the country— for the worse.*** Before Prohibition, Americans were mainly beer drinkers. Some consumed wine, but few were frequent distilled liquor drinkers. After Prohibition, however, more people drank hard liquor. Perhaps as a protest against the law, drinking became more open; the advent of the liquor flask can be traced to Prohibition. Alcohol became something to take along because one could not depend on finding a source at one's destination. Prohibition also changed drinking habits; whereas before, most beer drinking was done at home, now it became more popular in public places.

9. ***Prohibition contributed to cigarette smoking as a national habit.*** The original use of tobacco can be traced to the first colonists, but pipe and cigar smoking were the most popular forms of tobacco usage until about the turn of the century. Cigarettes grew in popularity after the Civil War, though there was both health and moral concerns about their use. These concerns led to legislation prohibiting cigarette smoking, particularly among young people. By 1921, cigarettes were illegal in 14 states and bills were pending in 28 others (McWilliams 1993, 77). During Prohibition, smoking had become a symbol of independence, glamour, and sophistication. By 1930, cigarettes were legal virtually everywhere—and as their consumption doubled

between 1920 and 1930, they became as irresistible as alcohol (Troyer and Markle 1983, 34).

10. ***Prohibition prevented the treatment of drinking problems.***
When the Prohibitionists succeeded in making alcohol illegal, there was no standard of moderate drinking; any drinking was considered deviant. As Timberlake (1963, 184) notes, "In trying to impose a rigid standard of sobriety on the entire nation by law they had undertaken something that the working classes would not accept and that they themselves would often not obey." Prohibition greatly undermined the notion of moderation, itself an important restraint on drinking.

11. ***Prohibition caused "immorality."*** Prohibition did not stop drinking, although it did put a dent in it. Not everyone violated the law, but many did. Drinking moved underground; it flourished in speakeasies, which were often not only taverns but also places of "ill repute," where the indulgence of other vices was possible, such as gambling, the use of other drugs, and prostitution. The availability and consumption of drugs other than alcohol also increased during Prohibition, largely because drinking had been outlawed.

12. ***Prohibition was very expensive.*** It is difficult to estimate accurately the costs of Prohibition. The total cost would include money used to find alternative employment for those put out of work by Prohibition and the criminal justice costs of enforcing the laws. One such estimate is that Prohibition cost one billion dollars at a time when assembly line workers at the Ford Motor Company were earning $5 a day.

Modern Legal Prohibitions

Prohibition was an expensive and disappointing experience for the United States. Although it probably did curtail drinking for many, including those who had problems with their drinking prior to its enactment, the overall costs of the policy appeared to outweigh the benefits. One lesson learned from Prohibition was the importance of using the law in instances in which public opinion is consistent with its dictates. Just like unpopular wars, unpopular laws are likely to encounter substantial difficulties.

Conventional images of the law as a powerful entity that can coerce conformity without popular support are incorrect. It is too simplistic to assert that law comes about because most people want it, but it does seem to be the case that there are many laws that cannot exist independently of the people whose behavior they regulate. Prohibition exemplifies this principle, and current drug laws may be another illustration of it.

Since 1970, drug penalties in many jurisdictions have abated, but only for marijuana. Penalty increases have been fast and furious for most other illegal substances, particularly heroin, cocaine, and methamphetamines. In the 1980s and 1990s, fueled by public fears of a drug "menace," many states and the federal government instituted mandatory penalties. These statutes were part of a larger movement to reform criminal justice sentencing procedures by reducing judicial discretion over sentencing. Many states shifted from indeterminate to determinate sentencing, with some establishing a set of sentencing guidelines to determine actual disposition. The effect in many states, as well as in the federal system, has been to lengthen actual time served in prison and to alter the demographic and offense-pattern composition of prison inmates.

In 1980, 57 percent of all state and federal prisoners were incarcerated for a violent crime. Thirty percent were in prison for property offenses, 8 percent for drugs, and 5 percent for public order crimes (Beck and Gilliard 1995). By 1993, only 45 percent of state and federal prisoners were incarcerated for violent crimes, 26 percent for drugs, 22 percent for property offenses, and 7 percent for public order crimes. The composition of inmates had changed because of alterations in sentencing practices that placed higher priority on drug offenders. Today, there are more inmates who are incarcerated for violent crimes than for any other offenses (47 percent), but there are fewer of them than in either 1980 or 1993; whereas, the number of drug offenders has more than tripled. The new drug laws have been a substantial contributor to prison overcrowding throughout the United States (Pollock 2004, 43).

Between 1980 and 1993, there was clear recognition that drug usage was related to other, more general conditions, and in fact, that those conditions—often called "root causes"—should really be the focus of intervention efforts. When asked to prepare a report on the root causes of drug abuse, William Bennett, the drug czar during President Reagan's administration, sidestepped the issue. The request recognized that drug use was related to larger problems of poverty, inadequate education, and a host of other social ills. Bennett replied, "We have a drug problem . . . [but] we don't have the time or authority to fix the housing or jobs or poverty problems" (Baum 1996, 302). Looking at the root causes of drug use would only dilute the focus on drugs, Bennett reasoned, and going beyond that focus was outside the mandate of the drug office. In addition, of course, focusing only on drugs was a good deal easier than trying to deal with the other social conditions that give rise to them.

The Netherlands' Approach to Drug Control

Drugs have long been regarded as a problem in the Netherlands, as in many other countries, but a different approach has been taken. The Netherlands has a population of 15 million people, 90 percent of whom live in cities. The largest city is Amsterdam, with a population of 700,000. There are an estimated 21,000 addicts in the Netherlands, 7,000 of whom are clients of methadone maintenance clinics. It appears that cocaine use is relatively low and has been stable over recent decades, and the use of "crack" cocaine is infrequent. Cocaine use is mainly experimental or recreational. Marijuana is the most frequently used illicit drug. The main objective of the Netherlands' drug policy is to restrict as much as possible the risks of drug use to the users themselves, their immediate environment, and society as a whole. Principle attention is directed toward the users. The policy appears to conceive of drug use in medical rather than legal terms. The law is obviously considered important in dealing with drugs in the Netherlands, but considerable value is likewise attached to strongly organized informal social control. Although risks to society are taken into account—and it is here where the law is most useful—the government attempts to ensure that drug users are not further harmed by prosecution and imprisonment. The Dutch policy continuously seeks to strike the right balance between protecting drug addicts and protecting the community.

This philosophy can be contrasted with American policy. In the United States, drug policy is driven by a similar goal, the reduction of use; but unlike in the Netherlands, the U.S. policy conceives of drug use as it does other crimes, as a freely chosen behavior that can be reduced by legal coercion. There is no recognition that conceiving drug use only in legal terms denies its medical and social context. There is also no recognition in U.S. policy that the use of the law can do harm to users.

The possession, transport, trafficking, manufacture, and sale of illicit drugs in the Netherlands is identified in the 1919 Opium Act, first revised in 1976. The consumption of illicit drugs is not illegal. The act attempts to distinguish users from traffickers. Possession of illegal drugs does not automatically involve a serious penalty in the absence of evidence of intent to sell.

The Dutch Code of Criminal Procedure has a provision called the "expediency principle," which provides the Public Prosecutions Department with the power to refrain from instituting criminal proceedings if there are believed to be weighty public interests against doing so. In the words of the Code, prosecution is to be avoided in certain cases "on grounds deriving from the general good." Guidelines have been established for detecting and prosecuting offenses under the Opium Act. The guidelines contain recommendations of penalties to be imposed and set out the priorities to be observed in detecting and prosecuting offenses. International drug trafficking has the greatest priority; possession of drugs the lowest. Whether possession cases should be prosecuted and, if so, to what degree, is a matter of discretion for the prosecutor. The Dutch Government directs responsibility for drug use to communities.

A major part of the Netherlands antidrug strategy is drug education. Information on the risks of drug use and the use of alcohol and tobacco are to be presented together. School prevention programs are directed toward potential drug users. Knowledge about the health risks of using certain drugs is often sufficient to prevent the drug's use. But drug education is not enough, and parents and the general citizenry are also requested to help potential drug users to identify drug risks.

Research conducted by the Dutch government on the lifestyles of heroin users has generated a new appreciation for the complexity of drug taking. While some people who use drugs will eventually become addicted to them, others are able to take drugs, including opiates, on an occasional, experimental, or recreational basis. This is similar to the observation about heroin use in the United States. There are clearly many different types of users with many different lifestyles. This Dutch research has also called into question the possibility of prevention of addiction by means of drug information only. Preventing occasional users from becoming frequent users or addicts is considered extremely important. The idea that preventing problems that accrue from the use of drugs is accordingly given at least equal emphasis as preventing the initial use of drugs.

A related problem is the spread of diseases, such as AIDS, among intravenous drug users. The Dutch government has instituted a clean-needle exchange to remove dirty needles from circulation. Needle exchanges are run from methadone maintenance programs, as well as by various municipalities. The report indicates that in 1992, one million syringes were exchanged in Amsterdam alone. While there is no illusion that needle exchange programs will alone contain AIDS cases among drug addicts, it is one avenue toward reduction. In addition to needle exchanges, "persuasive face-to-face counseling, in order to change addicts' risky behavior in favor of safer practices, is essential" (Ministry of Welfare, Health and Cultural Affairs 1994, 5).

In view of the greater sensitivity to various forms of drug taking, the report also says that "the Dutch government believes that drug use should be shorn of its taboo image and its sensational and emotional overtones. The image of the user and addict should be demythologized and reduced to its real proportions, for it is precisely the stigma, paradoxically enough, that exercises such a strong attraction on some young people" (Ministry of Welfare, Health and Cultural Affairs 1994, 5).

The primary weapon against drugs in the Netherlands is interpersonal intervention. Drug treatment for those who are addicted is considered essential. This treatment is administered outside the Dutch criminal justice system. The central agency for this work is the Medical Consultation Bureaus for Alcohol and Drug Problems (CADs). The CADs are autonomous, nongovernmental institutions, the entire costs of which are paid by the government.

The CADs are also active in the field of probation; one aspect is the initial reception of drug addicts in police stations, where an effort is made to establish contact that may lead to the acceptance of further aid during and after detention. Although the CADs primarily provide nonresidential mental health care, their services are oriented toward social work, as the majority of their staff (approximately 900 in all) are social workers. The objectives of individual CADs may vary from kicking the habit (drug-free) to stabilizing the functioning of addicts by supplying the substitute drug methadone on a "maintenance basis" (stable dosage). "Reduction based" methadone programs are also applied (gradually reduced dosages to nil). A variety of methods are used, including psychotherapy, group therapy, material assistance, family therapy, counseling, and advising groups of parents. An increasingly important area of the CADs' work is prevention, including AIDS control (i.e., needle exchange, information, and education). The Dutch approach thus employs a conception of drug taking, especially addiction, that does not fit the kinds of problems that the law typically addresses. Drug use is considered to be a community problem, and the solution must be sought via nonlegal means. Even those addicts who are in the Dutch criminal justice system are seen as candidates for intervention.

What Kind of a Problem Is 'Drugs'?

The Netherlands' approach is an example of a policy that conceives of drug usage as a problem more appropriate for other institutions and other social control mechanisms than law. Although most people in the United States would identify illicit drug taking as a problem, there is disagreement on what kind of problem it is. To some, drugs are a problem for criminal law, like theft, interpersonal violence, and fraud. To others, drugs represent more of a social or medical problem, one better addressed by community action, better parenting, and medical treatment. The appropriate policy follows from how one defines the problem.

Interestingly, although it might be expected that criminal justice officials advocate only a legal solution for drugs, this is not always the case. To inform policymakers about the law enforcement position on drugs, a "Law Enforcement Summit" was held in May

1995, involving the leaders of more than 50 law enforcement agencies. Former Secretary of State George Shultz and several federal judges spoke. Schultz denounced the Drug War as wrong-headed and not making sense economically.

Baltimore Mayor Kurt Schmoke, the main speaker, was invited because the city of Baltimore had decided to formulate its drug problem in terms that emphasized that drugs are a social, not a legal, problem. Joseph McNamara, former chief of police of both Kansas City and San Jose, asked Schmoke how a medical approach used in Baltimore went over politically in that city. The response was said to be as follows:

> I go to meet with people in the community, and I ask them three questions: Do you think we've won the Drug War? And people just laugh. Do you think we're winning the Drug War? And people just shake their heads. And the third question is, If we keep doing what we're doing now, in 10 years, will we have won the Drug War? Clearly, it is a rhetorical question. (*Baltimore Sun* January 24, 1996)

After this meeting, the Baltimore police commissioner announced that his department would de-emphasize arrests for possessing small quantities of drugs. Instead, the police would focus their energy on gun possession and gun violence. The commissioner was careful not to call his policy change an instance of decriminalization, but it was clearly based on the view that the war on drugs cannot be won by relying only on criminal law. "What impacts on the quality of life in this city," proclaimed a mayor's office spokesperson, "is not people taking drugs, but the violence associated with the drug trade" (*Baltimore Sun*, January 24, 1996).

Using the Baltimore approach as a focal point, the Law Enforcement Summit concluded with a survey of participants, of which more than 90 percent agreed that the legal war on drugs was a failure, a battle that could not be won with available resources. "The group was unanimous in saying," according to McNamara, "more treatment and more education would be more effective than more arrests and prisons." Furthermore, McNamara reported that "the group was unanimous in calling for a blue-ribbon panel to study the harm done by the Drug War and alternative methods of dealing with drugs" (*Baltimore Sun*, January 24, 1996).

The consequences of the drug war extend well beyond the immediate circumstances of making, selling, and using illegal drugs. One such consequence is the corruption that infests the criminal justice system as a result of the high profits in certain drugs. McNamara (1995) identified specific examples. The former police chief of Detroit was sent to prison for stealing drug funds. A number of sheriffs throughout the country have been convicted of dealing in drugs. The former untouchables, the "feds," now have officers in jail for drug offenses. The DEA agent who arrested General Noriega, the former leader of Panama who was implicated in drug trafficking, was arrested and imprisoned for stealing laundered drug money. In another case, an FBI agent stole drugs from the evidence room and mailed samples to regional drug dealers so they could determine the purity of the product and the appropriate price. McNamara (1995, 43) tells of other scandals:

> In New Orleans, a uniformed cop in league with a drug dealer has been convicted of murdering her partner and shop owners during a robbery committed while she was on patrol. In Washington, D.C., and in Atlanta, cops in drug stings were arrested for stealing and taking bribes. New York State troopers falsified drug evidence that sent people to prison.

Drugs are not only outlawed, they are outlawing and corrupting, much like alcohol during Prohibition. Clearly, the war metaphor has generated bad police practices, partly because everything is fair in war. The rationalization of crooked cops is that criminals are the enemy and should not profit. Some police feel justified in using questionable or illegal methods against drug dealers and users because, as McNamara says, "It's a war, after all" (1995, 57).

The consequences of the drug war are far-ranging and subtle. Increasingly, local and federal police agencies and other criminal justice organizations are being met with suspicion and distrust in the community. Some of this distrust involves high-profile cases, such as the Rodney King and O. J. Simpson cases. In the Rodney King case, the police were clearly involved in illegal activities against a defendant, whereas in the Simpson case, allegations of police misconduct by a racist police officer may have been instrumental in Simpson's acquittal. But a further cause of this distrust is related to the perceived unfairness of law enforcers, most of which is concentrated in groups against which the police have been the most aggressive: the inner areas of large metropolitan cities, mainly populated by African Americans. Confidence among whites has not declined as much, largely because the kinds of drugs that are the objects of current law enforcement are not found in white neighborhoods.

Further evidence of the ineffectiveness of current drug laws is reflected in a recent poll of policy administrators. Every three years or so, the National Institute of Justice conducts the National Assessment Program, which attempts to identify the needs and problems in criminal justice agencies around the nation. Almost all police chiefs and sheriffs (95 percent) claim that drug possession and sales are creating workload problems, primarily because of the increased number of cases (McEwen 1995). In most communities, the drug problem is coming to dominate law enforcement operations. More than 75 percent of police departments have created special community programs and crime units focusing on drugs. Not only is the war on drugs not being won, it has not even achieved a stalemate.

Decriminalization Does Not Solve the Problem of Drugs

One way to deal with the problems caused by the criminalization of drugs is to declare a truce: decriminalize drugs that are now illegal. Although such a policy might go a long way to reduce some problems, it leaves untouched those that gave rise to much legislation in the first place. Drug use has many undesirable consequences both for users and society at large, regardless of the particular substance. The use of some drugs involves health risks which are serious and of long-term duration. Some drug use interferes with the building and development of satisfying social and personal relationships with others. Some drug use interferes seriously with an individual's ability to find and hold meaningful employment, as well as reducing work productivity. Some drug use is associated with the commission of other crimes, some of which are the direct result of drug use (e.g., when the crime was committed because the offender was "high") while others are indirectly related to drugs themselves (e.g., an assault over a drug transaction). Some drug use is associated with a lifestyle from which most people wish to escape—polydrug use (alcohol, marijuana, tobacco, and others), poverty, discrimination, and living in crowded conditions.

Furthermore, the call to decriminalize often disguises troubling questions. Are all drugs to be legal? Even crack cocaine (Inciardi and Saum 1996)? Does decriminalization mean that now-illegal drugs can be sold openly on the marketplace, like cigarettes and alcohol? Would some drugs be regulated, much like prescription drugs now, and if so, which drugs would be handled this way?

Critics of decriminalization find important moral and practical messages in law that are not found elsewhere. Attacks on the policies of Mayor Schmoke of Baltimore, whose approach was detailed earlier, illustrate the criticisms. Bennett et al. (1996, 166) observe that emergency room admissions for serious health problems associated with drugs and drug overdoses rose significantly during the time when Schmoke was mayor of Baltimore. While Bennett and his colleagues cannot demonstrate that the increases were a direct result of the Baltimore policies, they do find that "it is at least fair to say that his [Schmoke's] policies did not prevent Baltimore from becoming far and away the national leader in drug-related emergency room admissions."

The consequences of drug use are not borne only by the users. Illicit drugs cost society billions of dollars each year. Employers lose money through reduced productivity and accidents on the job; banks lose money when addicted borrowers default on loans and forge checks; crime victims can lose not only money but their lives in attacks by people under the influence of drugs; criminal justice officials expend millions of dollars annually in processing drug- and alcohol-related cases through the police, court, and corrections systems; the health care system is put under increasing strain by accidents caused by drug use; and people in sensitive occupations who use drugs put many other lives at risk when they operate machinery, such as construction equipment and public transportation vehicles (Office of National Drug Control Policy 2004). Monetary estimates cannot account for the loss of human capital and the toll drugs and alcohol have taken on interpersonal relationships. The costs from drugs are so great overall that society has a strong impetus to somehow regulate their use.

We must also be sensitive to important differences among different kinds of drugs. Alcohol is a drug, but it differs from illegal drugs in some important ways. For example, alcohol is often taken socially and in moderation with no serious negative physical or social consequences. Red wine, for example, has been linked with reduced heart disease when it is used in relatively small quantities. There is also much more social support for the use of alcohol or tea, and these drinks are often consumed for reasons different from other drugs, such as the simple desire to quench one's thirst. Marijuana and LSD, on the other hand, are consumed to produce one effect only: getting high. Once the euphoria is no longer attained, for whatever reason, many marijuana users terminate their use.

Legalization of marijuana, heroin, cocaine, and other illegal drugs does not provide an easy—or perhaps any—solution to the nation's drug problems. Mario Cuomo, former governor of New York State, draws an analogy to a poisoned lake near a village:

> Imagine a village where more and more of the young people were being driven crazy by drinking from a poisoned lake in the hills. They storm the village night after night, creating mayhem. More and more of them are locked up. More and more executed. The villagers have to pay for more and more police and jail cells. Wouldn't someone say "Let's dry up the lake; let's find a new source of clean water?" (1995, 148)

This analogy considers the problem to be one of both supply and demand. The issue is two-fold: there is a poisoned lake, and the village's youth want the water. The law may be able to address, even if imperfectly, the former problem, but it is unlikely to be effective in dealing with the latter. The reasons for drug use are many, including experimentation, escapism, mood alteration, and habit. The law is unable to exert influence over virtually any of these reasons, let alone exert control over them.

But there are other issues. No one currently advocates legalizing drugs for children. Even under the most permissive system of law, therefore, there will be at least one group for whom the law will be used to prohibit drugs. This is essentially the system we presently have and enforce with respect to alcohol and tobacco.

Most people would also agree that the law has not been effective in keeping alcohol and tobacco away from children who really want them. And it may be that the law is as effective as it can be short of draconian measures that would be unsuitable in a free society. Furthermore, to say that alcohol is different from illicit drugs is not to condone its use. It is for this reason that many were disturbed in 1996 when the alcohol beverage industry appeared ready to end its self-imposed ban on advertising distilled spirits. In June 1996, a television station in Texas began showing ads for Seagram's whiskey, the first such ads in the media since the 1940s. Some media advertising specialists believe that the distillers want to put pressure on beer companies which run up a $626 million advertising bill annually. If networks refuse hard liquor ads, then a campaign could begin which seeks to ban beer commercials. Others claim that the distillers' long-term strategy is to get on television now so that when further technological advances occur in home electronics they will be guaranteed a place. Some distillers already advertise on the Internet.

It should be recognized too that the law has produced some important advances against illicit drugs. Interdiction measures have reduced the supply of certain illegal drugs, thereby reducing their use either by making them difficult to obtain or by increasing the price to render their use impractical. Yet although the law can slow the supply of drugs, there can never be enough law enforcement to stop that supply. Unless there is a change in the original conditions that bring about the decision to use illicit drugs, there will always be some groups eager to supply them for a profit.

Decriminalization is likely to increase the use of some drugs. Herbert Packer (1968) points out that the demand for some drugs is elastic, and the demand for other drugs is inelastic. By this, he means that the demand for some drugs can fluctuate widely over time, whereas the demand for other drugs is more stable and predictable. For example, most people do not use heroin because they do not wish to become addicts, not because they fear the law. The overall demand for heroin is therefore likely to remain relatively constant, regardless of its legal status. The demand for heroin is said to be inelastic. A drug like marijuana, on the other hand, which does not produce physical dependency, is likely to have a more elastic demand. Decriminalization will tend to increase use, because the law usually exercises a significant restraint both through its deterrent effect and by reducing the supply of the drug. Furthermore, there may be fewer other nonlegal sources of control for marijuana. Decriminalization is more likely to increase use—at least experimental use—of marijuana than heroin, if only because the law has a more significant control over marijuana than heroin.

There are some important trade-offs in the use of law to control drug behavior. Rand Corporation analysts, for example, estimate that a 25 percent reduction in funds currently used to cut the supply of cocaine would result in an 8 percent increase in cocaine use (Everingham and Rydell 1994; Rydell and Everingham 1994). If some of those saved funds were then spent on treatment programs, the current number of cocaine users could be substantially reduced, more than compensating for the 8 percent increase. Clearly, there is a need to balance those resources devoted to reducing supply and those to reducing the demand for cocaine. But it does not follow that all funds currently pouring into law enforcement to reduce supply should be diverted to treatment. Not all users will avail themselves of treatment, and not all those who do will finish treatment successfully. The law will be part of the overall system of control over illicit drugs for some time to come.

New treatments, such as immunotherapies and sustained release (depot) medications, may prove useful in the long term but their short-term effects are not fully known (National Research Council 2004). More sustained efforts toward constructing effective treatments would be an important component of reducing the demand for illicit drugs.

Conclusion

The campaign against drugs cannot be won if the law is the only weapon and complete repression is the only objective. The history of drug laws reflects a history of racist imagery, selective application, and uneven enforcement. No one doubts that drugs can ruin the lives of users and those around them, that drugs represent a loss to employers and communities, or that children need to be discouraged from drugs at an early age. None of these, however, render drugs a legal problem, as opposed to a family, community, or social problem. The real problem of drugs is their ubiquity in American life; our dependency on chemicals in subtle, everyday situations; and our inability to resolve our ambivalence about them: They are both wonderful and terrible—sometimes at the same time. This is a problem for which the law is inappropriate.

These are hardly new ideas, but until recently they have been heard only from the left end of the political spectrum. In recent years, political conservatives have also been expressing doubt about the effectiveness of a drug policy based on legal repression. Conservative skepticism about current drug policies increased significantly when the well-known conservative magazine *National Review* published a special issue on drugs in 1996, the title of which said it all: "The War on Drugs is Lost." The *Review's* editor, William F. Buckley, avowed that not only was the law ineffective, but it was counterproductive. Furthermore, the war has been far too expensive; more than $75 billion a year is spent on it, money that could be put to better use. The problem of drugs and the law had been dealt with before in the pages of *National Review*. In the July 10, 1995, issue, Michael S. Gazzaniga, director for the Center of Neuroscience at the University of California at Davis, suggested that people cannot be deterred by the law from using drugs, because the physiology of humans and the physical properties of drugs make the lure of drugs irresistible to some uncertain number of persons.

There are several policy alternatives, including regulation (manufacture and sale under controlled circumstances) and decriminalization (no regulation, whereby drugs are treated as any other legal commodity). Regulation is essentially the current policy with respect to alcohol and tobacco. Manufacture in accordance with government safety standards and distribution can both be accomplished competitively to keep prices down. Sales could be governed by laws as to time of sale, place of sale, and age of consumer, just as they are for alcohol. Furthermore, many of these decisions could be made at the local level to conform to local customs and social standards.

Drug policy continues to search for the most appropriate role for law. A national citizens' group advocating changes in the criminal justice system made the following recommendation: "Replace the war on drugs with a policy of harm reduction where the police work with public health and other professionals to stem substance use. Substance abuse would be treated as a public health challenge rather than a criminal justice problem" (Donziger 1996, 200–201). The notion of "harm reduction" means that the law should work cooperatively with other institutions to address problems. In this case, it refers to the importance of treatment facilities for addicts, the use of health professionals to administer drugs to addicts as part of a larger program of treatment, and needle exchange programs. Also recognized is the use of law to compel treatment for those who need and would benefit from it through such devices as drug courts.

Current skepticism about the role of law in controlling drugs is not motivated only by frustration with the law's apparent inability to reduce the supply of illegal drugs (Inciardi and Saum 1996). Rather, those who would decriminalize drugs have supplied a number of arguments, some sociological, others practical and philosophical. They include a review of the harmful consequences of employing law enforcement to control drug use, the inefficiency in deploying precious police resources, and the use of the law in circumstances in which it has little chance of overall success. Whether such reasons are persuasive depends, in part, on one's conception of the law and to what purpose it should be implemented.

References

Baum, Dan. 1996. *Smoke and Mirrors: The War on Drugs and the Politics of Failure.* Boston: Little, Brown.

Beck, Allen J., and Darrell K. Gilliard. 1995. *Prisoners in 1994.* Washington, DC: Bureau of Justice Statistics.

Bennett, William J., John J. DiIulio, and John P. Walters. 1996. *Body Count: Moral Poverty . . . and How to Win America's War Against Crime and Drugs.* New York: Simon and Schuster.

Brecher, Edward M. 1972. *Licit and Illicit Drugs.* Boston: Little, Brown.

Bureau of Justice Statistics. 1995. *Drugs and Crime Facts, 1994.* Washington, DC: Department of Justice.

Chambers, Carl D., and Michael T. Harter. 1987. "The Epidemiology of Narcotic Abuse Among Blacks in the United States, 1935–1980." 191–223 in Carl D. Chambers, James A. Inciardi, David M. Peterson,

Harvey A. Siegal, and O. Z. White, eds., *Chemical Dependencies: Patterns, Costs, and Consequences.* Athens: Ohio University Press.

Clinard, Marshall B., and Robert F. Meier. 2004. *Sociology of Deviant Behavior,* 12th ed. Belmont, CA: Wadsworth.

Cox, Terrance, Michael R. Jacobs, A. Eugene Leblanc, and Joan A. Marshman. 1983. *Drugs and Drug Abuse: A Reference Text.* Toronto: Addiction Research Foundation.

Cuomo, Mario. 1995. *Reason to Believe.* New York: Simon and Schuster.

Donziger, Steven R., ed. 1996. *The Real War on Crime: The Report of the National Criminal Justice Commission.* New York: HarperPerennial.

Everingham, Susan S., and C. Peter Rydell. 1994. *Modeling the Demand for Cocaine.* Los Angeles: Rand Corporation.

Federal Bureau of Investigation. 2004. *Crime in the United States, 2003.* Washington, DC: Department of Justice.

Friedman, Lawrence M. 2004. *Law in America: A Short History.* New York: Modern Library.

Goode, Erich. 2005. *Drugs in American Society,* 6th ed. New York: McGraw Hill.

Hill, Herbert. 1973. "Anti-Oriental Agitation." *Society,* 10:43–54.

Hunt, Leon Gibson, and Carl D. Chambers. 1976. *The Heroin Epidemics: A Study of Heroin Use in the United States, 1965–1975.* New York: Spectrum Publications.

Inciardi, James A. 1986. *The War on Drugs.* Palo Alto, CA: Mayfield.

Inciardi, James A., Dorothy Lockwood, and Anne E. Pottieger. 1993. *Women and Crack-Cocaine.* New York: Macmillan.

Inciardi, James A., and Christine Saum. 1996. "Legalization Madness." *The Public Interest* 123:72–82.

Johnston, Lloyd D., Patrick M. O'Malley, Jerald G. Bachman, and John Schulenberg. 2004. *Monitoring the Future: Overview of Key Findings, 2003.* Betheda, MD: National Institute on Drug Abuse.

Lindesmith, Alfred R., and John H. Gagnon. 1964. "Anomie and Drug Addiction." 162–178 in Marshall B. Clinard, ed., *Anomie and Deviant Behavior: A Discussion and Critique.* New York: Free Press.

McEwen, Tom. 1995. *National Assessment Program: 1994 Survey Results.* Rockville, MD: National Criminal Justice Reference Service.

McNamara, Joseph. 1995. *Address at the 9th International Conference on Drug Policy Reform.* Santa Monica, CA, October.

McWilliams, Peter. 1993. *Ain't Nobody's Business If You Do.* Los Angeles: Prelude Press.

Ministry of Welfare, Health and Cultural Affairs. 1994. *The Drug Policy in The Netherlands.* Amsterdam: The Netherlands.

Mokdad, Ali, James Marks, Donna F. Stroup, and Julie L. Gerberding. 2004. "Actual Causes of Death in the United States, 2000." *Journal of the American Medical Association,* 29:1238–1245.

Morgan, H. Wayne. 1981. *Drugs in America: A Social History, 1800–1980.* Syracuse, NY: Syracuse University Press.

Murr, David. 2004. "A New Menace on the Rez." *Newsweek,* September 27.

National Commission on Marijuana and Drug Abuse. 1972. *Marihuana: A Signal of Misunderstanding.* Washington, DC: Government Printing Office.

National Research Council. 2004. *New Treatments for Addiction: Behavioral, Ethical, Legal, and Social Questions.* Washington, DC: National Academy Press.

Office of National Drug Control Policy. 2004. *National Drug Control Strategy: Executive Summary.* Washington, DC: The White House.

Oliver, William. 1994. *The Violent Social World of Black Men.* New York: Lexington.

Packer, Herbert A. 1968. *The Limits of the Criminal Sanction.* Stanford: Stanford University Press.

Pollock, Joycelyn M. 2004. *Prisons and Prison Life: Costs and Consequences.* Los Angeles: Roxbury.

Reuter, Peter. 1995. *Cocaine: The First Decade.* Los Angeles: The Rand Corporation.

Rydell, C. Peter, and Susan S. Everingham. 1994. *Controlling Cocaine: Supply vs. Demand Programs.* Los Angeles: Rand Corporation.

Stephens, Richard C. 1991. *The Street Addict Role: A Theory of Heroin Addiction.* Albany: State University of New York Press.

Timberlake, James H. 1963. *Prohibition and the Progressive Movement, 1900–1920.* New Haven, CT: Yale University Press.

Trebach, Arnold S. 1982. *The Heroin Solution.* New Haven, CT: Yale University Press.

———. 1987. *The Great Drug War.* New York: Macmillan.

Troyer, Ronald J., and Gerald E. Markle. 1983. *Cigarettes: The Battle Over Smoking.* New Brunswick, NJ: Rutgers University Press.

Walters, John P. 1996. "Illegal Drugs and Presidential Leadership." *Wall Street Journal,* September 26:23.

Wolfgang, Marvin E. 1958. *Patterns of Criminal Homicide.* Philadelphia: University of Pennsylvania Press. ✦

Chapter 4

Homosexuality

They started lining up the night before. Hundreds of couples waiting patiently for the opening of the local town clerks' offices in the state of Massachusetts. The same-sex couples were waiting to fill out applications for marriage licenses. Those applications, along with the results of blood tests and fees, were all that was necessary to legally obtain a license to marry. They were in line because in November 2003, Massachusetts' highest court ruled that the state's constitution permitted gay couples to wed and authorized gay marriages beginning on May 17, 2004. Gay marriage opponents filed an appeal with the United State Supreme Court, but that court refused without comment to intervene. Previous appeals to a federal judge and the Boston-based First Circuit Court of Appeals upheld the original ruling.

But while these rulings implicitly adopted a particular moral position, they would not end the controversy because homosexuality is a topic about which there is substantial disagreement in the United States. Much of the dispute revolves around the extent to which homosexuality is immoral, a debate that has spilled out of the churches and into the legislatures, including, in 2004, the United States Congress. To some, there is substantial moral harm from homosexuality, which justifies using legal control; to others, homosexuality is an entirely private matter that should not be of concern to the criminal law. Homosexuals have faced both moral and legal censure. To be sure, most of the topics of current controversy—same-sex marriages, the role of homosexual personnel in the military, the ordination of homosexuals in churches, the identification of homosexuality as a protected category of citizens against discrimination, the ability of homosexuals to adopt and raise children—do not appear to touch on matters that involve criminal law. But law always lurks in the background, giving meaning to the issue and, in some instances, definition to a particular topic. There is much that is confusing about homosexuality, and only some of this confusion can be addressed scientifically. One observer, for example, views the origin of homosexuality like the development of any other habit:

> What deters young people from becoming emotionally committed to this form of release is doubtless its negative evaluation by peers and social rewards that are contingent on normal heterosexual relations. The few who turn into "true" homosexuals are presumably like the few drinkers who turn into confirmed alcoholics: they do so both because they drink too much and because they cannot make the normal adjustments in life. Once the homosexual habit is fixed by the reinforcement of frequent gratification, it becomes extraordinarily difficult to break. (Davis 1976, 255–256)

Such a statement is obviously too simplistic to persuade many observers today, but even more surprising is the tone of disapproval it conveys. Homosexuality, in this view, is merely a bad habit like alcoholism, and we are told that we are lucky that only a few persons are so afflicted. Strong opinions and polarized thinking have come to dominate discussions of homosexuality. To some, homosexuality is a lifestyle variation, freely chosen and largely, if not totally, immoral. To others, it is a biological condition over which the individual has no more control than he or she has over eye or skin color or reflex actions. Because neither science nor religion has yet resolved these opposing conceptions, it is understandable that the law has come to be used to both threaten and protect heterosexual interests. The law has become the battleground for opposing moral standpoints.

Whether homosexuality is viewed as choice or as condition is particularly important, because such conceptions have legal consequences. Criminal law cannot punish in the absence of intent to produce wrongdoing, and for this reason, the law recognizes various exceptions to criminal responsibility, such as compulsion, duress, and insanity. If homosexuality is the result of a conscious choice, as some believe, the law can be appropriately used. Yet, there is confusion even about the meaning of the term "homosexuality," which can refer both to a sexual orientation or preference and to sexual conduct between members of the same gender.

A note on usage: In this chapter, we follow the strict meaning of the term homosexuality—the prefix "homo" means "same," not "male." Thus, we intend the term to refer both to male homosexuality and lesbianism, although most of the writing and research on this topic has been done with respect to male homosexuality. This imbalance is reflected in the discussion in this chapter, but our intent is to treat both male and female homosexuality together.

Defining Homosexuality

There are several different definitions of "homosexual" that have given rise to different theories of the origin of homosexuality and differences in the estimates of the number of individuals who are homosexual. Homosexuality can be reflected in attitudes expressing sexual or erotic preference, the presence of a homosexual self-concept, or in actual sex behavior with members of one's own sex, whether male or female. These three connotations of the term homosexual—homosexual behavior, homosexual preference or orientation, and homosexual identity or self-concept—have different implications for our conception of homosexuality and its appropriateness under law.

Homosexual Behavior

Between males, homosexual behavior can be carried out physically in a number of ways: sodomy (anal), fellatio (mouth-genital), and mutual masturbation. Homosexual behavior between women can consist of oral stimulation of the clitoris (cunnilingus), mutual masturbation, and the use of objects such as vibrators or an artificial penis. People who engage in homosexual behavior, males and females, come from all social classes, have varying degrees of education, a wide range of occupations and professions, varied interests and avocations, and may be either married or single.

Homosexual behavior may seem to be the most obvious indicator of whether someone is a homosexual, but people can engage in homosexual behavior and still not consider themselves to be homosexual. They may participate in homosexual acts yet remain primarily attracted to persons of the opposite sex. On the other hand, some married males may feel more attracted to persons of their own sex and derive from them most of their sexual stimulation. The degree to which a person combines high levels of homosexual attraction and homosexual behavior may stem from one's participation in a homosexual subculture. For this reason, there is no such thing as *a* homosexual but rather differing degrees of a person's involvement with homosexuality at certain levels of behavior and attraction.

How common are homosexual experiences? No one knows for sure, but one estimate was obtained in an extensive survey of adult sexual behavior. Laumann and his colleagues (1994, 294) report that 2.7 percent of their sample of males and 1.3 percent of the females reported having sexual relations with someone of the same sex during the past year.

Homosexual Preference or Orientation

Homosexual preference refers to the subjective feeling that a person of the same sex is more sexually attractive than a person of the opposite sex. While the word "preference" may appear to denote some choice in which is preferred, we reject that notion here. Others do not (Nicolosi and Nicolosi 2002).

Considering homosexuality as sexual or erotic preference enables us to understand a number of different sexual behavior patterns (Langevin 1985, 2–3). According to Kinsey et al. (1948), in the best-known study of sexuality in the United States, 37 percent of a sample of American males had what they considered to be a homosexual experience at some time during their lives. But only 4 percent were exclusively homosexual and expressed an erotic preference for men throughout their adult lives. The others likely engaged in homosexual acts out of a desire for something different or while living with males in such situations as an all-male school or prison. In addition, there are some men who have had homosexual relations with male prostitutes—or have been male prostitutes themselves—though their involvement in this behavior is not necessarily the consequence of sexual preference (Luckenbill 1986). Similarly, there are some women who have had sexual relations with female prostitutes, but not all of these women are necessarily lesbians. Some, like the males, are bisexual; others are simply experimental. Having had homosexual relations does not constitute being a homosexual.

Homosexual Identity or Self-Concept

Yet another view of homosexuality derives its meaning from the self-conception of those who identify themselves as homosexuals. Traditionally, behavioral scientists have been more interested in the origins and consequences of the development of a homosexual self-concept than in homosexual behavior.

Using a self-concept measure yields different estimates of the prevalence of homosexuality. Although Kinsey's respondents were purposefully recruited and did not constitute a probability sample of adults, the participants in Laumann et al. (1994, 293) research were a representative sample: 2.7 percent of the men and 1.3 percent of the women reported some level of homosexual identity.

A few decades ago, little was known about the self-concept of homosexuals and the process by which it arose and changed. It was known that not all people who had homosexual preferences came to develop a corresponding self-concept, but the reasons seemed to extend beyond the powerful stigma that was associated with disclosing a deviant identity.

The key to this self-concept was believed to lie in the process by which homosexuals made public their orientation: the "coming-out" process. Analogous to debutantes who "come out" in polite society to publicly introduce their membership in the elite, the coming-out process for homosexuals entailed a public disclosure of homosexual orientation and a willingness to participate in public life as a homosexual. Once one left the closet, there was little possibility of turning back (but see Haley 2004). The sociological literature on the coming-out process is particularly extensive, in part because it deals with an intensely moving, high-risk public proclamation. The coming-out process further strengthens homosexual orientation that has already developed and been recognized by the individual as such.

Causes of Homosexuality

To ask about the origins of homosexuality means exploring the origins of all sexual preference. How is it that some people come to prefer sex with persons of the opposite sex, whereas others prefer it with members of the same sex? There remains much confusion about the origins of homosexuality, with some speculating that it has a genetic basis, others that it has psychological roots. According to a poll, many psychiatrists believe there is a biological basis to homosexuality (Vreeland et al. 1995), a view that has become very popular among homosexuals as well. Still others adhere to a more sociological foundation, which argues that homosexuality is learned, just as heterosexuality is learned. Although no one has yet definitively resolved such disputes, we can at least identify them.

The Biological Perspective

The biological perspective has gained support in recent years with research that has suggested, but no more than that, that homosexual orientation may be connected to or may reside in a particular gene or a particular physiological makeup. Some researchers have explored the chemical and hormonal bases of homosexuality. Roper (1996), for example, believes that homosexual orientation may be determined by testosterone action on the brain. A reduction in testosterone levels results in reduced proliferation of hypothalamic nuclei, which are said to play a vital role in psychosexual orientation.

LeVay also believes that brain development may determine whether a person has homosexual tendencies, and like Roper he has sought the answer in the hypothalamus. LeVay pinpointed a cell group called INAH3 (derived from "third interstitial nucleus of the anterior hypothalamus"). He points out that the INAH3 group is twice as large in men as in women. In autopsies of 19 homosexual and 16 heterosexual men who had died of AIDS, LeVay found that the cell group was two to three times larger in the heterosexual men than in the homosexuals and that in fact the group was altogether absent in some of the gays. He notes that the likelihood of such an outcome occurring by chance is about one in one thousand. This finding, nonetheless, has to be regarded as no more than a very tentative explanatory possibility; indeed, LeVay and Hamer note some of several possible interpretations:

> What might lie behind these apparent correlations between sexual orientation and brain structure? Logically, three possibilities exist. One is that the structural differences were present early in life—perhaps even before birth—and helped to establish the men's sexual orientation. The second is that the differences arose in adult life as a result of the men's sexual feelings or behavior. The third possibility is that there is no causal connection, but both sexual orientation and the brain structure in question are linked to some third variable, such as a developmental event during uterine or early postnatal life. (LeVay and Hamer 1994, 46)

The presence of the AIDS virus also represents a possible confounding variable, though the same phenomenon was found in a few non-AIDS cases autopsied. In the end, the conclusion remains that the researcher at the moment "cannot decide among the possibilities with any certainty" (LeVay and Hamer 1994, 46).

Other researchers have explored the genetic bases of homosexuality by examining the extent to which it is affected by genetic influences. A research team led by Dean Hamer has conducted perhaps the best-known work on this topic. Hamer and his associates (1994) concluded that there is a possibility of a genetic basis to sexual orientation, especially in the region of human DNA known as "Xq28."

Hamer's research was conducted at the National Cancer Institute, using a sample of 114 gay men. The investigators were intrigued that the families of 76 of these gay men included a higher proportion of homosexual male relatives than found in the general population. Because most of the homosexual relatives were on the mother's side of the family, the researchers concentrated on the X chromosome, which comes from the mother. "Using an approach called DNA linkage analysis, we found that a small region of the X chromosome, Xq28, appeared the same in an unexpectedly high proportion of gay brothers" (Hamer and Copeland 1994, 21). Specifically, DNA from 40 pairs of homosexual brothers was examined. The laws of inheritance indicate that two brothers have a 50-50 chance of inheriting the same single copy of their mother's X chromosome (the chromosome with the suspected

DNA "marker" for homosexuality). Thus, it was expected that, on average, 20 of the 40 pairs of brothers would have this chromosome. Instead, the researchers found that 33 pairs of brothers shared five different patches of the same genetic material, suggesting that they had all inherited the same X chromosome from their mother.

Hamer's research team concluded that there may be at least one gene that is inherited by a son from his mother that helps to determine whether the son is predisposed to be heterosexual or homosexual. Presumably, a common version of the gene increases the likelihood that the son will be heterosexual, and an uncommon version of the gene increases the likelihood that the son will be homosexual.

Other research has looked at heritability of homosexuality among identical twins or siblings. One study examined families that contained two gay brothers or two lesbian sisters, as well as heterosexual siblings (Hu et al. 1995). The researchers reported the existence of a linkage between the Xq28 markers and the sexual orientation for the gay male families, but not for the lesbian families. The researchers point out that although the results suggest some kind of X-chromosome linkage, they failed to find evidence of any direct inheritance (Hamer and Copeland 1994, 104).

Other studies have reported contradictory results (Whitehead and Whitehead 1999; Bailey, Dunne, and Martin 2000). It appears that every behavior may be attributed to inheritance at a certain level of probability, often cited as 50±20 percent, a large range indeed. So, even if 30 percent of siblings are gay given the presence of one gay sibling, this would not demonstrate that homosexuality was genetic or inherited. Continuing research may resolve some of the differences among studies, but it is also the case that different studies have used different methods (the solicitation of volunteers, the use of a twins registry, etc.) leading to different results.

At a more general level, sexual behavior has been said to develop in a biological, Darwinian framework. Some, for example, believe that sexual behaviors and functions coevolved, so that when females selected a particular trait in a male as desirable, other males eventually developed it (Rodgers 2003). Whether such a perspective is helpful in understanding the development and nature of homosexuality or responses to it remains uncertain.

The Learning Perspective

The learning perspective represents an alternative, but not completely separate, explanation of homosexuality. Because there is much we have to understand about the origins of homosexuality, it is possible that both biological and learning mechanisms are at work.

The learning of sexuality involves the acquisition of sexual norms and orientations, and this learning occurs throughout the lifecycle. Many social scientists believe that although it has a biological basis, sexuality is a social construction "that has been learned in interaction with others" (Plummer 1975, 30). It is not dictated by body chemistry or anatomical structures, but by experiences, social situations, and social expectations. "Male" and "female" are socially constructed categories, as is the conduct that arises from these roles.

One learns to be erotically responsive to some persons or objects but not to others. The process is not automatic, which is why some people are aroused by some objects to which others do not respond. One can learn that virtually anything is a sexual stimulus if it is paired with an appropriate sexual response. The sex drive, in other words, "is neither powerful nor weak; it can be almost anything we make it" (Goode and Troiden 1974, 15). The social meaning of sexuality, then, is attained in the same manner as the meaning of other social acts—as part of the overall socialization process that begins early in life (Akers 1985, 184–185). Sexuality is learned over a period of time and according to general principles of learning and social interaction. In other words, people learn to become homosexuals through the same general processes by which they learn to become heterosexual. It is the *content* of this learning that differs.

Virtually any object or person is capable of providing sexual satisfaction, but sexual behavior is always embedded in a web of normative constraints and other regulations that define only certain objects and persons as acceptable. Rewards and punishments from early childhood help the individual to define acceptable sexuality. Most people learn to adopt heterosexual roles and to derive sexual satisfaction from objects and people considered to be "conventional," that is, within the norms of their group.

But the learning of sexuality is not a uniform experience, because sexual socialization is an imperfect process and some individuals will come to derive sexual satisfaction from objects and people outside the group's normative structure. This can be expected for at least two reasons. First, the area of eroticism is an ambiguous one for socializers. Many parents and others feel uncomfortable about offering sex education that includes sex-specific information. For most socializers, the topic of sex is embarrassing. This seems to be particularly true for parents and children, as neither usually seems comfortable thinking of the other as sexual beings.

Second, the area of sexuality covers much ground, from appropriate partners to appropriate time, objects, places, and ages. In fact, sexual norms are among the most complicated of all social norms because of the different combinations of contingencies that one must learn. A woman, for example, might learn that males are appropriate sexual partners but only in certain relationships (e.g., after marriage) and certain places (e.g., private). It is not surprising, therefore, that there are instances in which the socialization process fails to adequately prepare individuals for sexual growth and maturation within the group. Some individuals will find themselves open to sexual alternatives, such as using a prostitute for sexual gratification or engaging in sexual practices such as sadism or masochism. For the same reason, it is not surprising that some people come to be attracted to members of the same sex. Even taking into account the complexity of sexual norms and the ambiguity of the socialization process, by far most people are socialized to become heterosexual.

Beyond these general statements, it is not possible at the present time to provide a definitive answer about the causes of homosexuality—or heterosexuality, for that matter. We continue to investigate the process of the acquisition of sexual orientation, and subsequent work may reach the conclusion that although sexual orientation is facilitated by certain chromosomal structures, it is basically a learned perspective.

To make matters even more complicated, many observers believe that not only is gender socially constructed, but that there are neither dichotomous distinctions between male and female, nor between heterosexual and homosexual (see Gamson and

Moon 2004, 48–49). So, while biological theorists implicitly point to physical causes that lead to distinct types of people, some social scientists believe that it is much more complicated than the biological model indicates.

Most homosexuals tend to lean toward the biological view to explain their own orientation, to some because it absolves them of the responsibility that may be imposed on them for having "chosen" this form of life; to others because they believe that heterosexuals have no right to condemn them for an inborn condition. But adherence to this biological view is not entirely motivated by a desire to deflect social stigma or counter condemnation. Many homosexuals report that their experiences were such that they had some inkling that they were "different" early in life. Many stories identify a turning point where homosexuals received an insight into the fact that they were not like others in their sexual orientation, seemingly before they had a chance to learn many sexual norms. One writer recounts how he disliked recess in elementary school because he didn't like to play soccer:

> [A] girl sitting next to me looked at me with a mixture of curiosity and disgust. "Why aren't you out with the boys playing football?" she asked. "Because I hate it," I replied. "Are you sure you're not a girl under there?" she asked, with the suspicion of a sneer. "Yeah, of course," I replied, stung and somewhat shaken. (Sullivan 1995, 3–4)

There seems to be little point in trying to discover the causes of homosexuality by relying on such authorities as the medical profession. The Committee on Public Health of the New York State Academy of Medicine declared authoritatively in 1964 that "homosexuality is indeed an illness," and that "the homosexual is an emotionally disturbed individual who has not acquired a normal capacity to develop satisfying heterosexual relationships" (New York Academy of Medicine Committee on Public Health 1964). A decade later, however, the American Psychiatric Association in its *Diagnostic and Statistical Manual* (DSM-IV) would proclaim that homosexuality is not an illness and that homosexuals are not in need of special services by virtue of their being homosexuals (Bayer 1981).

Public Opinion and Homosexuality

Psychiatrists are not the only people who change their minds. There are unmistakable signs of increased public tolerance of homosexuality, although the degree of shift is not dramatic over the short run. The difference is often attributable to how the questions are worded, but however questions are worded, most people in the United States still disapprove of homosexuality. A Kinsey Institute survey asked more than 3,000 adult respondents selected on a national basis about a variety of sexual acts, including homosexuality. The single most disapproved act involved homosexuality among partners who had no special affection for each other (Klassen, Williams, and Levitt 1989, 18). Of the respondents, 88 percent indicated that this was "always wrong" or "almost always wrong." Fewer respondents found homosexual acts between parties who were in love as "always wrong" or "almost always wrong," but the percentage was still high: 79 percent.

In another national survey, investigators asked young men about their attitudes toward homosexuality and found that 89 percent found sex between two men to be "disgusting," and only 12 percent thought they could be friends with a gay male (Marsiglio 1993). These views were related to perceptions of the traditional male role, religious fundamentalist beliefs, and upbringing by a parent with few formal years of education.

Evidence indicates that public disapproval of homosexuality has declined from previous decades (Stephan and McMullin 1982). The percentage of people who favor legalizing homosexual relations between consenting adults increased slightly from 43 percent in 1977 to 47 percent in 1989 (cited by Posner 1992, 202). This means, of course, that more than half of the respondents do not favor such measures. In 1986, 54 percent agreed that homosexual relations between consenting adults should be illegal. This negative opinion was even stronger for older age groups, but there is also evidence that the majority of college students have negative views of homosexuality (Endleman 1990, 52). In the 1986 poll, 51 percent believed that the Constitution of the United States does not protect private homosexual acts (Gallup Poll 1986), a position that was consistent with an important U.S. Supreme Court ruling that same year.

The Gallup organization has asked the following question each year: "Do you feel homosexuality should be considered an acceptable alternative lifestyle or not?" The question is badly worded and suggests that one becomes homosexual only by exercising some choice in adapting a particular lifestyle. That aside, the percentage of respondents who considered homosexuality "acceptable" rose from 34 percent in 1982 to 54 percent in 2003. Then, the U.S. Supreme Court (*Lawrence et al. v. Texas*), in the summer of 2003, announced a decision that overturned a Texas law that prohibited sodomy between same-sex couples. While a measure of this question after that ruling showed that the level of public acceptance had decreased, it bounced back up the following May (2004) to 54 percent (Moore 2004).

The increase in tolerance of homosexuality among the general population has occurred in most groups, although there remains stronger condemnation of homosexuality among religious Christians than among others. The issue there remains a divisive one, whether over a broad topic, such as the morality of homosexuality in general, or a narrow one, such as the appropriateness of allowing known homosexuals to become clergy. And, in spite of increasing tolerance, a substantial majority of Americans do not agree that homosexuality is just another lifestyle. When 70 percent of a sample of Americans respond to a poll that homosexuality is immoral (Shapiro 1994), one might reasonably question whether all respondents are using the same definition of "morality."

There has long been an uneasy relationship between homosexuality and Christianity. Historically, most of the objections to homosexual behavior that have been raised in the larger society can be traced to religious prohibitions (Crompton 2003). One common objection is that homosexual conduct cannot lead to reproduction or to the development of a "normal" family. Homosexuality certainly cannot lead to human reproduction, but reproduction is increasingly seen as only one purpose for sex. Most heterosexual people also engage in sexual relations for purposes other than reproduction. Indeed, the purpose of birth control is precisely to avoid reproduction. Even the Roman Catholic Church, though it discourages birth control devices, endorses timed birth control to avoid ovulation, the so-called "rhythm" method.

Some Christians have accepted homosexuals as full church members, but others oppose such religious liberalization. During the 1990s, the issue that was contested most strenuously was whether homosexuals could be ordained as clergy. The Episcopal Church, like many Protestant denominations, had been wrestling with the question for a number of years, largely without resolution. When an openly gay man was ordained in May 1990, the church had to confront the issue in a more direct manner. Six years later, a special church court ruled that there was no church doctrine against ordaining noncelibate homosexuals (*Des Moines Register* May 20, 1996). The court ruled further that the Episcopal Church was in a period of indecision about homosexuality, which triggered a series of debates as local churches wrestled with the meanings of the ruling. For some, the decision was evidence of further liberalization; for others, it represented a reasonable compromise on the issue, so that local churches could decide for themselves whether to ordain homosexuals. The debate continued in June 2003 when Gene Robinson, an openly gay man, was elected bishop of New Hampshire. Bishop Robinson's subsequent confirmation gave rise to substantial debate and schism. The matter is likely to be a topic of controversy for some time.

The Regulation of Homosexuality

Religious objections to homosexuality are but one part of a larger context of social regulation of sexuality. One of the most distinctive features of human societies is the variety and strength of controls that govern sexual behavior. Sex is one of the most strongly regulated acts of human beings; even in relatively permissive societies, sexual activity nonetheless receives special social attention. Even those individuals who regard sex between consenting adults as natural and private have had to recognize the powerful social pressures, norms, attitudes, and taboos on sex, independent of legal restrictions.

Homosexuality is perhaps most visible in social settings that encourage sexuality but are one-sexed in composition, such as in the military, boarding schools, prisons, and other societies in which sexuality may be encouraged—or tolerated—but where there is no opportunity for heterosexual activity. This is not to say that homosexuals are merely heterosexuals who do not have a heterosexual outlet; homosexuality is obviously much more complex than that. But it should be recognized that homosexuality is often neither permanent nor invariant, and that many people are able at different times to adapt to changing sexual circumstances.

Legal prohibitions regarding sexuality, of course, do not take into account such variation, although social norms are able to accommodate situational contingencies. Laws against unwanted sexual aggression (e.g., rape), specific forms of sexual behavior (e.g., sodomy), and sexuality with commercial intent (e.g., prostitution) apply to everyone in all social situations. The social regulation of sexuality, however, is more complicated because it is often difficult to determine the content of norms and where or when they might apply.

The Social Regulation of Sexuality

As pointed out earlier, sexuality is not just a biological fact or condition; it is a learned and constructed one as well. This means that people learn sexual content in the larger and more general process of socialization. There is much that people must learn: appropriate norms, objects, relationships, times and places for sex, situations, and partners. This learning takes place over an extended period of time, but it suffers from a serious handicap in our society: People do not like to talk much about sex in personal and intimate terms. Sex is considered impolite and intensely private in some groups. Many believe that sex should be discussed only in the context of a family. Consequently, the sexual socialization process tends to be imperfect and overburdened with misinformation or noninformation concerning sexuality, the result of which much is misunderstood. The process involves not only sex education but also the communication of norms and values that pertain to the sex act in its social and religious context. This is obviously a very subtle process.

One reason that the norms governing sex hold such power is that sexual drive itself can be very powerful. Sexual gratification is not required for individual survival in the same way as the alleviation of hunger, thirst, or fatigue. As a result, restrictions on sexuality are often more absolute than those governing, for example, ingesting food which would be more likely to permit exceptions necessary for survival (Davis 1976, 223). When one includes the fact that sexuality is experienced mentally and visually, as well as behaviorally, and that sexual behavior can take many different forms, one can realize that there is an enormous variety of sexual behaviors, conditions, and situations to regulate.

Sexual norms are linked with reproductive norms because sexual intercourse has the potential to create a new human being. This means that the social regulation of sexuality is often considered part of the regulation system that relates to the bearing and rearing of children. Child rearing is obviously a fundamental societal need, and every society has an interest in ensuring that child bearing and rearing are performed in a way that is believed to most benefit the society. This is why many modern discussions of homosexuality often revolve around family issues, as well as why there is a strong temptation to use the criminal law as a backup to existing social attitudes.

Religious and Legal Regulation of Sexuality

There are a number of sexual acts that appear to demand a legal response, such as those with involuntary partners and those with children regardless of their consent. Our concern in this chapter is not with such acts, which would affect both heterosexuality and homosexuality and about which there is widespread agreement. Rather, we are concerned with consensual homosexual relations involving adults. One question is whether, and to what extent, the law should be involved in regulating the sexual relations of consenting adults, whether the behavior is homosexual or heterosexual. Despite one's opinion on that issue, the fact is that sexual acts associated with homosexuality have been subject to criminal law in the United States and elsewhere, and this situation has existed for a long time.

Early religious codes were very influential on the content of laws regarding homosexuality, but this influence was not as simple as it might seem. The Christian Church adopted ancient Jewish regulations on sex. These regulations were incorporated into ecclesiastical laws that influenced thinking about homosexuality during the medieval ages and later provided the basis for the legal condemnation of homosexuality in English common law (see Katz 1976; 1983). There were a number of prohibitions in the Old Testament concerning a variety of acts and conditions, but all of them were eliminated except for homosexuality. Lesbianism is not mentioned in the Talmud, suggesting that it was permitted (Crompton 2003, 46). The prohibition against homosexuality was retained in the Christian tradition, and expanded to include lesbianism.

Before this time, the concept of homosexuality did not exist as it does now. The Hebrews and the Greeks had no word for homosexuality (Hubbard 2003). Ancient Greek and Roman cultures permitted sexual activity with either sex, although exclusive sexuality with the same sex may have been rare and considered a bit unusual (McWilliams 1993, 605). In their now-famous survey, Ford and Beach studied 76 folk societies and found that among 49 of them, or 64 percent, "homosexual activities of one sort or another are considered normal and socially acceptable for certain members of the community" (Ford and Beach 1951, 130).

Some observers hold that the negative position of the Christian Church on homosexuality has been longstanding and consistent (Soards 1995). Others claim that homosexuality was tolerated in the Christian tradition until the mid-thirteenth century, at which time the church adopted a more negative view (Boswell 1980), a viewpoint still others (Crompton 2003) find untenable. This is not to say that homosexuality was encouraged in earlier periods. Soards (1995, 38–40) points out that regulations in Spain about 700 A.D. held that homosexuals were to be castrated, an edict reinforced later by declarations of the King of Spain at the Council of Toledo. By the twelfth century, homosexuals were ordered to show through confession and penance that they were worthy of redemption from their "shameful sin of sodomy."

Homosexuality did not play a prominent role in ecclesiastical debates during the Reformation, but by the twentieth century, Protestant thought underwent a marked change. Increasingly, homosexuality was referred to as a moral perversity. Theologian Karl Barth (cited in Soards 1995, 43) described homosexuality as a "physical, psychological, and social sickness, the phenomenon of perversion, decadence, and decay, which can emerge when man refuses to admit the validity of the divine command." A similar transformation took place in the Latter Day Saints (Mormon)

Church, in which homoeroticism was tolerated until the mid-1950s, when the church expressed strong condemnation (Quinn 1996).

Eventually, the language of illness and therapy began to replace and challenge the tone of moral condemnation. Much of this change occurred in the context of "hate the sin, love the sinner," an approach that has generated confusion among many Christians, if only because the distinction between "homosexual" and "homosexual behavior" is no sharper than it is between "heterosexual" and "heterosexual behavior." In each instance, peoples' sexual orientation does not provide enough information to define or categorize them. Furthermore, it may make little sense—except perhaps to a few—to proclaim that one has a sexual orientation that is not acted upon. In those instances where there is a separation of sexual behavior from sexual orientation (e.g., as with priests under a vow of celibacy), it is recognized that the individual has had to make a remarkably strong and unusual commitment. To some, including fundamentalist Protestants, such a separation is itself often seen as unnatural.

The most basic division in debates about homosexuality "is between those who maintain that homosexuality is proscribed by Scripture and by God's design for human sexuality and those who argue that the love of God surely must embrace the lifestyle of those who discover that by nature they are homosexuals" (Baird and Baird 1995, 18). Those who adhere to the former view are more punitive than those who express the latter position. Combatants often appeal either to Scripture or church law or policy for guidance. Some assert that the Bible's few explicit prohibitions on sex between men is evidence that such behavior is permissible (Bawer 1996, 240–242), whereas others derive no such insight from the absence of categorical prohibition.

But although religious disapproval of homosexuality has seemingly increased over time, legal censure has declined. As with the religious courts, early legal prohibitions were strict. Emperor Justinian condemned homosexual offenders to death in 538 A.D., and this portion of the Justinian Code served as the basis for the punishment of homosexuality in Europe for the next 1,300 years. During most of this time, homosexual acts were dealt with by ecclesiastical, but not government, courts in England, often with torture followed by death. By 1533, the jurisdiction of such offenses was vested in royal courts, and the English statute enacted at that time provided for death "without benefit of clergy." Claiming "clergy" was typically allowed for offenses deemed less serious. The offender had to demonstrate an ability to read, a condition then found almost exclusively among church officials. Later, a particular biblical passage ("the hanging verse") had to be recited, and illiterate offenders often memorized the verse beforehand. This punishment remained until the nineteenth century when it was reduced to life imprisonment. In France, as late as the mid-eighteenth century, homosexuals were burned at the stake. The Napoleonic Code, enacted after the French Revolution, omitted mention of homosexual acts, a situation that still prevails in many European countries. During the course of this century, other European countries maintained strong legal prohibitions against homosexuality, but they were infrequently enforced.

Today, although laws seek to protect young people from homosexual acts and to protect "public decency," most continental European countries do not consider homosexual acts committed in private by consenting adults to be criminal. Even in those countries where the behavior is defined by law as criminal, violators are generally not prosecuted.

Much of this trend can be traced to the 1950s, when a British governmental committee was charged with the task of examining the laws relating to homosexual behavior and prostitution. The committee was created because there was concern that the penalties for many sexual acts were too severe. Under the British law of 1956, for example, sodomy with a person under age was punishable by life imprisonment; the sentence for the same crime committed with adults was imprisonment. The Wolfenden Report, issued in 1957, recommended the cessation of penalties for homosexual acts between consenting adults. After long debate, penalties in England for homosexual acts in private between adults over 21 were removed in 1965. Sanctions remained for acts with those under age and for persons who procure others for homosexual acts.

As in Europe, American laws were heavily influenced by religious admonitions. The law of criminal sodomy in colonial Connecticut's statute, for example, followed closely the wording of Leviticus 18:22:

That if any man shall lie with mankind, as he lieth with woman-
kind, both of them have committed abomination; they shall be
put to death, except it shall appear that one of the parties was
forced or under 15 years of age. (cited in Dworkin 1987, 153)

Other American statutes maintained a similar moral outrage,
if not the precise wording of biblical injunctions. The 1837 North
Carolina statute makes reference to "the abominable and detest-
able crime against nature, not [to] be named among Christians"
(cited in Dworkin 1987, 153). Although many state laws would
not subsequently contain such preachy embellishments, it was
clear that sodomy was generally considered to be a crime both
against law and against nature. It was not until 1962 that Illinois
became the first American state to repeal the criminal sodomy
statute and it was not until 2003 that the U.S. Supreme Court declared all sodomy laws to be unconstitutional.

In 1998, police in Houston, Texas, responded to a possible
weapons disturbance. Upon entering the residence, they observed the resident, John Lawrence, and another man, Tyron Gar-
ner, engaging in a sexual act. The men were arrested, charged, and
convicted by a justice of the peace under a Texas statute of engaging in "deviate sexual intercourse with a member of the same sex"
(Texas Penal Code Ann. § 21.06 (a) 2003). In other words, the two
men were convicted of engaging in anal sex.

The U.S. Supreme Court issued its ruling on June 26, 2003, in
Lawrence et al. v. Texas. In a 6–3 vote, the court sided with an appeal
court in overturning the convictions, ruling that the petitioners
have the right to engage in private conduct, in this case consensual sexual behavior, without government intervention. The ruling essentially struck down as unconstitutional all state statutes
that prohibited sodomy, even sodomy between a man and a
woman. Prior to the *Lawrence* ruling, 14 states, Puerto Rico, and
the United States military had sodomy laws.

The Consequences of Legal Regulation

Few homosexuals regard themselves as criminals or deviants,
as being "sick" or immoral. The negative views of others as expressed in stigmatizing efforts, however, are not without their effect. Many homosexuals believe it is necessary to conceal their
homosexuality. They report that they sometimes feel guilty for

their behavior and fear negative social sanctions from family, friends, and employers with whom they wish to continue to associate. Often, the homosexual may be outwardly gregarious and popular but inwardly feel rejected and alone (Harry 1982).

There is little doubt that most homosexuals have experienced negative stigma because of their homosexuality, and there is little doubt that such censure has much of its roots in legal measures to control homosexuality. Most of this stigma has been generated in social situations by heterosexuals and has ranged from mild expressions of disapproval to assault, or "gay bashing." Between these extremes, homosexuals have experienced ridicule and scorn, moral condemnation, and social avoidance. Some say that many of these sanctions reflect homophobia, the fear and misunderstanding of homosexuality. Whatever their origins, the sanctions experienced by homosexuals have been substantial, although variable, during different historical periods. There is no known society that values homosexuality, though some have tolerated it at different times, in different individuals, and under different circumstances.

One consequence of both legal and social regulation in the 1990s was the increased militancy of some homosexuals. Not content to be the objects of society's disapproval, some gays declared a new view of homosexuality as nondeviant, acceptable behavior. Bolstered by recent biological work that suggests a chromosomal basis for at least some portion of sexual preference, militant gays have attempted to "take back" the conception and language of homosexuality from the larger society (Browning 1994). Groups such as Queer Nation often protest conventional normative definitions by affirming gayness.

These very activities, however, demonstrate the power and impact of the stigma on homosexuality. Gay men and women are often put in the position of asserting that they are "normal" and everyone else is out of step. On the one hand, militant gays deny that homosexuality is deviant; on the other, they experience substantial discomfort trying to live in a heterosexual world that generally disapproves of them. Not wishing to accept the larger community's social and legal definitions of their sexuality, many of them rebel against the labels in ways that often accentuate their differences rather than their similarities. Such efforts are not individualistic responses but represent a collective reaction that stems from a political movement.

The Gay Movement and Gay Communities

The gay movement became politically visible on June 28, 1969, when patrons of Stonewall, a gay bar in New York City's Greenwich Village, refused to cooperate with police who were carrying out a routine raid (Carter 2004). The patrons, composed mostly of flamboyant drag queens and prostitutes, escalated their protests against the police into nearly five days of rioting that eventually involved hundreds of sympathetic supporters. The rioting appeared to accomplish little; no laws were changed, gays continued to be "bashed," and homosexuals continued to be regarded as socially and sexually marginal people. The significance of this resistance was in the imagination it sparked in gay people throughout the United States and elsewhere. Many gays became eager to reject the social stigma and shame heaped upon them by conventional society (Bawer 1996, 4–15). Stonewall became synonymous with any resistance to that oppression.

The rioting galvanized gay opinion like no other event. Gays had witnessed the success of the women's movement, which grew out of a similarly felt oppression. But gays and lesbians had obstacles beyond traditionally held prejudices, reinforced by two of the most powerful institutions of social control in society: religion and the law. The women's movement had to confront antiquated tradition and stodgy beliefs about gender roles but not moral condemnation or nightsticks, as did the gay movement.

Only the cleverest and most energetic strategies would stand a chance against such puissant foes. Yet:

> . . . gays developed a territorial base, with a matrix of bars, associations, publications, theaters, churches, writers, comedians, professional services, and eventually political representatives. Gayness became a sort of ethnicity with its own codes of recognition, rituals, parades, sacred days, even its own flag with a rainbow motif. (Gitlin 1995, 142–143)

The first generation of gays after Stonewall worked hard to produce such a community, but the effort was thought to require extremism and aggressiveness. It was to be a public community, which meant that homosexuals would have to be enticed to come out of the closet. Gay pride marches, celebrations of Stonewall, and organized events were meant to shock, annoy, retaliate, and educate—all at the same time. There was a portion of the gay community that "developed a radical direct-action movement among men and women who are no longer interested in dwelling only within the safe ghettos of gaydom" (Browning 1994, 25). The closet was defined as only a transient haven from the political realities of the movement and the drive for eventual freedom.

As in the women's movement, the gay movement produced a gulf among different generations, antagonisms among leaders and followers over points of ideology, and gender segregation. The movement was and continues to be far from monolithic. Some leaders oppose discrimination in any form; others preach the politics of sexual identity in which gayness must be affirmed as something special and distinctive. Some gays are willing to live peaceably in the absence of overt discrimination; others want no less than a social recanting of previous wrongs done to gays. Some wish only that gay bashing would be eliminated; others are more militant in demanding retributive—and in some cases—retaliatory justice.

The women's movement can appeal to both men and women and, hence, can lay theoretical claim to a large segment of potential supporters in the population, but the gay movement cannot assert itself on the basis of numbers only. Rather, it has to rely, ironically, on the moral strength and legal correctness of its position. Such a strategy involves a tricky balancing performance, in which previously denigrated acts and conditions are reclaimed from the oppressors and reaffirmed. The first target was language. The words "gay," "homosexual," and "lesbian" had served their purpose well for those before Stonewall, but they seemed old-fashioned by 2000. These were terms for the closet, not for public discourse. More suitable to the militants were the previously hated expressions of "queer," "faggot," and "dyke." By claiming such words as their own and providing them with a positive connotation, the movement believed that it would liberate the terms from their oppressors. Frank Browning (1994, 34) summarizes the strategy:

Steal back all the hateful epithets thrown at gay people over the decades, turn them inside out, and celebrate them. If homophobes and fundamentalist preachers rant on about homosexuals recruiting the young because it's the only way to replenish their unholy ranks, then steal the language back. Yes, queer people want to recruit the young, not by kidnapping young men as Chicago serial killer John Wayne Gacy did, but by being mentors and role models who would show gay and lesbian adolescents that they are not alone, that they are not freaks, that they need not continue committing suicides at three times the rate of straight teenagers.

So gay activists took one of two directions. The first direction was found in the first-generation gay activist after Stonewall, a militant who exaggerated gayness for effect. "Fag power, Dyke Power, Que-e-e-e-r Nation!" was the shout. Or "We're Queer! We're Here! Get Used to It!" signs, outrageous clothes, public displays of sexuality—anything that was acceptable to get across the message that the days of passivity—the closet—were over. The militant, dissatisfied with continued discrimination and social censure, would demand equality by highlighting the differences between gays and straights. One writer recounts that some gays were able to read a manifesto that advised:

> The next time some straight person comes down on you for being angry, tell them that until things change, you don't need any more evidence that the world turns at your expense. You don't need to see only hetero couples grocery shopping on your TV. . . . You don't want any more baby pictures shoved in your face until you can have or keep your own. No more weddings, showers, anniversaries, please, unless they were our own brothers and sisters celebrating. And tell them not to dismiss you by saying, "You have rights," "You have privileges," "You're overreacting," or "You have a victim's mentality." Tell them, "GO AWAY FROM ME, until YOU can change." (Browning 1994, 27)

While most gays would reject this statement as little more than a perhaps understandable but politically ineffective tantrum, rage is an important component of the gay agenda. Unmistakable gains have been attained politically and socially, and many gays have experienced what one writer called "virtual equality" (Vaid 1995), a condition of being almost there, almost equal. By the mid-1990s, gays were said to be "virtually normal" (Sullivan 1995). But "virtually" would be insufficient for many.

The second, more recent direction was that of the subdued activist who saw political extremism as part of a short-term agenda. More meaningful change would involve direct education, modeling, and quiet conformity. The gay educator didn't want to shake the boat, only to make sure there was room for everyone on board. He or she was interested in the more subtle, longer-term strategy of convincing straights that gays were very much like them in most of the ways that count. The moderate was convinced that the key to social change was political activism that, in turn, required a resolution of the basic conflict in the gay movement. The question needing resolution was whether gays were different from straights of whatever race and gender so that they required special status, or whether gays were just like everyone else except in sexual orientation.

Things have changed little in the new millennium. The presentation of this conflict now determines the direction of the gay movement. What is required is not merely agreement on a political strategy but discussion and resolution of many issues, involving the extent to which homosexuality is deviant and according to whom, the degree to which gays can be accepted in straight society, and the role of law in liberating or repressing them.

Two Additional Issues

As public opinion expresses more toleration toward homosexuality, two recent issues continue to polarize people. These issues are the acceptability of same-sex marriages and the extent to which homosexuality should be considered a protected status for purposes of law and public policy.

Same-Sex Marriages

We began this chapter by talking about one of the most divisive issues in contemporary society: same-sex marriage. While there has been considerable legal activity on this issue since the turn of the century, the issue first moved into the legal arena in 1995 when a special commission appointed by the Hawaiian legislature recommended the legalization of same-sex marriages. The legal proceedings had begun in 1990, when a Hawaiian lower court heard a case in which three gay couples claimed that the state's constitution afforded them the right to obtain marriage licenses. One of the couples, Ninia Baehr and Genora Dancel, had met only a few months before they decided to get married. The couple had strong emotional feelings about each other, but they were specifically motivated when Baehr sustained a serious ear infection and her medical bills mounted. "I wanted to get her on my insurance, but only married people can do that," said Dancel, a television station engineer (Barrett 1996). When denied the licenses, the couples filed a lawsuit against the state of Hawaii. In 1993 the state Supreme Court, in *Baehr v. Lewin*, agreed with the couple.

The following year, the state legislature passed a law defining marriage as a union solely between a man and a woman. The Hawaiian Supreme Court delayed rehearing the *Baehr* case until a special commission report was issued. The commission in December 1995 recommended legalizing same-sex marriages, saying in effect that there was no reason not to recognize them.

Up to this point, no case concerning gay marriages had progressed so far in the court system of any state or the federal government. Although the case originated in Hawaii, the issue has had national significance because the "full faith and credit clause" of the U.S. Constitution requires other states to recognize marriages sanctioned in other states. In other words, if you are married in Hawaii, you are married in the other 49 states as well. This is the same situation for divorces; a divorce in one state is recognized in all other states.

As a result of the Hawaiian ruling, some states introduced legislation withholding recognition of same-sex marriages. Utah, which has a long history of dealing with nontraditional marriages such as polygamous ones, passed a law in 1995 that denies recognition of marriages that do not conform to Utah law. In 1996, South Dakota defined marriage in that state as a union between a man and a woman. Legislation of this sort is typically justified with the rationale that the state has an interest in encouraging heterosexual marriages to best guarantee a satisfactory environment for raising children.

The ruling in *Lawrence* in 2003 did not provide for same-sex marriage, but it clearly opened the door for such marriages. Later that year, the notion of same-sex marriage was again tested in the courts. Two lesbian partners in Massachusetts (Julie and Hillary Goodridge) and six other gay or lesbian couples filed a lawsuit that led to a landmark ruling by the Massachusetts Supreme Judicial Court that same-sex marriage was legal under the state's constitution. The Goodridges claimed they were being discriminated against and being denied equal protection guaranteed under the state's constitution. They won. The Massachusetts court subsequently underscored that ruling by indicating in February 2004 that only marriage, not "civil unions," would satisfy the constitutional requirement. The law took effect May 17, 2004. More than 2,400 same-sex couples filed for marriage licenses during the first week in which it was legal in Massachusetts, as same-sex couples from throughout the United States went to Massachusetts.

So heated has been the concern over same-sex marriage that in the summer of 2004 a proposed amendment to the United States Constitution designating marriage as limited to a man and a woman was debated in the halls of the U.S. Congress. The proposed amendment, which would require a two-thirds approval in both the Senate and House, was brought to a vote on July 15, 2004. The vote in the Senate was 38 in favor of the amendment and 50 against. The bill did not pass. But similarly worded bills did pass in the state of Missouri in July 2004 and in Louisiana in September of that year. In each case a bill amended the state constitution to define marriage as only between a man and a woman.

By the time of the elections of November 2004, similar amendments to state constitutions were referred to the voters in 11 states. By November 3, it was clear that all 11 of them had been approved, making, in each instance, marriage recognizable only between a man and a woman. Most of the states passed these amendments by wide margins. The closest margin was in Oregon where the amendment passed by 57 percent to 43 percent (Graves 2004).

While legal developments in the United States have gone against those who favor same-sex marriage, that is not the case in some other countries. In December 2004, Canada's Supreme Court ruled that proposed legislation allowing gay marriage is constitutional, although it also cautioned that the government cannot force religious officials to perform unions that were against their beliefs (*USA Today* December 10, 2004). The Supreme Court's opinion is strictly advisory, however, and a bill would have to be introduced in the House of Commons. If such a bill were passed, Canada would join Belgium and the Netherlands in allowing same-sex marriage.

The Issues. There are two kinds of marriages, civil and religious. Civil marriage is a legally sanctioned relationship available to all within a political jurisdiction, subject to constitutional standards and procedures. Religious marriage involves church recognition of a union and is subject to the rules and policies of individual churches, as well as those of the state. The boundaries of what constitutes an acceptable civil marriage have changed considerably through our history. There was a time when African Americans and Asian Americans were not permitted to marry at all; until 1967, laws in some states provided for criminal prosecution of those who married someone of the "wrong" race; and in earlier times women who married were considered the property of their spouses. All of these civil marriage policies have changed.

The differences between civil and religious marriages do not invalidate the marriage. The Roman Catholic Church, for example, does not recognize a second marriage after divorce, although the marriage will be recognized under civil law. It is also the case that many gay couples have been "married" in religious ceremonies conducted in churches and temples in many states. The issue with respect to the Hawaii case discussed earlier is not whether individual churches will recognize same-sex marriages, but whether they will be recognized in the civil realm.

Most objections to same-sex marriages reflect negative social attitudes toward homosexuality. Some people are concerned that official recognition of same-sex marriage might be construed as a societal endorsement of homosexuality and perhaps even sodomy. Such a concern, of course, assumes that the issuance of a marriage license entails something more than merely filling out a form. State issuance of licenses to ride a bicycle on public streets, operate a chauffeur service, or run a restaurant is not an endorsement of those activities; it is merely an effort to make them more orderly and controlled. It is debatable whether state-sanctioned same-sex marriage would make society more civilized, as argued by Eskridge (1996), but it is certainly the case that obtaining a marriage license is easier than obtaining a driver's license, which involves long lines and a test. State interest in marriage has erected no such concern or barriers.

One persuasive argument is that the equal protection clause of the Fourteenth Amendment requires that only in cases of "compelling state interest" should the government be legally allowed to prohibit marriage among consenting adults. The issue is sex discrimination, because to prohibit homosexual marriage is by definition to limit the choice of marriage partners. A woman cannot marry a woman, and a man cannot marry a man. Appiah (1996, 54) points out the following:

> Some will object that this is preposterous: the current law treats men and women equally in requiring both to marry someone of the other gender. But, by that line of reasoning . . . we could defend anti-miscegenation laws: for all those require both whites and blacks to marry within their "races."

Clearly, this is a line of reason that has long been rejected in the United States, but the legal system has yet to fully embrace its implications for homosexuality.

Homosexuality as a Protected Status

The law is a powerful resource that can be employed to confer political advantages on groups. It is not surprising to find that the law has been used to restrict and regulate homosexual conduct because it is a resource homosexuals as well as other groups can use, as in the case of antidiscrimination legislation. The importance of such legislation is unmistakable to those affected by it. One letter writer responding to a newspaper editorial on same-sex marriages took issue with the position that gays were asking for special rights:

> I am a 43-year-old gay man in a committed relationship who is raising an 18-year-old straight son. Currently I do have special rights because I am gay. I have the right to be fired from my job and be denied housing in 41 states without legal recourse simply because I am gay. I have the right to be denied custody of my son in most legal jurisdictions, regardless of my parenting capabilities. I have the right to be denied visitation of my lover in a hospital's intensive care unit because we are not legally considered

to be family. I have the right to incur large legal bills and suffer great uncertainty in an estate settlement if he dies before I do, despite any wills that we might prepare. I also have the very special right to have my lover (a non-American) deported, as he is in the U.S. on a temporary work permit; if we were able to legally marry, a green card could be easily obtained.

I don't want these special rights or any others. I just want the right to be able to lead a happy, healthy, peaceful and legally committed life with the person that I happen to love. I want the right to marry him. These rights seem to be the same rights that any loving, committed couple desire and deserve. In my mind, they have a "family values" ring to them. (*Wall Street Journal* March 22, 1996)

Because rights are not absolute and must be interpreted within moral and political contexts (Dworkin 1977), what sometimes appears to be a right for one group looks like the deprivation of a right for another. And this is more than an academic discussion. On November 3, 1992, Colorado voters were asked to consider a referendum which, if passed, would alter the state's constitution. The amendment stated the following:

Neither the State of Colorado, through any of its branches or departments, nor any of its agencies, political subdivisions, municipalities or school districts, shall enact, adopt or enforce any statute, regulation, ordinance or policy whereby homosexual, lesbian or bisexual orientation, conduct, practices or relationships shall constitute or otherwise be the basis of or entitle any person or class of persons to have or claim any minority status quota preferences, protected status or claim of discrimination.

The amendment passed by a vote of 53 percent to 47 percent. This passage meant that all state and local government units were barred from providing any protection to homosexuals, lesbians, and bisexuals against discrimination. It also resulted in substantial legal maneuvering. A state court invalidated the amendment, allowing ordinances or policies prohibiting discrimination based on sexual orientation to remain intact in Denver, Boulder, Aspen, and several other Colorado cities.

The central argument was whether homosexuals were entitled to the category of protected status. Colorado state officials argued that the amendment merely denied "special rights" to homosexuals and put them in the same legal and social position as everyone else. Members of the homosexual community and others argued that the amendment itself was discriminatory since it removed homosexuals, but no other group, from legal protections in housing, insurance, health benefits, welfare, private education, and employment.

It was on the basis of this argument that the case eventually wound its way to the Colorado Supreme Court (see *Evans v. Romer*). There, the justices ruled the law was unconstitutional because the Equal Protection Clause of the United States Constitution protects the fundamental right to participate equally in the political process. Any legislation or state constitutional amendment which infringes on this right by "fencing out" an independently identifiable class of persons must be subject to strict judicial scrutiny.

An appeal was made to the U.S. Supreme Court, which subsequently ruled on May 21, 1996, in a 6–3 vote, that the Colorado amendment was indeed unconstitutional. The Supreme Court decision, of course, did not settle the larger issue of whether homosexuals constitute a group in need of special protection. Continued legal action and social debate is guaranteed.

Conclusion

Homosexuality has been tolerated in many societies, but it has never been respected or held as an ideal of sexual relations. In ancient Greece and Rome, homosexuality was permitted but not particularly valued. There is no reliable way, however, to gauge public opinion in such societies, nor is it possible to know accurately whether homosexuality, although tolerated, was viewed negatively or positively. Finding instances in which homosexuality was tolerated is quite different from claiming that it was esteemed.

Viewing homosexuality negatively, however, does not necessarily mean that it is an appropriate candidate for criminalization. All sexual behavior is socially regulated and only some is legally regulated. Recent changes in opinion and law may reflect fundamental changes in the way in which homosexuality is regarded, but the process of greater open-mindedness is indeed slow. The Wolfenden Report that recommended the decriminalization of homosexuality in Great Britain in the 1950s generated considerable controversy. Though the recommendation was eventually enacted into law, the British public continued to oppose the legislation. A Gallup Poll taken after the report was issued showed that 38 percent of the respondents favored the legislation, 15 percent were uncertain, and 47 percent were against it (Williams 1960).

It is doubtful that legal prohibitions can be more effective than religious and historical restrictions in regulating sexual conduct. Yet curiously, there are contemporary legislators who seem to find more power in the law than it can legitimately possess. In the summer of 1994, the family of a deceased woman was shocked to witness a man in a funeral home fondling her dead body. Their outrage, along with the fact that the Iowa criminal code did not prohibit such behavior, prompted action at the next legislative session. A law prohibiting sexual acts with a corpse was championed by the chair of the Senate Judiciary Committee, who reported that he was surprised to learn of the law's failure to prohibit this behavior, a situation that represented to him an obvious omission. "From time to time," he said, "we find that even though the Iowa code is as large as it is, some individuals have a way of finding that one niche it doesn't cover" (*Des Moines Register* February 22, 1996). It could be argued that the reason there is not more of this kind of aberrant behavior is not that most people are deterred by the law, but that most find such behavior highly objectionable, regardless of its legal status.

The norms that govern sexual behavior are usually powerful and broad. Some societies also have a system of laws that bolster these social restrictions. The difficulty is that although social regulation varies from group to group, legal prohibitions apply to all within a political jurisdiction. This means that the law may not be consistent with the content of the sexual norms of any given individual's group. In some cases, the law may be just the opposite of the group's edicts. Homosexuality has been subject to legal prohibition for a long time in the Western legal tradition, but the content and perhaps the intent of that law has changed over time. So too has public opinion, which in the end is a notably formidable force in the efforts to shape that law.

References

Akers, Ronald L. 1985. *Deviant Behavior: A Social Learning Approach*, 3rd ed. Belmont, CA: Wadsworth.

Appiah, K. Anthony. 1996. "The Marrying Kind." *New York Review of Books* 43 (June 20):48–54.

Baehr v. Lewin. 1993. 74 Haw. 645, 852 P.2d 44.

Bailey, J. Michael, Michael P. Dunne, and Nicholas G. Martin. 2000. "Genetic and Environmental Influences On Sexual Orientation and Its Correlates in an Australian Twin Sample." *Journal of Personality and Social Psychology* 78:524–536.

Baird, Robert M., and M. Katherine Baird, eds. 1995. "Introduction." *Homosexuality: Debating the Issues*. New York: Prometheus Books.

Barrett, Paul M. 1996. "How Hawaii Became Ground Zero in Battle Over Gay Marriages." *Wall Street Journal*, June 17, 1996, pp. 1A, 5A.

Bawer, Bruce. 1996. *Beyond Queer: Challenging Gay Left Orthodoxy*. New York: Free Press.

Bayer, Ronald. 1981. *Homosexuality and American Psychiatry: The Politics of Diagnosis*. New York: Basic Books.

Boswell, John. 1980. *Christianity, Social Tolerance, and Homosexuality*. Chicago: University of Chicago Press.

Browning, Frank. 1994. *The Culture of Desire*. New York: Simon and Schuster.

Carter, David. 2004. *Stonewall: The Riots That Sparked the Gay Revolution*. New York: St. Martin's Press.

Crompton, Louis. 2003. *Homosexuality and Civilization*. Cambridge, MA: Belknap Press of Harvard University Press.

Davis, Kingsley. 1976. "Sexual Behavior." 219–261 in Robert K. Merton and Robert Nisbet, eds., *Contemporary Social Problems*, 4th ed. New York: Harcourt Brace Jovanovich.

Dworkin, Andrea. 1987. *Intercourse*. New York: Free Press.

Dworkin, Ronald. 1977. *Taking Rights Seriously*. New York: Oxford University Press.

Endleman, Robert. 1990. *Deviance and Psychopathology: The Sociology and Psychology of Outsiders*. Malabar, FL: Robert Krieger Publishing.

Eskridge, William N. 1996. *The Case for Same-Sex Marriage: From Sexual Liberty to Civilized Commitment.* New York: Free Press.

Evans v. Romer. 1993. 854 P.2d 1270, Colo.

Ford, Clellan S., and Frank A. Beach. 1951. *Patterns of Sexual Behavior.* New York: Harper and Row.

Gallup Poll. 1986. "Sharp Decline Found in Support for Legalizing Gay Relations." *The Gallup Report,* Report No. 254, November:24–26.

Gamson, Joshua, and Dawn Moon. 2004. "The Sociology of Sexualities: Queer and Beyond." *Annual Review of Sociology,* 30:47–64.

Gitlin, Todd. 1995. *The Twilight of Common Dreams.* New York: Henry Holt.

Goode, Erich, and Richard T. Troiden, eds. 1974. *Sexual Deviance and Sexual Deviants.* New York: Morrow.

Graves, Mark. 2004. "Oregonians Vote Against Land Rules, Gay Marriage." *The Oregonian,* November 3, found at *http://www.oregonlive. com/news/oregonian/index.ssf?/base/front_page/1099486714212580.xml*

Haley, Mark. 2004. *101 Frequently Asked Questions About Homosexuality.* Eugene, OR: Harvest House.

Hamer, Dean, and Peter Copeland. 1994. *The Science of Desire: The Search for the Gay Gene and the Biology of Behavior.* New York: Simon and Schuster.

Harry, Joseph. 1982. *Gay Children Grown Up: Gender Culture and Gender Deviance.* New York: Praeger.

Hu, Stella, Angela M. L. Pattatucci, Chavis Patterson, Lin Li, David W. Fulker, Stacy S. Cherny, Leonid Kruglyak, and Dean H. Hamer. 1995. "Linkage Between Sexual Orientation and Chromosome Xq28 in Males But Not in Females." *Nature Genetics* 11:248–256.

Hubbard, Thomas K. 2003. *Homosexuality in Greece and Rome: A Sourcebook of Basic Documents.* Berkeley: University of California Press.

Katz, Jonathan, ed. 1976. *Gay American History: Lesbians and Gay Men in the U.S.A.* New York: Cromwell.

Katz, Jonathan. 1983. *Gay/Lesbian Almanac: A New Documentary.* New York: Harper and Row.

Kinsey, Alfred C., Wardell B. Pomeroy, and Clyde E. Martin. 1948. *Sexual Behavior in the Human Male.* Philadelphia: Saunders.

Klassen, Albert D., Colin J. Williams, and Eugene E. Levitt. 1989. *Sex and Morality in the U.S.* Middletown, CT: Wesleyan University Press.

Langevin, Ron. 1985. "Introduction." 1–13 in Ron Langevin, ed., *Erotic Preference, Gender Identity, and Aggression in Men: New Research Studies*. Hillsdale, NJ: Lawrence Erlbaum Associates.

Laumann, Edward O., John H. Gagnon, Robert T. Michael, and Stuart Michaels. 1994. *The Social Organization of Sexuality: Sexual Practices in the United States*. Chicago: University of Chicago Press.

Lawrence et al. v. Texas. 2003. 41 S.W. 3rd 349.

LeVay, Simon, and Dean H. Hamer. 1994. "Evidence for a Biological Influence in Male Homosexuality." *Scientific American* 270:44–45.

Luckenbill, David F. 1986. "Deviant Career Mobility: The Case of Male Prostitutes." *Social Problems* 33:283–293.

Marsiglio, William. 1993. "Attitudes Toward Homosexual Activity and Gays as Friends: A National Survey of Heterosexual 15- to 19-Year Old Males." *Journal of Sex Research* 30:12–17.

McWilliams, Peter. 1993. *Ain't Nobody's Business If You Do*. Los Angeles: Prelude Press.

Moore, David. 2004. "Modest Rebound in Public Acceptance of Homosexuality." *The Gallup Organization*, at: *http://www.gallup.com*

New York Academy of Medicine Committee on Public Health. 1964. "Homosexuality," *Bulletin of the New York Academy of Medicine* 40:576.

Nicolosi, Joseph, and Linda Nicolosi. 2002. *A Parent's Guide to Preventing Homosexuality*. Downers Grove, IL: InterVarsity Press.

Plummer, Kenneth. 1975. *Sexual Stigma: An Interactionist Account*. London: Routledge and Kegan Paul.

Posner, Richard A. 1992. *Sex and Reason*. Cambridge, MA: Harvard University Press.

Quinn, D. Michael. 1996. *Same-Sex Dynamics Among Nineteenth Century Americans: A Mormon Example*. Urbana: University of Illinois Press.

Rodgers, Joann Ellison. 2003. *Sex: A Natural History*. New York: Owl Books.

Roper, W. G. 1996. "The Etiology Of Male Homosexuality." *Medical Hypotheses* 46:85–88.

Shapiro, Joseph P. 1994. "Straight Talk About Gays." *U.S. News and World Report* July 5:47.

Soards, Marion. 1995. *Scripture and Homosexuality: Biblical Authority and the Church Today*. Louisville, KY: Westminster John Knox Press.

Stephan, G. Edward, and Douglas R. McMullin. 1982. "Tolerance of Sexual Nonconformity: City Size as a Situational and Early Learning Determinant." *American Sociological Review* 47:411–415.

Sullivan, Andrew. 1995. *Virtually Normal: An Argument About Homosexuality.* New York: Knopf.

Vaid, Urvashi. 1995. *Virtual Equality: The Mainstreaming of Gay and Lesbian Liberation.* New York: Anchor Doubleday.

Vreeland, Carolyn N., Bernard J. Gallagher III, and Joseph A. McFalls, Jr. 1995. "The Beliefs of Members of the American Psychiatric Association on the Etiology of Male Homosexuality: A National Survey." *Journal of Psychology* 129:507–517.

Williams, J. E. Hall. 1960. "Sex Offenses: The British Experience." *Law and Contemporary Problems* 25:354–364.

Whitehead, Neil, and Briar Whitehead. 1999. *My Genes Made Me Do It.* Lafayette, LA: Huntington House. ✦

Chapter 5

Abortion

On Sunday, April 24, 2004, an estimated 800,000 persons paraded in Washington, D.C., along a route that led to the National Mall, the mile-long stretch between the Capitol and the Washington Monument, in what they called the March for Women's Lives. They had gathered because they believed that there had been a continuing erosion of the right to an abortion that was decreed by the United States Supreme Court in its 1973 decision in *Roe v. Wade.* Speakers at the rally protested President George W. Bush's reinstatement of what the marchers labeled the "Global Gag," an edict that bans overseas health workers from receiving American funds if they include abortion in campaigns advocating family planning. Typical signs held aloft by the marchers included one that said: "My body is not public property" and another that proclaimed: "Not the Church, Not the State/Women Will Decide Their Fate" (Toner 2004, A16).

The march was staged in an attempt to counteract the efforts of groups battling to eliminate or at least to reduce the right to an abortion. "Shame on you," chanted a chorus of voices among the 1,500 protesters lining the march route, many of whom knelt in prayer as members of the pro-abortion group went by. A leader of the anti-abortion forces called the rally a "Death March," declaring that he was there to extend the protection of the law to all unborn human beings. He believed that stepping stones were currently being put in place that would pave the way toward that result. A California woman in the ranks of the anti-abortion group explained that she had undergone an abortion eighteen years earlier. "They just said, 'You have to do this,' and at the time I thought, I'm so glad that it's legal. But if women knew the physical and emotional ramifications of abortion there would be a lot less suffering for years" (Venzer 2004, News 2; see generally Maxwell 2002).

Today, abortion stands high on the list of moral issues and criminal justice concerns that divide people in the United States (Risen and Thomas 1998) and in many other parts of the world. In July 2004, for instance, the European Court of Human Rights concluded that there was "no European consensus on the scientific and legal definition of the beginning of life" (Dyer 2004, 11) and therefore it rejected a criminal charge of involuntary manslaughter brought by a 36-year-old woman whose fetus had been aborted when a physician ruptured her water sac after confusing her with a patient who was to have an intrauterine contraceptive device removed. As we will see, an individual's view about abortion depends on what the person believes in regard to a range of semantic, religious, political, philosophical, emotional, and historical matters, rather than on what the person knows or can scientifically prove.

In the political realm, persons nominated for appointment to the United States Supreme Court have to field confrontational questions posed by members of the Senate Committee on the Judiciary who want to learn how the candidate will rule if a case concerning abortion comes before the court. Depending on what the answer is, some senators will vote for or against the confirmation solely on that basis.

The problem politicians face is trying to determine how many people will allow their opinions about abortion to dominate their decision regarding who to vote for. It is believed that those opposing abortion are more likely to vote for a candidate because of his or her views on the subject while many of those who favor abortion are more likely to find other issues more compelling when they go to the polls (Saad 2002).

Both sides in the abortion debate are well aware that the public responds to evocative slogans. Thus, one calls itself "pro-life" (after all, who can be against life?) while the other side defines its position as "pro-choice" (after all, who in a democratic society can be against free choice?). In the semantic arena at least, the pro-life group holds a tactical edge, because it is apparent that those things we are allowed to "choose" will always be limited by many conditions, such as our ability to afford what we want. In addition, there is an edge of selfishness attached to favoring "choice" over "life." It is likely that an awareness of these considerations has moved pro-choice advocates to begin to stress what they call "reproductive liberty" in their campaign literature. They also have abandoned a phrase much employed in earlier days—"abortion on demand"—presumably because it struck others as too inflammatory. Other examples of the semantic and pictorial battle abound:

- Pro-life advocates use the word "baby" to describe all stages of development in a pregnancy. They frequently call women who choose abortions and doctors who perform them "baby killers." To spread the antiabortion message, bloody pictures of aborted fetuses give the impression that abortions result in babies hacked to pieces.
- Pro-choice advocates are also selective in their language. They usually use the word "embryo" or "fetus" or other medical terms to refer to stages of pregnancy. Frequently the pro-choice message is accompanied by pictures of back alleys, dirty restrooms, and dead women to warn that if abortions become illegal again they will take place under unsafe and life-threatening conditions (Williams 2002).

Theology and Abortion

Roman Catholicism

The most intense debates over abortion are often related to religious doctrine, most notably that of the Roman Catholic Church which, with its 50 million adherents in the United States, embraces 23 percent of the country's population. The core issue for the church is "ensoulment," a concept that refers to the moment when an embryo or fetus becomes a human being with a God-given right to life.

The historical record shows that in early times Roman Catholic doctrinal authorities held that abortion during the early months of pregnancy did not constitute an ecclesiastic offense. St. Augustine, following the writings of Aristotle, declared in the fourth century that the soul did not enter the unborn until the time of fetal quickening, which usually occurs in the fifth month of pregnancy with the development of the spinal cord. Therefore, abortion prior to that time did not constitute the destruction of human life. Pope Innocent III, the church leader from 1198 to 1216, set the dividing line between "early" pregnancy (when abortion was permissible) and "late" pregnancy (when it was a mortal sin) at 40 days after conception for a male fetus and 80 days for a female fetus, numbers based on the times when it is possible to discern genital development in spontaneously aborted fetuses. In practice, because it was impossible to determine the gender of the fetus, 80 days became the latest time for sanctioned abortions (Asma 1994). The early Catholic position on ensoulment was codified as official doctrine during the Council of Trent in the mid-sixteenth century (Schroeder 1941). After persisting for more than two centuries, the position was abandoned in 1859, when Pope Pius IX promulgated the doctrine of "immediate ensoulment" of the fetus and declared that both early and late nonspontaneous abortions were acts of murder.

The position of the Roman Catholic Church was emphatically restated by Pope John Paul II in his 1995 encyclical *Evangelium Vitae* (The Gospel of Life), which condemned abortion and euthanasia, "crimes which no human law can claim to legitimate." The Pope wrote: "I declare that direct abortion, that is, abortion willed as an end or as a means, always constitutes a grave moral disorder since it is the deliberate killing of an innocent human being." The Pope warned against the "profound crisis of culture," which he said was caused by the exaltation of the freedom of individuals at the expense of their personal responsibility, a matter the Pope believed had caused "a veritable structure of sin" (John Paul II 1995).

The use of abortion as a "means," noted in the Pope's message, aroused considerable debate. If there is a situation in which a woman will likely perish during the birth process unless the fetus is destroyed, the Pope's position is that it would be immoral to kill the fetus. Those differing offer the argument that if the woman is allowed to survive she can bear other children at a later time. Similarly, church doctrine declared it impermissible to kill the woman prematurely, even if she is doomed, in order to save the fetus. The end of life, the church believes, is a matter of God's will, not human decision. The effort must be to try to keep both the woman and the fetus alive, not to choose between them.

The ranks of Catholic communicants are far from solid in terms of adherence to the Church's policies on abortion. As we shall see, proportionately more women who identify themselves as Catholics opt for abortions than the percentage of Catholics in the population. In Brazil, where abortion is illegal and 80 percent of the population is Catholic, a study of 2,074 women admitted in a single year for complications following self-induced abortions found that 91.6 percent were Catholic (Fonseca et al. 1996).

In the United States, Cardinal Richard Cushing of Boston declared that "Catholics do not need the support of civil law to be faithful to their religious convictions, and they do not seek to impose by law their moral views on other members of society" (Lader 1966, 60). This position has generally lost favor in the face of the pro-life emphasis that abortion is a form of homicide. If so, it is intolerable to stand by and let others kill, even though they may not agree with your position. In 2004, the matter erupted into public controversy when some bishops announced that Catholic public officials who disagree with the church's teachings on abortion should not take communion. One went so far as to extend that edict to voters. To support abortion was said to be a matter of "obstinately persevering in manifest grave sin" (Ostling 2004).

Categoric theological attitudes regarding abortion can become complicated when a pregnancy is caused by rape. The general pro-life position has been that regardless of the manner in which the child was conceived, a woman is morally obligated to bear the child. Pro-choicers often challenge this position with specific examples: if the impregnated victim of rape is a 13-year-old girl, should she be required to give birth to the child or should she be allowed to decide to have it aborted? They favor the latter interpretation.

Judaism

Jewish thought on abortion mirrors the deep divisions on the subject in American society. For one thing, Jews divide into three major sects—Orthodox, Conservative, and Reform—each with different abortion positions. Besides, there is no one person in Judaism, such as the Pope, who enunciates dogmas that all believers are expected to echo. As one writer has observed, among Jewish leaders "clarity has proven difficult to attain. This reality makes the thought of the rabbis—as they grapple with a delineated textual tradition, wrenching actual moral dilemmas, and a diversity of developing responses—intriguing" (Schiff 2002, vii).

Orthodox Jews oppose abortion (Lapin and Fuller 2003), but some Jewish theologians teach that a fetus becomes human only at the time that some part of its body appears in sight. Until that point, abortion is permissible, though Jewish leaders are reluctant to encourage its practice because of the dwindling number of communicants. The Jewish out-marriage rate is very high—as many as half of all Jews in the United States marry outside their religion—and the group's birth rate is below the level required to keep their numbers stable.

Jewish theology takes a view opposite to that of Catholic doctrine on the priority of mother and fetus in circumstances in which a choice seems called for. Moses Maimonides (1135–1234), a renowned Jewish philosopher, indicated that when a pregnancy is endangering the health or life of a woman, the fetus can be regarded as an aggressor and can be killed as an act of self-defense. The rule in this regard again reflects the view on when life begins: "If a woman suffered hard labor in travail, the child must be cut up in her womb and brought out piecemeal, for her life takes precedence over its life; if the greatest part already has come forth, it must not be touched, for the claim of one life can not supersede that of another life" (Zoloth 2003, 40–41).

Abortion Before It Became Legal

Before the nineteenth century, abortions performed by midwives, herbalists, and rogue doctors, who advertised their services in the newspapers, were readily available in the United States. There also was recourse to a considerable number of self-induced abortion tactics, some reasonably effective, others based on inadequate folklore, and others very dangerous to the pregnant woman.

In the mid-nineteenth century, the medical profession launched a crusade to drive other practitioners out of the abortion trade, a move that is generally interpreted both as an effort to upgrade patient care and to monopolize it. Religious groups took little part in this antiabortion campaign that between 1859 and 1900 saw many states enact laws allowing abortion only when a pregnancy threatened a woman's life and only by a medical doctor (Tribe 1991).

Doctors then found themselves with patients who desired to end a pregnancy but who did not meet the legal standard for an abortion. This group included teenagers, unmarried women with "too many" children, women who for personal reasons (such as a job or an unhappy marriage) did not wish to raise a child, as well as women who did not want to carry a child for nine months and then place it out for adoption. Women who had the wherewithal and the proper connections could arrange for allegedly therapeutic abortions. "I had a legal abortion in a city hospital," one women observed, reflecting back on those times. "My parents paid two board-certified hospital psychiatrists to testify that I was too mentally unstable to bear a child. I wasn't mentally unstable, I just didn't want a baby" (Brownmiller 1999, 5). The less fortunate had to resort to illegal back alley operators, who sometimes botched the surgeries so badly that their patients suffered severe injuries or died (Messer and May 1994; Polgar and Fried 1976; Howell 1969).

In one instance, a law clerk who had been having an affair with a married woman told his superior in the firm where he worked about the dire condition of the woman after a mismanaged abortion. The two men hastened to the apartment where the woman lay bleeding severely. They summoned discrete medical aid to save her life and her reputation. The older man involved in this episode, Lewis Powell Jr., later indicated—by then he was a justice on the United States Supreme Court—that this episode was a major consideration in his vote in favor of legalizing abortion in the Court's *Roe v. Wade* decision (Roy 2003; Jeffries 1994).

Given the secretive and illegal nature of abortions, there exist no reliable figures on the number performed before the Supreme Court made it a permissible operation. There is inferential evidence, however, that the approximate rate was somewhat lower before the *Roe* decision. For one thing, the cost of an abortion was much higher than today, adjusting for inflation, which kept many women from securing illegal abortions. In addition, there was a dramatic decline in the number of children put up for adoption after abortion was permitted. Almost 9 percent of premarital births resulted in adoptions before 1973, a number that fell to 4 percent between 1973 and 1981 (Stolley 1993).

Frederick J. Taussig (1936, 422), a leading authority on abortion, observes that he knew of "no other instances in which there had been such frank and universal disregard for a criminal law." Statisticians monitoring crime sometimes point out that if all women who committed the criminal offense of having an abortion were counted in the tallies of illegal behavior, the female crime rate would have come much closer to or exceeded that of males, and generalizations about criminal tendencies by gender would have to be thoroughly altered. In practice, sanctions were not applied to the women in abortion cases but to the person who performed the abortion. Most often, this happened when after-effects of the procedure brought a woman to the attention of medical authorities. Under such conditions, she sometimes was persuaded or offered to testify for the state against the abortionist.

Roe v. Wade and Its Progeny

As with so many highly controversial issues in the United States, such as school desegregation, it was the judicial branch of the government that took the lead in decreeing change. Part of the explanation is that federal judges hold their position for life and need not be too concerned about public disfavor with their decisions. Legislators and governors and presidents, on the other hand, if they want to remain in office, cannot afford to alienate too significant a portion of their constituency, and often decide to stay on the sidelines when issues that split the public are involved.

Roe v. Wade *(1973)*

The issue of privacy was the lynchpin of the *Roe v. Wade* decision to freely permit abortions during the first trimester of a pregnancy, as well as the decision in the companion *Doe v. Bolton* ruling that abortion was permissible after the first trimester if a woman's health was at risk (Garrow 1994). The *Doe* opinion also declared that a Georgia law that required that a doctor's decision regarding an abortion had to be confirmed by another doctor or a committee and that all abortions must be performed in a hospital was unconstitutional. There is no specific mention of privacy in the U.S. Constitution, but in *Roe v. Wade* the majority opinion declared that the right to privacy was implicit in the fourteenth amendment to the Constitution, approved after the Civil War, which guarantees to all citizens the right to be protected by a system of "ordered liberties."

The earliest judicial usage of the principle of privacy appeared as far back as 1834 when a Supreme Court ruling noted of a defendant in a copyright case that "he didn't ask nothing—wants nothing but to be left alone until it can be shown that he has violated the rights of another" (*Wheaton v. Peters* 1834, 834). The privacy principle was thrust into the limelight in a path-breaking article in the *Harvard Law Review* by Samuel Warren and Louis D. Brandeis (1890, 193) which argued that "political, social, and economic changes entail the recognition of new rights, and the common law [ancient English law upon which American law is based], in its eternal youth, grows to meet the demands of society." Though the precise nature of what constitutes an unacceptable invasion of privacy is far from crystal clear, the principle became a formidable cornerstone of important judicial decisions (for a thorough analysis of the history of the doctrine see Gormley 1992).

The *Roe v. Wade* ruling, made by a 7–2 vote, drew heavily upon *Griswold v. Connecticut* (1965) in which the Supreme Court had invalidated a Connecticut law that prohibited the use of contraceptives by married couples (and thus their sale in the state), a ruling that seven years later was extended to unmarried persons (*Eisenstadt v. Bard* 1972). The court in *Roe v. Wade* cited three guiding principles that underlay its conclusion: the protection of life, the safeguarding of health, and the preservation of the standards of the practice of medicine. It harked back to a dissenting opinion by one of its luminaries to provide a context for its decision which it knew would produce strong political and emotional reactions. Justice Oliver Wendell Holmes had written in *Lochner v. New York* (1905, 76) a sentence that cuts to the core of many of the moral issues that we consider in these pages:

> The Constitution is made for people of fundamentally different views, and the accident of our finding certain opinions natural and familiar or novel and even shocking ought not to conclude our judgment upon the question of whether statutes embodying them conflict with the Constitution of the United States.

It is not a simple matter to pinpoint reasons that led to so sweeping a change in the law on abortion. Certainly, the vigor of the women's movement played a very large part, particularly as a growing number of women moved into the work force. Also, revived Malthusian fears of overpopulation led legal abortion to be redefined in some instances as part of a war to be waged against a presumed demographic threat. Birth control pills, which allowed a greater degree of interference with conception than ever before, called into question the inviolability of the birth process, since it could readily have been prevented even before it began. A research report maintains that the pill is largely responsible for the fact that 36 percent of women held professional jobs in 1988 and 25 percent were in what were defined as "high-powered professional positions," compared to 18 and 5 percent, respectively, 30 years earlier (Goldin and Katz 2000). The public nature of birth control also brought into the limelight once taboo subjects. Inserting a diaphragm is a very private process, whereas birth control pills can sit on the kitchen counter, waiting to be gulped down with orange juice at the family breakfast.

The Webster Decision (1989)

Sixteen years after ruling in *Roe v. Wade*, the U.S. Supreme Court upheld the constitutionality of a Missouri statute that prohibited the use of public facilities, such as municipally owned hospitals, to perform abortions, except when necessary to save a woman's life. The Missouri law also disallowed public funding for programs that included abortion counseling. The court further agreed that a doctor could be required to inform a pregnant woman seeking an abortion whether her fetus was viable and might possibly survive if delivered prematurely.

The court reasoned that prohibiting use of public funds and facilities for abortion "leaves the pregnant woman with the same choices as if the state had chosen not to operate public hospitals at all" (*Webster* 1989, 509). Nothing in the Constitution, the court declared, required the state to enter or remain in the business of performing abortions. Justice Antonin Scalia dissented only because he believed that the court should have gone much further and repudiated *Roe v. Wade,* and that the ruling would "needlessly prolong this court's self-awarded sovereignty over a field where it has little proper business since the answers to most of the cruel questions posed are political and not just juridical" (*Webster* 1989, 532).

On the other side, also in dissent, Justice Harry Blackmun took strong issue with the restrictions the *Webster* decision placed on free access to abortion:

> The plurality discards a landmark case of the last generation, and casts into darkness the hopes and visions of every woman in this country who has come to believe that the constitution guaranteed her the right to exercise some control over her unique ability to bear children. The plurality does so either oblivious or insensitive to the fact that millions of women, and their families, have ordered their lives around the right to reproductive choice, and that this right has become vital to the full participation of women in the economic and political walks of American life. . . . The plurality would clear the way again for the state to conscript a woman's body. (*Webster* 1989, 557)

The Casey *Decision (1992)*

The ruling in the *Planned Parenthood v. Casey* case found the U.S. Supreme Court justices divided 5 to 4 in favor of upholding a Pennsylvania law that required a woman seeking an abortion to listen to a lecture or watch a film about fetal development, and then wait a day before undergoing the procedure. In the lecture, the doctor was obligated to provide information about alternatives to abortion, the procedure's medical risks, and the probable gestational age of the fetus. The physician also had to alert the woman to the availability of printed materials published by the state that described the fetus, told about medical benefits for prenatal care, childbirth, and neonatal assistance, and offered information regarding the father's legal responsibility to assist with child support (Wells 1995). The waiting period, those arguing against the law declared, imposed an unreasonable cost on women who had to travel a long distance to reach an abortion facility or had to pay for overnight lodging. It was also noted that the waiting period had at times been used by pro-life groups to trace the abortion seeker's car license plate and telephone her parents to announce that their grandchild was about to be murdered.

There was only one part of the Pennsylvania law in which inroads against *Roe v. Wade* failed to carry the day. This involved a requirement that a woman seeking an abortion must sign a statement that she had informed her husband of the situation, though she could avoid that stipulation by filing an alternative document indicating any of the following: that her husband was not the man who impregnated her, that her husband could not be located, that the pregnancy was the result of spousal abuse which she had reported, or that she believed that notification would cause her husband or others to inflict bodily injury on her. The judges in the minority offered the following justification for their position:

> First, a husband's interests in procreation within marriage and in the potential life of his unborn child are certainly substantial ones. In our view, the spousal notification requirement is a rational attempt by the State to improve truthful communication between spouses and encourage collaborative decision making and thereby foster marital integrity. (*Planned Parenthood* 1992, 974–975)

The winning side, by a margin of one vote, rejected the old principle that "a woman had no legal existence separate from her husband, who was regarded as her head" (*Bradwell v. State* 1872, 141). The majority declared that women had attained a right to "bodily integrity" and that states "may not give to a man the kind of dominion over his wife that parents exercise over their children" (*Planned Parenthood* 1992, 806–897).

The Partial-Birth Abortion Act (2003)

There is no medical procedure known as "partial-birth abortion." Yet the accepted medical terms "dilation and evacuation" (D and E) and "dilation and extraction" (D and X) fail to convey the strong emotional overtones that have dominated discussions of this issue. The legal ban on what popularly came to be known as "partial-birth abortion" designated as a criminal offender anybody who (a) deliberately and intentionally vaginally delivers a living fetus which, in the case of a head-first presentation, the entire fetal head is outside the body of the mother, or, in the case of a breech presentation, any part of the fetal trunk past the navel is outside the body of the mother, for the purpose of performing an overt act that the person knows will kill the partially delivered living fetus; and (b) performs the overt act, other than completing the delivery that kills the partially delivered living fetus.

The procedure outlawed in the 2003 law generally is employed after 20 weeks of pregnancy. Its performance is made a felony that carries a possible prison sentence of not more than two years and/or a fine of not more than $250,000. If a man is married to the woman who underwent the procedure and if he did not give his consent, he may sue the doctor for damages. So too can the maternal grandparents if the woman had not passed her 18th birthday.

Description of the dilation and evacuation procedures involves unappetizing prose. The woman's womb is dilated, followed by puncturing and draining of the fetal sac, and then crushing the unborn fetus' head so that it can more easily pass through the cervical opening. The body is then dismembered and removed with suction and forceps. In the year 2000 about 2,200 of these procedures took place in the United States.

A Nebraska statute similar to the one later enacted by Congress was struck down by the U.S. Supreme Court in 2000 on the grounds that it failed to allow the procedure in order to preserve a woman's physical or emotional and mental health, as required by *Roe v. Wade*. In the Nebraska case, the court noted "reasonable differences" among "highly qualified knowledgeable persons on both sides of the issues" regarding the medical efficacy and importance of dilation and evacuation (*Sternberg v. Carhart* 2000, 297). The Congressional committee that had considered the partial-birth abortion ban, for its part, concluded that D and E was "gruesome and inhumane" and "never the most appropriate procedure" and, therefore, despite the Supreme Court ruling, no exception was placed in the law to allow partial-birth abortion to be employed to protect a woman's health.

Successful challenges to the 2003 law were immediately launched in three federal district courts. In a 92-page opinion, a New York judge ruled that the Congress might disagree with the Supreme Court about the constitutional necessity to allow such abortions to protect the mother's health, but that it had no authority to ignore that ruling (*National Abortion Federation v. Ashcroft* 2004). Similar conclusions were reached in California (*Planned Parenthood v. Ashcroft* 2004) and Nebraska (*Carhart v. Ashcroft*

2004). Ultimately, the issue will return to the Supreme Court, with pro-life forces hoping that new appointments will bring about a reversal of the *Sternberg* decision. But there is no question that public discussion of the partial-birth matters has strengthened the pro-life forces. The impact on overall approval for abortion (though other things besides partial-birth matters have played into the figures) is reflected in the fact that 56 percent of respondents in a 1995 Gallup poll identified themselves as pro-choice, a figure that had dropped to 48 percent by the end of 2003. Particularly notable was the fact that only 34 percent of respondents in the 18 to 28 age bracket were pro-choice (Mannies 2004).

Unborn Victims of Violence Act (2004)

Legislators are wont to react to a heinous occurrence that gains media notoriety by passing a law that defines what happened as a criminal offense if the event had not specifically been outlawed. And so it was with the killing of 27-year-old Laci Peterson of Modesto, California, who was pregnant with a fetus that she had named Conner. Peterson's body was dropped into San Francisco Bay on Christmas Eve 2002 and was not found until it washed ashore four months later. Her husband, Scott, who had been having an affair, was convicted and sentenced to death for the murder of his wife and also of the unborn child, California being one of the 29 states that define the killing of a fetus as a criminal offense. Sixteen of these states embrace the entire time of pregnancy, while in the remaining 13 states the law applies only after a specified length of gestation.

The Peterson killing provided the impetus for passage in 2004 of the federal Unborn Victims of Violence Act, also known as Laci and Conner's Law. The law makes it a crime to injure or kill a fetus during the course of an act of violence that violates federal law, though the death penalty may not be imposed for an offense against an unborn child. It need not be proven that the offender was aware that the woman was pregnant. The law specifically states that prosecution cannot occur for conduct relating to an abortion for which the consent of the pregnant woman had been obtained or for an abortion resulting from a medical emergency. Also exempt are harmful behaviors inflicted by a woman on her unborn child.

The response to the passage of the law was predictably partisan. Cathy Cleaver Ruse, speaking on behalf of the U.S. Bishops' Secretariat for Pro-Life, noted that now "a woman who loses her child to a brutal attacker in a federal jurisdiction will no longer be told that she has lost nothing." Ms. Ruse charged that "abortion activists recoil from any acknowledgment of a child's existence before birth, whatever the context, and however bizarre the argument, in order to protect the 'logic' of *Roe v. Wade.*" She pointed out that unborn children are often recognized by the law in other contexts. Most states, for instance, allow them legal recourse for prenatal injuries, unborn children can inherit property, be represented by a guardian, sue for the wrongful death of a parent, and be recipients of state-funded health insurance.

For its part, the Planned Parenthood Federation of America denounced the Unborn Victims of Violence Act. "The Act is not intended to protect pregnant women from domestic violence or punish individuals who harm them," said Gloria Feldt, president of the federation. "It is part of a deceptive anti-choice strategy to make women's bodies mere vessels by creating legal personhood for the fetus."

RU-486 (Mifepristone)

For a time, it appeared that the introduction of nonsurgical abortion procedures might de-escalate the intense emotions that have characterized the debate about abortion. RU-486, named after Roussel Uclaf, the French company that introduced the drug, can be used within 49 days following a woman's previous menstrual period and is 93 percent effective in ending a pregnancy. The process requires three visits to a physician, one for counseling and administration of RU-486, which is marketed as mifeprex, a second visit two days later for a dosage of misoprostol, which induces uterine contractions, and a final visit two weeks later to ascertain that the fetus has been aborted and that there are no medical complications (Raymond, Klein, and Dumble 1991).

The Federal Drug Administration approved RU-486, whose technical name is mifepristone, in 2000 after 17 years of review. About 6 percent of abortions result from the drug's use and it has been estimated that since it became available it has accounted for about half of the drop in the total number of surgical abortions in the United States. Only 6 percent of gynecologists and 1 percent of family practitioners will administer the drug, with particular reluctance found among younger practitioners. The doctors' hesitation stems from the number of visits involved, the expense of the drug—about $270—and, for some, moral objections to the procedure.

Plan B: The Morning After Pill

Considerable controversy has swirled about what is called Plan B, the so-called "morning-after pill." The 8 percent likelihood of pregnancy from sexual intercourse without contraceptive protection is reduced to 1 percent if the pill is ingested within 72 hours following the sexual act. The pill, whose proper chemical designation is synthetic progestin levonorgesterel, is made up of concentrated doses of the hormones found in birth control pills. It prevents pregnancy by delaying ovulation, blocking fertilization, and/or inhibiting uterine implantation. Its sponsors call it "emergency contraception," but the U.S. Conference of Bishops maintains that Plan B is unacceptable because in some cases it may destroy an already implanted fetus.

The major American pharmaceutic companies, fearing adverse publicity that could affect the sale of their other products, declined to market the drug. A consortium called the Women's Capital Corporation (WCC) was organized in 1997 specifically to import and sell the morning after pill, which was approved by the Food and Drug Administration (FDA) in 1999 for prescription by a physician. In 2003, the WCC sold its exclusive rights to the drug to Barr Laboratories, located in Pomona, New York. Barr's application to the FDA to allow the drug to be sold over-the-counter in pharmacies was rejected in April 2004, a move that many thought was dictated by politics, not by science. The advisory board of the FDA had recommended approval of Barr's application by a 23–4 vote and that decision was endorsed by relevant FDA staff members after they had reviewed 40 studies and 15,000 pages of data regarding the drug. Old-timers in the federal agency could not remember when such a strong endorsement had been rejected by the head of the agency. At the time, five American states allowed the drug to be sold over-the-counter. In one of those five, California, however, only 14 percent of the pharmacies stocked the pill. Around the world, 36 of the 101 countries where the drug is available allow pharmacists to prescribe it, while three countries—Norway, Sweden, and Israel—permit over-the-counter sales.

The reason given for the unwillingness to approve over-the-counter sales was that Barr had failed to demonstrate satisfactorily that the drug would not become readily available to girls and young women in the 13- to 17-year age range and that it would encourage promiscuity. The FDA also argued that the morning-after pill might lead to less use of birth control because of a belief that a possible pregnancy could readily be terminated.

This last point had been the subject of a research experiment by Melanie Gold and her colleagues who set out to determine if advance provision of morning-after emergency contraception pills to a group of young women would be related to more sexual and contraceptive risk-taking. They concluded that "providing advance emergency contraception to adolescents is not associated with more unprotected intercourse or less condom or hormonal contraception use" (Gold et al. 2004, 88; see also Raine et al. 2005).

One person who objected to the FDA's position and the logic behind it noted that it was unlikely that the agency would reject an application by the makers of an anticholesterol drug on the grounds that people would eat more cheeseburgers when such a drug became available. His position was countered by a pro-life spokesperson associated with the Concerned Women for America who thought the analogy flawed: "One cheeseburger is not going to kill you," she said, "while sex can be life-threatening in one instance" (Harris 2004, A13; Kemper 2004).

Parental Notification and Abortion

Should minors—that is, girls and young women under the age of 18—be required to notify a parent and secure permission in order to be allowed to obtain an abortion? After all, say those who advocate this requirement, minors must obtain parental permission for most medical and dental treatments, for a permanent tattoo, for marriage, and for a driving license. Supporters of parental notification rules maintain that underage girls are not sufficiently mature to make so vital a decision. Besides, if the minor decides to go ahead with the procedure, parental involvement could change what might be a lonely and alienating experience into a more relaxed endeavor.

Those taking a contrary position say that parents often are part of the problem and not the desired solution to it. When the pregnancy is the result of sexual assault within the family it is obvious that parental involvement in an abortion decision is not likely to be a reasonable option.

Thirty-three states now require parental consent or notification before an abortion is legally permissible. The U.S. Supreme Court has ruled, however, that minors must have the alternative option of seeking a court order authorizing the procedure (*Belloti v. Baird* 1979; see also Ehrlich 2000). The argument against the approval requirement is that some girls who prefer an abortion nonetheless will not seek it because they are unwilling to notify their parents or to be involved in a court procedure, despite the fact that judges almost never deny permission. California judge Joyce Kennard observed that appearing in court in regard to what might be considered a private, intimate issue, could be "unbearably intimidating" and "humiliating" so that young women "will risk their lives with illegal or self-inflicted abortions or opt for bearing a child that they cannot care for" (*American Academy of Pediatrics v. Lungren* 1997, 932). Opposing the California notification law, which was ruled unconstitutional by state courts, Justice Kennard further quoted Justice Thurgood Marshall who had pointed out in *Hodgson v. Minnesota* (1999, 467) that "a minor's overall risk of dying in childbirth is over nine times greater than the risk of dying from a legal abortion" (citing Greydanus and Railsback 1985, 213).

Susanna Ehrlich conducted a comprehensive study of 26 young women, with an average age of 16.3, who chose the court option approach instead of parental notification. About one-third were Hispanic, one-third Anglos, and one-third African Americans. Most were Catholics, and three-quarters were living at home and attending school. The major reasons for not informing their parents were that they felt their parents would be extremely upset and that they feared an adverse reaction, such as being kicked out of the house or physically harmed. Underlying these reasons was the desire not to damage their relationship with their parents. Two-thirds said they had conferred with a "responsible adult"—a professional, a relative, a foster parent, or the parents of their boyfriend. After intensive personal discussion with her study subjects, Ehrlich (2003, 145) concluded they were capable of deciding sensibly for themselves whether or not they wanted to have an abortion.

Two events illustrate how the parental notification requirement can engender further disputes about abortion. The first took place in Houston in 2004 when a 21-year-old woman and her father sued an abortion clinic and a physician on the grounds that she had received an abortion when they accepted as proof that she was 18 years old a supermarket identification card on which she had misrepresented her true age—she was seven weeks short of 18. Texas requires notification by people under 18 of their parents at least 48 hours before an abortion can be performed. The young woman had secured the abortion because she believed that telling her father, a fundamentalist minister, that she was pregnant would "break his heart." The father testified that had he known he would have given her love and encouraged her to have the baby. She has since married the man who had first impregnated her and has given birth to two children (Nissinov 2004).

How would you have decided this case? The jury ruled that the plaintiff deserved no compensation, apparently on the grounds that she had intentionally deceived the clinic authorities.

In a 1996 case, an older woman who drove a 13-year-old Pennsylvania girl to New York, where there is no parental notification law, for an abortion without informing the girl's mother was fined $500 and sentenced to 150 hours of community service. The woman's 18-year-old stepson, who had impregnated the girl, was convicted of statutory rape.

How Many Abortions Are There?

There are a large number of important consequences of *Roe v. Wade* that cannot be calculated numerically, including, for example, the effect of the Supreme Court's decision on the movement of women into the work force and the spacing of children and, perhaps, even on the divorce rate. Many other matters contribute to these developments and there is no way to disaggregate them.

We can measure with some reliability the number of legal abortions that have been performed since 1973. Unfortunately, the federal Centers for Disease Control (CDC), which usually is the prime source for such information, comes up short in regard to abortion figures. They have placed the number at 857,475 for 2001, the most recent figure currently available. Reporting to the CDC is voluntary and four states—Alaska, California, New Hampshire, and Oklahoma—have chosen not to supply information to the federal agency. Since California has one-eighth of America's population and an abortion rate almost double that for the nation, the absence of its data skews the centers' total significantly.

The best statistics on abortion numbers and trends come from the Alan Guttmacher Institute, a nonprofit organization for reproductive health research, policy analysis, and public education. It reports that the abortion rate for the year 2000 was 21.3 per one thousand women of child-bearing age, the lowest rate since 1975.

The institute estimates that there were 1.31 million legal induced abortions in 2000. This total compares to an estimated 800,000 illegal abortions in the year that *Roe v. Wade* was decided. The number of legal abortions rose to 1.6 million through much of the 1980s before beginning to move downward in the 1990s (Finer and Henshaw 2003). The abortion rate for teenagers, females age 15 to 19, has shown the same pattern of decline, though the rate for Hispanic women has been increasing during the past decade. Hispanic women have an abortion rate 2½ times higher than Anglos, while the African-American rate is three times that of the white rate. Poor and low-income women account for more than half of the abortions performed (Jones, Darroch, and Henshaw 2002). Women who identify themselves as Protestants are involved in 43 percent of the abortions and Catholics in 27 percent. More than 80 percent of women having abortions are unmarried; two-thirds of the women have never been married. A majority of all women having abortions have given birth previously, and about 45 percent of the 1.3 million abortions involve women who have had a previous abortion. The three reasons given for securing an abortion are, in descending order: (1) a child would interfere with work, school, or other responsibilities; (2) I cannot afford a child; (3) I do not want to be a single parent; and (4) I am having trouble with my husband or partner.

By far the largest number of abortions are performed in clinics and not by private doctors in hospitals or in their offices. Many gynecologists refuse to do abortions because they believe that they would gain an unfavorable reputation in the community. Others resent being put in a position in which they say they can be treated as hirelings, mere providers of a service on demand (Imber 1986). In addition, some doctors avoid performing abortions because they fear harassment or physical harm from militant antiabortionists (on this last point see Baird-Windle and Bader 2001).

In general, physicians often oppose abortion because, politically, they tend to align themselves with conservative positions. Also, physicians are committed by oath to the preservation of life, and might well regard abortion as a violation of their professional duty. One doctor claims to know another reason why obstetricians remain wary of doing abortions:

> Ob-Gyns are mama's boys. They go into obstetrics because they identify with women and the whole reproductive process. Now ask them to do an abortion and it's against what they're psychologically attuned to. They're trained to deliver babies and put them at the mother's breast. The woman who doesn't want to go through the natural birth bit and nursing—why, she's a tramp to them. (Scott 1970, 69)

The refusal and reluctance of physicians to provide abortion treatment, particularly marked with younger doctors, is one of the reasons offered for the decline in the number of abortions. Other explanations include: (1) teenagers are increasingly postponing or avoiding sexual intercourse; (2) the growing success of the pro-life forces in persuading women to give birth and retain the child or place it out for adoption; (3) the new restrictive state laws, especially those that deny payment for abortion procedures to people on welfare rolls; (4) the reduced number of women in the prime childbearing age range of 20 to 29; and (5) more effective use of birth control methods, especially the use of condoms (Bosanko 1995; Matthewes-Green 1995). Not too long ago, condoms had never been discussed in "polite" society. With the advent of AIDS, they began to be sold in dispensers in college dormitories, restrooms, and gas stations, among other places. It used to be that teenage males proclaimed loudly to a pharmacist that they wanted to purchase a pack of cigarettes, then whispered that they also needed some condoms. Today, the reverse may well be true.

Abortion Views in Context

There is majority support in the United States for permissive abortion policies, but it should not be presumed that the majority is made up solely of persons who reject theological doctrines, such as those of the Catholic faith. Nor is it correct to identify pro-choice advocates with a range of other viewpoints that would be regarded as liberal on the American political spectrum (Saletan 2003). This being so, support for abortion is by no means unalterable, and the manner in which the debate is framed can significantly shift the amount of support for *Roe v. Wade*.

Most importantly, a large number of persons who lean toward the pro-choice view do so because they prefer limited government interference in their lives. Their motto is: Who Decides, You or Them? This was brought home forcefully when two questions were put to a national sample. The first, asking whether poor women should be allowed to have abortions, received strong support. But when the question was altered to inquire whether Medicaid, the program of government subsidy for medical care for the poor, should pay for abortions, the answers moved strongly to the negative side. Obviously, many of those who hold pro-choice views do so only as long as the policy does not cost them money.

Kimberly Cook's (1998, 187) research discovered that pro-lifers as a group have no interest in returning to illegal back-alley abortions, but that they hope for "social change that will occur to transform the minds and hearts of women, and make abortion unthinkable." But among a fringe group of those in favor of both capital punishment and making abortion illegal there were some who advocated the death penalty for persons who performed abortions.

Arguments: Pro and Con

There is no way that the core of the abortion debate can be resolved except in terms of what an individual believes, not what that person can demonstrate scientifically—that is, can demonstrate in a manner that the legitimacy of the conclusion will have to be conceded by any reasonable person.

In addition, much of the empirical evidence in the abortion controversy can be judged only in terms of our own personal values and how much importance we attach to the information set before us. Consider, for instance, findings on the psychological consequences of abortion. A review by Nancy Adler and her colleagues (Adler et al. 1990) concluded that for those who have abortions, the psychological distress is generally greater before the abortion than subsequently, and that the incidence of severe negative responses is "low." Seventy-five percent of women who had an abortion indicated a feeling of relief and happiness, while the most common negative emotion—guilt—was reported by 17 percent. These figures cannot be judged merely in terms of the majority opinion. Is a 17 percent "guilt" response high enough to support a view that favors outlawing the procedure? If the death rate were that high, then assuredly the procedure would be banned. But guilt is not death. Nonetheless, the figures only provide information that has to be evaluated in terms of our basic conceptions of what element of the findings is "important."

Even more treacherous are findings in which respected investigators report contradictory results. Take the matter of the alleged link between abortion and breast cancer, especially if the abortion takes place before a first birth. Joel Brind and his coworkers (1996) have sought to prove such a linkage and have cited a plethora of studies from various parts of the world to support their position. The Brind research team maintains that there is a 30 percent greater likelihood of a woman getting breast cancer if she has had an abortion. But there exists substantial research on the other side that denies any such connection. In 2004, the respected British medical journal *Lancet* published the results of a survey of 53 studies conducted in 16 countries and involving 83,000 women that concluded that an abortion slightly reduced the likelihood of subsequent breast cancer (Collaborative Group 2004). Many of the published studies are somewhat suspect because they rely on self-reports of abortion experiences. Danish researchers, however, reviewed the hospital records of more than 1.5 million women and found no increase in breast cancer associated with abortion, even if a woman had two or more abortions (Melbye et al. 1997). Nonetheless, Montana state law requires doctors to tell women seeking abortions about "the particular medical risks associated with the particular abortion procedure to be employed, including, when medically accurate, the risks of infection, hemorrhage, breast cancer, danger to subsequent pregnancies, and infertility" (Montana Code Annotated 2003:s.50-20-104 (5)(a)(i); see also Kindley 1998).

Historical annals offer little material with which to determine the impact on social vitality, if any, of diverse kinds of abortion policies. The early Greeks and Romans condemned abortion. The Roman poet Ovid (43 B.C.E.–18 A.D.) wrote a mournful verse concerning a woman fighting for her life after a self-induced abortion:

> Aiming to end her pregnancy—so rashly—
> Corrina lies exhausted, life in doubt
> To run such fearful risks without my knowledge
> Should make me rage, but fear's put rage to rout
> O Isis . . .
> Turn your eyes here on her—and me—have mercy;
> You will give life to her and she to me
> You too, kind Ilithyia, who take pity
> When girls are locked in labor, and relieve
> Their hidden load, be present, hear my prayer.
> (quoted in Kapparis 2002, 17)

Isis was the nature goddess, considered to be one of the most powerful of the Roman deities; Ilithyia was the goddess of childbirth, presumably the figure best placed to intervene successfully in an abortion trauma.

Middle Assyrians impaled women on stakes if they were found guilty of abortion. But the demise of these civilizations can hardly be tied to their abortion practices. Among preliterate societies, policies run the gamut. Some groups impose no penalties for abortion; others, such as the Truk islanders, resort to mild scolding; still others, such as the Jakuns, exact the penalty of death for abortion (Devereux 1960).

Arguments Against Legalized Abortion

1. It is argued by pro-lifers that to allow legal abortion represents a wedge into more drastic reinterpretations of what

it means to be "human." Permitting a fetus to be legally aborted, they insist, provides a precedent for the killing not only of unwanted fetuses, which are defined as "non-human," but of infants themselves who could also be declared to lack adequate humanity before they reach their first birthday or if they suffer from a serious physical or genetic defect. Legal abortion is said to make actions such as fetal experimentation and human cloning more acceptable. The belief here is that morally wrong laws and court decisions, such as *Roe v. Wade*, poison the value system and sow degradation throughout the country's political system.

2. Pro-life advocates maintain that many women who undergo abortions later come to regret their decision. They note that children who are seen before birth as "unwanted" often turn out to be cherished when they become part of a family. The British novelist Margaret Drabble offers a portrait of such a situation:

> After thirteen months [of marriage] we had Flora. I was furious; she was David's responsibility, we owed her to his carelessness. I was appalled by the filthy mess of pregnancy and birth, and for the last two months before she was born I could hardly speak to him for misery.
>
> But somehow, after she was born, and this again is a common story, I am proud of this commonness, things improved out of all recognition. We changed. I can see that it was as simple as that. I was devoted to Flora, entirely against my expectations, so that every time I saw her I was filled with delighted and amazed relief. What I had dreaded as the blight of my life turned out to be one of its greatest joys. David too reacted overwhelmingly strongly toward the child, and in the shock of our mutual surprise at this state of affairs we fell once more into each other's arms. (Drabble 1966, 29)

3. Relatively few persons, pro-lifers point out, no matter how wretched their lives may be, choose to end their lives themselves, although they always have that option. Nor do many people truly wish that they had never been born. The argument is made that the fetus whose existence

hinges on the abortion decision has no way of registering his or her view on the matter.

4. Pro-lifers believe that legal abortion encourages behavior that they see as immoral and unacceptable. They argue that it contributes to casual sexual encounters between unmarried people. More fundamentally, they believe that a woman who becomes pregnant has the duty—not as a penalty but as a moral obligation to the unborn child—to carry the fetus to term.

5. The term "genocide" is sometimes used to discredit abortion, with parallels being drawn between what is declared to be the murder of the innocent unborn (almost 40 million cases of legal abortion in the United States since 1973) and the Holocaust (involving the slaughter of 6 million Jews).

6. It is maintained that the Supreme Court put its nose into business that is far from its legitimate concern when it delivered the *Roe v. Wade* decision. That decision is deemed at fault as well for relying on the concept of "privacy" which is not found in the Constitution and is defined so loosely as to be virtually meaningless. In *Doe v. Bolton* the definition of the pregnant woman's health also is deemed by pro-lifers to be ill-defined, since it includes emotional, psychological, familial, and other factors that are believed to be relevant to the well-being of the patient.

7. Pro-lifers insist that the issue of abortion should be left to the states, whose legislators are responsible to the people, and not to the courts.

8. With ultrasound techniques now able to determine the sex of a fetus, pro-lifers note that abortion is likely to be used to discriminate against female fetuses, skewing the population ratio and in time having far-reaching detrimental consequences for social arrangements (Sanger 2004, 211). Research shows that for unmarried couples, having a son makes it 35 to 40 percent more likely for the parents to marry than having a daughter (Lundberg and Rose 2003). Also, parents of girls are more likely to divorce than parents of boys (Dahl and Moretti 2004). Given these circumstances, women seeking to wed their child's father or to

remain married to him might elect abortion if they learn that they are carrying a female fetus.

Arguments for Legalized Abortion

1. Pro-choice advocates emphasize that making abortion illegal has significant racist implications. They point out that when abortion was against the law fatalities from the procedures were primarily found among poor minority group women. In New York in one year, 56 percent of such deaths involved Puerto Rican women, compared to less than half as many among Anglo women ("Abortion and the Changing Law" 1970; Nelson 2003).

2. Research by John Donohue III and Steven D. Levitt suggests that legalized abortion serves to reduce the rate of crime and juvenile delinquency decades later by reducing the number of unwanted children who disproportionately get into trouble with the law. The decline in the number of adopted children effected by the *Roe v. Wade* decision also significantly reduced another group at high risk for delinquent behavior (Donohue III and Levitt 2003; see also Donohue III and Levitt 2001; for a supporting study see Sorenson et al. 2003; while Joyce [2003] provides a critique).

3. More generally, there is the view that if women bear children they do not desire to have, this will severely undermine the quality of life in store for those children and impose social costs upon others.

4. Pro-choicers dispute the claim that there exists biblical justification for a crusade against legal abortion. They maintain that the text in Numbers 3:40 is the nearest reference to the question of the humanity of a fetus. Instructing Moses regarding how to conduct a census, God says that he should count only those firstborn males "a month and upward." Pro-choicers disclaim any idea that newborns and females and later-born children are not full-fledged human beings, but argue that to oppose abortion on the basis of biblical teachings is a feckless enterprise.

5. Pro-choicers argue that it is condescending and discriminatory not to allow women to make their own decisions about abortion.

Conclusion

The fight (battle is probably a better term) over abortion shows no signs of abating, and it is difficult to think of a compromise that would appease either side. The pro-life side, generally the more vociferous of the two because it is seeking change in the status quo, pickets abortion clinics and lobbies to jettison the law that permits abortion. It advocates that, as a minimum, individual states should be allowed to legislate as they see fit on abortion. Clearly, some states would enthusiastically embrace a ban on abortion, while others would not. This would allow those who could afford it to seek out a pro-abortion jurisdiction to accomplish what they desire. For the more ardent pro-lifers, the call is for a constitutional amendment to ban abortion throughout the country, a move that seems unlikely to be successful in the foreseeable future.

The conflict over abortion has been aptly summarized in the following way:

> The issue of abortion has grown increasingly difficult. Few issues have more thoroughly fragmented contemporary America. Operation Rescue and Rescue America, large antiabortion organizations, have organized thousands of actions against clinics that perform or refer for abortions, against physicians who perform abortions, and against organizations even indirectly supportive of the practice of abortion. The people in these organizations act with the fervor of absolute moral conviction. Likewise, women and men with equal fervor vow they will not allow abortion again to become a "back alley" activity requiring women to risk their lives to obtain what should be a safe and simple surgical procedure. So far as one can estimate such things, sincerity and integrity appear in equal measure on both sides. (Baird and Rosenbaum 2001, 9)

Perhaps the best shorthand summary of the abortion debate is that by Laurence Tribe, a preeminent constitutional law professor. What we have, Tribe observes, is "a clash of absolutes" (1991, 6).

References

"Abortion and the Changing Law." 1970. *Newsweek,* April 13:53–61.

Adler, Nancy E., Henry P. David, Brenda N. Major, Susan H. Roth, Nancy F. Russo, and Gail E. Wyatt. 1990. "Psychological Responses After Abortion." *Science* 6 (April):41–44.

American Academy of Pediatrics v. Lungren. 1997. 940 P.2d 797.

Asma, Stephen T. 1994. "Abortion and the Embarrassing Saint." *Humanist* 54 (May–June):30–33.

Baird, Robert M., and Stuart E. Rosenbaum. 2001. "Introduction." 9–15 in Baird and Rosenbaum, eds., *The Ethics of Abortion: Pro-Life vs. Pro-Choice.* Amherst, NY: Prometheus Books.

Baird-Windle, Patricia, and Eleanor J. Bader. 2001. *Targets of Hatred: Anti-Abortion Terrorism.* New York: St. Martin's Press.

Belloti v. Baird. 1979. 443 U.S. 662.

Bosanko, Deborah. 1995. "Abortion's Slow Decline." *American Demographics* 17:20–22.

Bradwell v. State. 1872. 83 U.S. (16 Wall) 130.

Brind, Joel, Vernon M. Chinchilli, Walter B. Severs, and Joan Sunny-Long. 1996. "Induced Abortion as an Independent Risk Factor for Breast Cancer: A Comprehensive Review and Meta-Analysis." *Journal of Epidemiology and Community Health* 50:481–486.

Brownmiller, Susan. 1999. *In Our Time: Memoir of a Revolution.* New York: Dial Press.

Carhart v. Ashcroft. 2004. 331 F. Supp. 2d 805 (D. Neb.).

Collaborative Group on Hormonal Factors in Breast Cancer. 2004. "Breast Cancer and Abortion: Collaborative Reanalysis of Data from 53 Epidemiological Studies, Including 83,000 Women With Breast Cancer in 16 Countries." *Lancet* 363:1007–1016.

Cook, Kimberly J. 1998. *Divided Passions: Public Opinions on Abortion and the Death Penalty.* Boston: Northeastern University Press.

Dahl, Gordon B., and Enrico Moretti. 2004. *The Demand for Sons: Some Evidence from Divorce, Fertility, and Shotgun Marriage.* Cambridge, MA: National Bureau of Economic Research.

Devereaux, George. 1960. *A Study of Abortion in Primitive Societies.* London: Yoseloff.

Doe v. Bolton. 1973. 410 U.S. 179.

Donohue, John, III, and Steven D. Levitt. 2001. "Legalized Abortion and Crime." *Quarterly Journal of Economics* 116:379–420.

———. 2003. *Further Evidence That Legalized Abortion Lowered Crime: A Reply to Joyce.* Cambridge, MA: National Bureau of Economic Research.

Drabble, Margaret. 1966. *The Garrick Years.* Harmondsworth, Middlesex, UK: Penguin.

Dyer, Clare. 2004. "Ruling on Foetus Saves Abortion Laws." *The Guardian* (London) July 9:11.

Ehrlich, J. Shoshanna. 2000. "Minors as Medical Decision Makers: The Protextual Reasoning of the Court in the Abortion Cases." *Michigan Journal of Law and Gender* 7:65–106.

———. 2003. "Grounded in the Reality of Their Lives: Listening to Teens Who Make the Abortion Decision Without Involving Their Parents." *Berkeley Women's Law Journal* 18:61–180.

Eisenstadt v. Bard. 1972. 405 U.S. 438.

Finer, Lawrence B., and Stanley K. Henshaw. 2003. "Abortion Incidence and Services in the United States in 2000." *Perspectives on Sexual and Reproductive Health* 35:6–15.

Fonseca, Walter, Chiyuru Misago, Luciano L. Correia, Joan A. M. Parente, and Francisco Olivereira. 1996. "Determinantes de Aborto Provacado Entre Mulheres Admitadas en Hospitals en Localidade de Regiao Nordeste de Brasil." *Revista de Saúde Pública* 30:13–38.

Garrow, David J. 1994. *Liberty & Sexuality: The Right to Privacy and the Making of Roe v. Wade.* New York: Macmillan.

Gold, Melanie, Jennifer E. Wolford, Kym A. Smith, and Andrew M. Parker. 2004. "The Effects of Advance Provision of Emergency Contraception on Adolescent Women's Sexual and Contraceptive Behaviors." *Journal of Pediatric and Adolescent Gynecology* 17:87–96.

Goldin, Claudia, and Lawrence F. Katz. 2000. "Career and Marriage in the Age of the Pill." *American Economic Review* 90:461–465.

Gormley, Ken. 1992. "One Hundred Years of Privacy." *Wisconsin Law Review* 1992:1335–1466.

Greydanus, Donald E., and L. D. Railsback. 1985. "Abortion in Adolescence." *Seminars in Adolescent Medicine* 1:214–215.

Griswold v. Connecticut. 1965. 381 U.S. 479.

Harris, Gardiner. 2004. "Morning-After Pill Ruling Defies Norm." *New York Times,* May 5:A13.

Hodgson v. Minnesota. 1999. 497 U.S. 47.

Howell, Nancy Lee. 1969. *The Search for an Abortionist.* Chicago: University of Chicago Press.

Imber, Jonathan B. 1986. *Abortion and the Private Practice of Medicine.* New Haven: Yale University Press.

Jeffries, John Jr. 1994. *Lewis F. Powell, Jr.* New York: Scribner's.

John Paul II. 1995. *Evangelium Vitae.* Boston: Pauline Books and Media.

Jones, Rachel K., Jacqueline Darroch, and Stanley K. Henshaw. 2002. "Patterns in the Socioeconomic Characteristics of Women Obtaining Abortions in 2000–2001." *Perspectives on Sexual and Reproductive Health* 34:226–235.

Joyce, Theodore. 2003. "Did Legalized Abortion Lower Crime?" *Journal of Human Resources* 18:1–37.

Kapparis, Konstantinos. 2002. *Abortion in the Ancient World.* London: Duckworth.

Kemper, Vicki. 2004. "FDA Drug Chief Says He Made 'Morning After' Pill Decision." *Los Angeles Times,* May 8:A17.

Kindley, John. 1998. "The Fit Between the Elements for an Informed Consent Cause of Action and the Scientific Evidence Linking Induced Abortion With Increased Breast Cancer Risk." *Wisconsin Law Review* 1998:1595–1644.

Lader, Lawrence. 1966. *Abortion.* Indianapolis: Bobbs Merrill.

Lapin, Daniel, and Adam L. Fuller. 2003. "LeChayim—to Life!: Judaism is for Life." 239–245 in Teresa R. Wagner, ed., *Back to the Drawing Board: The Future of the Pro-Life Movement.* South Bend, IN: St. Augustine's Press.

Lochner v. New York. 1905. 198 U.S. 45.

Lundberg, Shelly, and Elaina Rose. 2003. "Child Gender and Transition to Marriage." *Demography* 40:333–349.

Mannies, Jo. 2004. "Abortion Rights March Mobilizes Young Women." *St. Louis Post-Dispatch* April 23:A1.

Matthewes-Green, Frederica. 1995. "Embryonic Trend: How Do We Explain the Drop in Abortion?" *Policy Review* 73:55–58.

Maxwell, Carol J. C. 2002. *Pro-Life Activists in America.* New York: Cambridge University Press.

Melbye, Meda, Jan Wohlfart, Jorgen H. Olsen, Morton Frisch, Tine Westergaard, Karin Helwig-Larsen, and Per Krogh Andersen. 1997. "Induced Abortion and the Risk of Breast Cancer." *New England Journal of Medicine* 336:81–85.

Messer, Ellen, and Kathryn E. May. 1994. *Back Room: Voices in the Illegal Abortion Era.* Buffalo, NY: Prometheus.

Montana Code Annotated. 2003. *Health & Safety,* Title 50, Chapter 20, section 104(5)(a)(i).

National Abortion Federation v. Ashcroft. 2004. 330 F. Supp. 2d 436 (S.D.N.Y.).

Nelson, Jennifer. 2003. *Women of Color and the Reproductive Rights Movement.* New York: New York University Press.

Nissinov, Ron. 2004. "False ID Card at Center of Abortion Clinic Suit." *Houston Chronicle,* April 13:A111.

Ostling, Richard N. 2004. "Questions and Answers on Catholic Politics, Abortion and Communion." *Associated Press* (May 20).

Planned Parenthood of Southeastern Pennsylvania v. Casey. 1992. 505 U.S. 833.

Planned Parenthood v. Ashcroft. 2004. 320 F. Supp. 2d 957 (N.D. Cal.).

Polgar, Steven, and Ellen Fried. 1976. "The Bad Old Days: Clandestine Abortion Among the Poor in New York City Before Liberalization of the Abortion Law." *Family Planning Perspectives* 8:125–127.

Raine, Tina R., Cynthia C. Harper, Corinne H. Rocca, Richard Fisher, Nancy Padian, Jeffrey Klausner, and Philip D. Darney. 2005. "Direct Access to Emergency Contraception Through Pharmacies and Effect on Unintended Pregnancies and STIs: A Randomized Controlled Trial." *Journal of the American Medical Association* 293:54–62.

Raymond, Janice G., Renate Klein, and Lynette J. Dumble. 1991. *RUR: Misconceptions, Myths and Morals.* Cambridge, MA: Institute on Women's Technology.

Risen, James, and Judy L. Thomas. 1998. *Wrath of Angels: The American Abortion War.* New York: Basic Books.

Roe v. Wade. 1973. 410 U.S. 413.

Roy, Lisa Shaw. 2003. "Roe and the New Frontier." *Harvard Journal of Law & Public Policy* 27:339–383.

Saad, Lydia. 2002. "Public Opinion About Abortion—An In-Depth Review." Princeton, NJ: Gallup (January 22).

Saletan, William. 2003. *Bearing Right: How Conservatives Won the Abortion War.* Berkeley: University of California Press.

Sanger, Alexander. 2004. *Beyond Choice: Reproductive Freedom in the 21st Century.* New York: Public Affairs.

Schiff, Daniel. 2002. *Abortion in Judaism.* New York: Cambridge University Press.

Schroeder, H. J. 1941. *Canons and Decrees at the Council of Trent.* St. Louis: Herder.

Scott, Lael. 1970. "Legal Abortion: Ready or Not." *New York* (May 25):70–75.

Sorenson, Susan, Dawn Upchurch, Douglas Kliebe, and Richard A. Berk. 2003. "Youth Homicide and the Legalization of Abortion." *Analysis of Social Issues and Public Policy* 3:45–64.

Sternberg v. Carhart. 2000. 520 U.S. 914.

Stolley, Kathy S. 1993. "Statistics on Abortion in the United States." *The Future of Children: Adoption* 31:26–42.

Taussig, Frederick J. 1936. *Abortions, Spontaneous and Induced: Medical and Social Aspects.* St. Louis: C. V. Mosby.

Toner, Robin. 2004. "Abortion Rights Marchers Vow to Fight Another Bush Term." *New York Times,* April 6:A1,A16.

Tribe, Laurence H. 1991. *Abortion: Clash of Opposites.* New York: Norton.

Venzer, Ted. 2004. "New Impetus Swells March." *Orange County (CA) Register* April 6:News 1, 7.

Warren, Samuel D., and Louis D. Brandeis. 1890. "The Right to Privacy." *Harvard Law Review* 4:193–220.

Webster v. Reproductive Health Services. 1989. 492 U.S. 490.

Wells, Christina E. 1995. "Abortion Counseling as Vice Activity: The Free Speech Implications of *Rust v. Sullivan* and *Planned Parenthood v. Casey.*" *Columbia Law Review* 95:1724–1764.

Wheaton v. Peters. 1834. 33 U.S. 591.

Williams, Mary E., ed. 2002. *Abortion: Opposing Viewpoints.* San Diego: Greenhaven Press.

Zoloth, Laurie. 2003. " 'Each One an Entire World': A Jewish Perspective on Family Planning." 21–53 in Daniel C. Maguire, ed., *Sacred Rights: The Case for Contraception and Abortion in World Religions.* Oxford: Oxford University Press. ◆

Chapter 6

Pornography

No one doubts that sexual materials in movies, magazines, videos, and computer sources are of great interest to people. But evaluating the popularity of sexually explicit materials is an uncertain endeavor. One estimate (Malamuth and Donnerstein 1984, xv) indicates that the adult male readership of the two most popular sexually oriented magazines (*Playboy* and *Penthouse*) is higher than the combined readership of the two most popular news magazines (*Time* and *Newsweek*). Even if these particular publications do not fit a strict definition of pornography, such figures, if true, reflect strong interest in sexually oriented materials.

Pornography has been at the center of debates concerning the relationship between morality and law for a long time. The issue for some people is that pornography is, by itself, immoral and should be banned, both by church and state. For others, the issue is that pornography has deleterious effects and it would be immoral for the law not to protect us, and especially children, from those effects. But what if the effects of being exposed to pornography are, as some claim, positive? Moreover, what if one does not regard pornography as immoral at all? Should the law be used to enforce the morality of only some people?

Definitions

Obscenity is a term that has multiple meanings. Displaying obscene images on a website is against the law in the United States, but the definition of what is and what is not obscene varies from community to community, and determining the meaning in any given community may be virtually impossible. Obscenity suggests something that is repulsive to a viewer or reader, but obscenity doesn't have to relate to sex or even to physical phenomena. Some people can conclude that the genocide in Rwanda is obscene and others might judge the behavior of a serial murderer obscene.

But we must eventually wrestle with the term *obscenity* because it is part of most legal definitions of pornography. While legal definitions vary, there is an even greater lack of consensus in nonlegal definitions of pornography. It is simply insufficient to use the measuring rod of "I know it when I see it" (*Jacobellis v. Ohio* 1964, Stewart, J., concurring).

The term *obscenity* has been approximately defined in law, but there are problems in applying this definition. In the 1973 *Miller v. California* case, the United States Supreme Court ruled that states can classify material as obscene and ban it if an average person, applying contemporary community standards, would find that it (1) appeals to "prurient interests in sex," (2) describes sexual conduct "in a patently offensive way," and (3) "taken as a whole, lacks serious literary, artistic, political, or scientific value."

This conception of obscenity would permit the use of legal sanctions only for materials that meet all three conditions. The Supreme Court clearly indicated that local tribunals, applying community standards rather than national or federal ones, are the final judges of obscene material. Obviously, San Francisco would use different standards than would Lebanon, Illinois. The problem with this definition is that there is no obvious best way by which to determine what local community standards exist.

The word pornography stems from the Greek word *porne*, which refers to a "buyable woman" or prostitute and *graphos*, meaning writing. In antiquity, the term was used in a limited manner, meaning a writer or painter of prostitutes. Over time, the term was broadened to include the display of sexual organs and sexual activity. The *Oxford American Dictionary*, for example, defines pornography as "printed or visual material containing the explicit description or display of sexual organs or activity, intended to stimulate erotic rather than aesthetic or emotional feelings." Whether that definition is useful, of course, depends on whether the word pornography involves only sexual or erotic stimuli. What is sexual or erotic to some may not be to others. Consider, briefly, fetishes. A fetish is the attachment of sexual or erotic meaning to an object that is otherwise nonsexual. Feet aren't sex organs, but some people become aroused by them. Women exercising physical domination over men may excite some folks but repulse others. In any case, no definition can make pornography moral or immoral, legal or illegal. Only people can do that.

Another definition, this one from the *Encyclopedia of Ethics*, suggests that pornography "is the sexually explicit depiction of persons, in words or images, created with the primary, proximate aim and reasonable hope, of eliciting significant sexual arousal on the part of the consumer of such materials" (van de Beer 1992, 991). What this and the earlier dictionary definition share is that pornography has something to do with things sexual and it is intended to sexually stimulate its consumer.

This is consistent with the definition of pornography of the Home Office Departmental Committee on Obscenity and Film Censorship, a British committee charged in 1977 with examining pornography in the media:

> A pornographic representation combines two features: it has a certain function or intention, to arouse its audience sexually, and also a certain content, explicit representation of sexual materials (organs, postures, activity, etc.). (Home Office 1979, 103)

The Ubiquity of Pornography

People in the United States, like those in many other nations, are exposed to many sexually explicit materials in everyday life. Mass media outlets, such as films, novels, television shows, periodicals, and newspapers, graphically portray sexual images and behaviors today that never appeared in those media in earlier times. Are these images pornographic? According to our definition, not if the intent is to sell a product rather than produce sexual arousal. Many advertisers will attempt to associate their product with something else that is attractive, such as sexy people, but to call a picture of a woman in a low-cut dress holding a bottle of dish soap pornographic would stretch the meaning of that term too far.

Some industries have been sensitive to the necessity of self-regulation. The motion picture industry instituted a rating system in 1968 to regulate access to sensitive images in films and to alert potential viewers to their sexual and violent content. That system was changed in 1990 to eliminate the X rating, which limited access to patrons 18 years old or older, and substituted NC-17, indicating materials not suitable for children under 17. The motive behind the change in the rating system was to attempt to remove the stigma of pornography from films whose contents had earned an X rating. The ratings provide potential viewers with some information about the contents of the film so that they may make more informed choices.

Network television has also practiced self-regulation by assigning in-house censors to evaluate program content and ensure compliance with federal regulations. In 1997, the television industry launched a program-rating system much like that for motion pictures. The ratings reflect the producers' judgments of the appropriate ages for the programs rather than specific types of content. Cable television systems, which are not subject to the same Federal Communications Commission regulations as broadcast or network television, permit more latitude in presentations of sexually explicit materials.

The spread of cable television, along with the wide availability of videocassette recorders (VCRs), broadened the market for pornography. By renting or buying X-rated and NC-17-rated videocassettes, people could view pornography in any dwelling equipped with a suitable player. Many video retail outlets maintained "adult" sections full of sexually explicit movies. Just as printing technology expanded the market for printed pornography a couple of hundred years ago, home video systems and cable television technology have expanded the availability of video pornography during the past decade.

While the innovation of VCR tapes and Digital Versatile Discs (DVDs) made possible more private viewing of pornography, a more recent innovation has further decentralized pornography. Technological developments have brought pornography to myriad computer systems. Communications networks can transmit digital images in the same way that they handle data, from one computer to another. Appropriate software then translates this data into on-screen images. It is not difficult to find pornography on the Internet, although many such sites are now using age-check systems to try to ensure that viewers are adults. But some sites will display various images or stories that are pornographic, with little or no attempt made to check the age of the viewer.

The data for such images fill large files, sometimes creating storage problems. In the last decade, the advent of the DVD, the fastest adopted medium in the history of video, has helped to solve this problem by offering large storage capacity. Companies now sell pornographic DVDs much as they sold magazines only a few years ago.

The use of computers to display pornography led naturally to the development that people who had been consumers of pornography could become producers. Requiring only a computer, a web camera, and a working knowledge about creating and maintaining a website, amateurs who were not associated with the pornography industry could, and did, start producing their own pornography.

Danni Ashe, who was not an industry insider, decided that there was money to be made by having her own X-rated website. It appears that Danni's website has thousands of visitors a month. Basic membership is $19.95 a month and VIP membership, which entitles the viewer to higher resolution pictures, is $29.95 a month. And how is business? According to HBO, Danni made more than $5 million in 2003.

On July 3, 1995, *Time* magazine ran an article titled "On a Screen Near You: Cyberporn." It alerted readers to the existence and dangers of Internet pornography. Although many pieces of information in the article were inaccurate or misleading (Wilkins 1997), the issue of accessible pornography took on a life of its own.

Those who have free web-based e-mail accounts, such as Yahoo and Hotmail, know how easy pornography is to locate. It literally comes to them in the form of uninvited, explicit spam. Much of the spam comes from places other than the traditional movie-making area of California. The advent and rapid growth of Internet porn sites has shifted the industry from a concentration of companies to a widely dispersed set of groups and individuals.

Pornography, in some cases, seems to find us or, at least, the in-boxes of our e-mail programs. What had been confined to special movie theaters, and then to videotapes, has now been thoroughly democratized on the Internet. While consumption used to be limited only to those who braved possible identification in theaters, and then to those willing to visit retail pornography establishments, today everyone with an Internet connection can access pornography in the privacy of their homes. No need to worry about being identified in the wrong place at the wrong time. The Internet provides virtual companionship 24-7.

The Pornography Industry

Pornography is big business. The multimillion- and perhaps multibillion-dollar pornography industry is largely located in southern California and has experienced growth in sales each year (Attorney General's Commission on Pornography 1986, 285). Estimates of the size of the pornography industry range from $400 million a year (Lane 2001) to perhaps greater than $10 billion a year (Sullivan 2004).

Professional companies may employ 50 or more employees for production, advertising, and sales (Abbott 2000, 18). Each company may release 20 or more titles a month and use the most glamorous and popular talent in the industry. Although laws no longer prohibit this activity, a substantial portion of the pornography industry still operates "underground." Many companies are amateur and operate on low budgets; a single person frequently performs the functions of writer, producer, and director. In larger companies, teams of writers often generate text for sexually explicit novels, pooling different sections of the old book and often reusing old material by altering it slightly to fit circumstances and characters in the new stories.

The industry has little to do with the mainstream film industry, and performers in X-rated movies rarely become well known for mainstream movie roles. Ron Jeremy, an icon in the pornography industry, has made several legitimate films only to find himself on the cutting room floor at the end of the shooting or cast in the most minor of roles. While there is no formal relationship between the porn industry and the legitimate film industry, the porn industry has emulated many of the features of the legitimate film industry, including marketing strategies, production values, and awards to recognize achievements.

Some actors and actresses do pornographic work because they have failed to obtain work in the legitimate film industry. As one actor put it:

The legitimate film industry is so dog-eat-dog, the openings so miniscule, that it's like trying to squeeze yourself into a fine pipe. If you're lucky, you might be able to squish your head in. But then you see that you'll probably never get your shoulders in, and that's when you can fall prey to the Big X. It's quick money, and it's kind of a camouflage Hollywood. You're on film, you're acting but you're also not acting, in the sense that you are really having sex, really feeling . . . emotions you get from having sex with another person. (Butler 1990, 298)

Actors and actresses are drawn to this type of work for a variety of reasons. Like prostitution, some actresses earn quite a bit of money, but most make meager wages. Actresses are paid by the "scene," and fees vary with the popularity of the performer and the nature of the scene. An average scene will earn an actress $500, which amounts to a high hourly wage but fails to take into account the long periods of time between working opportunities (Abbott 2000, 20). Nevertheless, actresses can make $5,000 a month in the beginning and more later if they become popular. There are many expenses that must be borne by actresses, including the costs of cosmetic plastic surgery (liposuction and breast augmentation are the most common) and HIV testing, which must be done every month in order to work for large film companies. Other reasons for working in the pornography industry include freedom, flexible hours, and fun. And the sex.

There is also at times a psychological motivation to becoming a performer in the porn industry. As one performer put it:

Pornography is a boarding house for people running away from themselves. Oh, you wear nice clothes, have your picture in glossy magazines, see yourself on video. But porno people are out of step with the rest of the world. We say, "Love me. Well, at least like me." Taking our clothes off, we're not only baring our skins, but we're baring our souls and making ourselves more vulnerable. We have to sacrifice our bodies to gain affection. (Butler 1990, 161)

Actors and actresses in the porn industry must inevitably deal with the stigma that comes with this work. After all, like prostitutes, porn actors and actresses are paid to have sex. No money, no sex. One method of dealing with the stigma is to dissociate oneself from the negative side of the business. Christi Canyon (2003, 167) recounts an incident where a photographer touched her groin. She was furious and screamed at the man. He explained that he wasn't trying to rape her and that she was a porn star after all.

> I was shaking with rage. "So that gives [you] the right to invade my body?" I picked up the office chair and threw it against the Hawaiian backdrop [that was serving as the scene for the photography]. "IT'S MY JOB!! IT'S NOT WHO I AM!" [emphasis in original]

Because most pornography is marketed for straight males, it is the women who drive the pornography industry. They are the real stars. Women are paid more than men and while "boy-girl" scenes pay more than "girl-girl" scenes, women can do more "girl-girl" scenes in any given day. Almost all pornography scenes that are girl-girl are performed for men, not women. Girl-girl scenes for women consumers are a niche market and those movies involve a greater amount of character development and plot complexities. Gay porn is also a niche market and is performed both by gay and straight males.

The road to stardom in the pornography industry is elusive and the perils along the way are great. This is an industry that values youth above all. Therefore, there is less time to make a mark than in the legitimate film industry where there are more roles for older actors and actresses.

It seems common among successful porn stars to have had family problems or to have experienced abuse before joining the industry. Jenna Jameson (2004) reports that she was raped by a relative of a boy she was seeing at the time, and that she started stripping in clubs when she was 16, using moves learned while cheerleading. Traci Lords (2003) also reported being raped when she was younger and started working in the industry when she was 15. Christi Canyon (2003) was a young runaway before becoming a big star who earned over $100,000 as a teenager. These actresses were highly successful, but their success—like their counterparts in the "legitimate" movie industry—is not often duplicated. Lesser talents also may have gravitated to the industry from personal tragedies. For example, "Angel's" parents died when she was very young and she was taken in by an older man who made her do "awful things" (Butler 1990, 119).

Porn work can be used to meet psychological needs. Traci Lords says her work helped her enormously to meet various demands.

> [Porn] allowed me to release all the fury I'd felt my entire life. And that's what got me off. Freedom, peace, revenge, sex, power. I'd finally found a place to put my energies—I was vengeful, even savage, in sex scenes, fully unleashing my wrath. At the ripe old age of sweet sixteen, I was nothing short of a sexual terrorist. (Lords 2003, 88)

One complaint against the porn industry is that women are said to be coerced into performing, but there is little evidence for this. Feminist Wendy McElroy (1995, chapter 1) concluded that there is no coercion in a physical or emotional sense. In fact, since the great majority of porn is for men, the women are more valued. Not surprisingly, women's participation in the industry is strongly driven by monetary incentives.

There are several connections between the pornography industry and organizers of other forms of vice and between the pornography industry and organized criminal syndicates. Many retail pornography stores visited in one observational study in Philadelphia also provided prostitution, illegal gambling, and illicit drug sales (Potter 1989). In nearly 40 percent of the stores, customers could gamble or find referrals to gambling operations, and in 70 percent they could obtain drugs or information on where to get them. Many of the establishments offered prostitution services on-site. Their owners often carried on other related businesses, including publishing a sex tabloid that carried explicit personal advertisements, managing a massage parlor, and running an escort service.

Clearly, things are thriving in the porn industry. There are a number of reasons for this and they appear to revolve around the extensive and expanded use of the Internet. First, it appears that porn websites are more adept at getting and keeping customers. The use of multiple styles of advertising and a tolerance for pop-ups and other gimmicks that are shunned by conventional sites helps to generate interest.

Second, porn sites will cooperate with each other. Other sites are not regarded as competition but as potential allies. If one site doesn't have what a potential customer wants, they can be channeled to one that does. It helps business to have links to so-called "rival" sites. You won't find a link on the J.C. Penney's website to redirect customers to Sears.

Third, the pornography industry has become technologically sophisticated. Websites are regularly upgraded and broadband increased to make it easier and quicker for customers who enter sites that are heavily graphic.

Fourth, new websites featuring a different kind of sexual stimulation can be created very quickly, especially compared to the delays found in magazine production. Once a website developer learns there is a market for, say, sexy people sitting on John Deere tractors, all you need is a digital camera, some models, and a farmer acquaintance. Bam! You're in business.

For all these reasons, pornography creators and consumers have moved closer together and the volume and visibility of pornography has increased. Is this a bad thing? It depends on whom you ask.

The Pornography Commissions

Concern over the potential for harmful effects of exposure to obscenity (a legal term) and pornography (a popular term) has built over time. During the late 1960s and early 1970s, interest in the harm that might result from viewing pornographic movies and magazines led to the formation of a national commission to study the nature and effects of pornography (Commission on Obscenity and Pornography 1970). In addition, the subsequent Supreme Court decisions set guidelines for regulating pornography within constitutional guarantees of free expression. A surge of interest during the 1980s resulted in the formation of yet another national commission to examine changes in pornography since the time of the previous commission and to make another set of recommendations regarding its uses and regulation (Attorney General's Commission on Pornography 1986).

The 1970 commission attributed many problems of pornography to a less-than-open prevailing atmosphere regarding sexual matters. It recommended more systematic public discussion of the subject as well as programs of sex education in the schools. This tone is conveyed in an important statement:

> The Commission believes that much of the "problem" regarding materials which depict explicit sexual activity stems from the inability or reluctance of people in our society to be open and direct in dealing with sexual matters. This most often manifests itself in the inhibition of talking openly and directly about sex. Professionals use highly technical language when they discuss sex; others of us escape by using euphemisms—or by not talking about sex at all. Direct and open conversation about sex between parent and child is too rare in our society. Failure to talk openly and directly about sex has several consequences. It overemphasizes sex, gives it a magical, nonnatural quality, making it more attractive and fascinating. It diverts the expression of sexual interest out of more legitimate channels. Such failure makes teaching children and adolescents to become channels for transmitting sexual information and forces people to use clandestine and unreliable sources. (Commission on Obscenity and Pornography 1970, 53)

The 1986 pornography commission did not concur with this conclusion. It took a more serious view of pornography, with numerous statements about potentially harmful effects and language promoting greater, not less, regulation (Attorney General's Commission on Pornography 1986). The differences of opinion between these two national commissions can be best understood within the larger context of pornography and social reactions to it. It was no accident that the two commissions reflected the mood and tone of the presidential administration in power at the time each commission met (see also Hawkins and Zimring 1988).

One particular issue that each commission examined was the relationship between exposure to pornography and rape. Their conclusions could not have been more different. The Commission on Obscenity and Pornography (1970, 27) reported: "The Commission cannot conclude that exposure to erotic materials is a factor in the causation of sex crimes." However, the Attorney General's Commission on Pornography reported:

> We have reached the conclusion, unanimously and confidently, that the available evidence strongly supports the hypothesis

that substantial exposure to sexually violent materials as described here bears a causal relationship to antisocial sets of sexual violence and, for some subgroups, possibly to unlawful acts of sexual violence. (1986, 326)

A British commission, which met between the times of the two American commissions, also examined the relationship between erotica and sexual violence and concluded:

We unhesitatingly reject the suggestion that the available statistical information for England and Wales lends any support at all to the argument that pornography acts as a stimulus to the commission of sexual violence. (Home Office 1979, 80)

Public Concern Over Pornography

Some evidence indicates narrowing social conceptions of pornography and increasing tolerance for materials universally considered pornographic only a few decades ago. One national survey found increasing acceptance by many adults of access to and displays of materials depicting genitalia and many kinds of sexual activity (Winick and Evans 1994). Whether this finding reflects an emerging national consensus for acceptance remains to be seen. The National Health and Social Life Survey (NHSLS) found that men viewed pornography more often than women did. Those results revealed that 23 percent of the men, but only 11 percent of the women, reported seeing X-rated movies or videos, and 16 percent of the men, compared with only 4 percent of the women, indicated that they had read sexually explicit books or magazines (Laumann et al. 1994, 135).

Outrage about indecency in the media may have increased, but appearances may be deceiving. While off-color comments by such celebrities as Howard Stern may not be approved by many, it is another thing to make a formal complaint to the Federal Communications Commission, the federal oversight agency. In 2004, the FCC was deluged with complaints following a "wardrobe malfunction" during the Super Bowl, according to FCC chairman Michael Powell who appeared before Congress that year. However, what Powell didn't say was that 98 percent of those complaints were filed by one organization, the Los Angeles–based Parents Television Council (Del Colliano 2005).

Let's dispense with one consideration immediately. No one advocates that children be exposed to pornography. While there may be some differences surrounding at what precise age people are old enough to be exposed, even advocates of the possible beneficial effects from pornography rule out children.

So where do the disagreements lie? The first concern is outcome from being exposed to pornography. Does exposure have negative, benign, or positive outcomes? A second area of disagreement has to do with the degree to which pornography is associated with the exploitation of women. A third is how best to regulate pornography in a free society that permits free speech.

The Regulation of Pornography

There are disagreements about the role of law in regulating pornography. Again, no one questions whether children should be exposed, but there are many questions about such matters as what kinds of pornography should be regulated and the best manner to do so. Pornography does not represent the same kind of threat to the community as do interpersonal violence or the theft of personal property. Should the police be used to enforce pornography laws or should the duty be assigned to special units in prosecutors' offices?

Historically, pornography, like all sexuality, has been regulated. One can find examples of explicit sexual references intended to entertain or arouse audiences in many forms created by diverse societies throughout history, including Greek and Roman mosaics, poetry, and drama; Indian writings such as the *Kama Sutra;* medieval ballads and poems such as those by Chaucer; farcical French plays of the fourteenth and fifteenth centuries; and Elizabethan poetry and art. Only fairly recently, however, have governments begun trying to regulate such references and themes by law (Attorney General's Commission on Pornography 1986, 235). Medieval religious institutions—such as the Catholic Church—established the first formal regulations, applicable only to descriptions of sex that accompanied attacks on religion or religious authorities. Even common law courts in England were reluctant to directly address the issue of pornography (see Clinard and Meier 2004, 395–396).

Contemporary legal concern with pornography dates from the early 1800s in England. As changing technology allowed increasingly economical printing, thereby increasing the availability of printed materials to the masses, sexually explicit materials that once achieved only limited circulation began to reach wider audiences. This growing exposure boosted demand, which in turn prompted an increase in the supply (Attorney General's Commission on Pornography 1986, 241). These changes, occurring before the Victorian era, accompanied an increasing willingness to condemn perceived violations of sexual morality. The development of citizens' groups, such as the Organization for the Reformation of Manners and its successor, the Society for the Suppression of Vice, reflected this emerging social concern.

In the United States, the same concerns motivated organizations such as the New York Society for the Suppression of Vice to press for legislation tightening restrictions on pornography. Such groups succeeded in securing legislation against sexually explicit materials, forcing the pornography industry to become almost entirely clandestine through the first part of the twentieth century. Subsequent legal skirmishes raised issues of First Amendment protections of free speech. The most recent laws governing pornography have reflected the outcomes of these disputes. They also reflect deep ambivalence regarding pornography and questions about how or whether society should regulate it.

The Law and Pornography

U.S. Supreme Court decisions on pornography have often reflected close votes among the justices, suggesting that jurists themselves have not uniformly resolved the disputes about what is and what is not pornography that still divide segments of the public. Among U.S. states, Massachusetts in 1811 enacted a statute prohibiting distribution of pornography, and Vermont followed suit in 1821. The first federal statute prohibiting importation of pictorial pornography was enacted in 1842. An 1865 federal statute forbade distribution of obscene materials through the mail. Later legislation coincided with a wider social decline in the direct influence of religion over community life, a spread of free universal education, and increases in literacy.

Two Supreme Court decisions, both from 1973, embody modern U.S. legal opinion on regulation of pornography. Important standards emerged from *Paris Adult Theatres v. Slaton* (1973) and *Miller v. California* (1973). The court decided that public displays of pornography represented appropriate candidates for regulation, while displays in one's own home did not. It also established local community standards, as explained earlier, as the appropriate criteria for determining obscenity. These decisions returned the questions of what is and what is not pornography and what to do about it back to local jurisdictions. As a result, some local officials pursued prosecutions, while others declined to do so, for the same material. Controversies continue over such matters as what constitutes local community standards.

The *Miller* cases involved the mass mailing of brochures to people who had not requested the material. The brochures advertised the sale of four books with the titles *Intercourse, Man-Woman, Sex Orgies Illustrated*, and *An Illustrated History of Pornography*. Their content mostly took the form of pictures and drawings of group sexual activities with prominent displays of genitalia. A restaurant owner in Newport Beach, California, with his mother looking on, had opened the mail, was appalled, and complained to the police. Miller, who had sent the brochures, was arrested and convicted in a jury trial in Orange County, California. He appealed to the U.S. Supreme Court which, in a 6–3 decision, upheld the conviction. The judges on the majority side sought valiantly to formulate a new standard by which material could or could not be regarded as obscene. Besides the matter of sexual explicitness, they enunciated the idea that what was involved had to be "utterly without redeeming value," hardly a clearcut criterion that would readily create consensus regarding whether this or that piece of evidence was pornographic. Indeed, the judges had to decide if a quotation from Voltaire, the distinguished French philosopher, on the flyleaf of the brochure constitutionally removed it from the realm of pornography. They thought not. For the three dissenting jurists, the matter could have been more easily resolved. As they saw it, pornography, in this case the advertising brochure, was protected by the first amendment guarantee of free speech and Miller was innocent of any criminal behavior.

The *Paris Theatre* case involved an Atlanta, Georgia, movie house that was closed down temporarily for showing to a consenting adult audience, that included two detectives from the police force, films with the titles *Major Mirror* and *It All Comes Out in the End*. The films, the Supreme Court decision declared, showed scenes of simulated fellatio, cunnilingus, and group sex, which the Georgia Supreme Court had denoted as "hard-core pornography" leaving "little to the imagination." (*Paris Adult Theatres v. Slaton* 1973). The judges in the non-jury trial declared that the theater's rights to show the films were protected by the free speech doctrine of the first amendment. The state Supreme Court disagreed and the U.S. Supreme Court upheld its line of reasoning, though the 5 to 4 split demonstrated that such exhibits had their judicial supporters. The majority opinion granted that the film audience had some prior notice of what they were going to view. A sign outside the theater read: "You must be 21 and able to prove it. If viewing the nude body offends you—please do not enter." It declared that there was no need in such a case to prove conclusively that there existed a connection between such films and antisocial behavior.

A claim of protection under the doctrine of privacy failed to convince the majority of the court justices who found that in this instance it was neither a necessary nor legitimate pleading. There is no privacy protection, the court observed, for marital intercourse on a street corner or on a theater stage. This last observation provides insight about how much standards of obscenity have changed in the three-plus decades since the court's ruling. Today, actual or simulated sex on a theater stage probably would not create much of a stir in a cosmopolitan area. The court offered an observation that applies importantly both to pornography and to our earlier discussion of abortion:

> Like the proscription of abortion, the effort to suppress obscenity is predicted on unprovable, although strongly held, assumptions about human behavior, morality, sex, and religion (*Paris Adult Theatres v. Slaton* 1973, 110)

There appears to be little interest at the federal level in attempting to control pornography, but some states and communities have used the law to regulate at least some aspects of pornography. For example, in 2004 the California Division of Occupational Health and Safety (CDHS) fined two adult film companies more than $30,000 each for permitting actors and actresses to perform without condoms. Susan Gard, spokesperson for the CDHS, said, "Any bodily fluid is considered infectious. That means barrier equipment must be used" (*Newsweek* September 27, 2004). Notice, however, that the fine was not for engaging in sex for money but for engaging in sex without protection.

More recent legal developments have been concerned with pornography on the Internet. The Communications Decency Act (CDA) of 1996 was enacted as part of the Telecommunications Act of 1996. The CDA sought to protect minors from harmful material online by criminalizing Internet transmission of "indecent" materials to minors. The following year, the Supreme Court ruled 9–0 in *Reno v. American Civil Liberties Union* (1997) that CDA was an unconstitutional restriction on the Internet which, in the opinion of the court, deserved full First Amendment protection. Because only obscenity can be regulated, the rules would effectively reduce the constitutionally protected material available to adults to only that which would be appropriate to children. The unique characteristics of Internet communications, including its ready availability and ease of use, were central to the decision. Because it is possible to warn viewers about potential indecent content, and because alternatives exist, at least in theory, the court believed that CDA's provisions would hamper free speech.

In 1998, Congress passed the Child Online Protection Act (COPA), which was designed to succeed the CDA. It was challenged almost immediately as to its constitutionality. In 1999, a federal circuit court ruled that to protect minors from potentially harmful content would deprive adults of lawful Internet content. Another federal court affirmed this judgment in 2000 indicating that since the Internet was world-wide, the community standards test of *Miller v. California* would have to be a world standard, which would certainly be the most restrictive standard possible. Finally, in June 2004, the Supreme Court affirmed the lower court rulings in *Ashcroft v. ACLU* (2004) that there is not only the possibility of harm but also a serious chill on protected speech if the bill were to be ruled constitutional. In other words, COPA would prohibit adults, as well as children, from going to the pornographic website. "A law intending to protect children ended up infringing on the rights of adults" (Goodale 2004, 3).

The Effects of Pornography

Observers have divided the effects of pornography into two classes: direct and indirect effects. Direct effects might include arousal of the pornography's audience and changes in their behavior that result from exposure to it. Studies have examined the relationship between exposure to pornography and sex crimes, for example, looking specifically for direct effects. Indirect effects would include subtle, long-term changes caused by exposure to pornography, such as redefinitions of sexual objects or sexual accessibility. Some observers argue that there are long-term consequences that strengthen the identification of women as objects for sex or violence and weaken their identities as people. Another indirect effect might be a divorce of the context for sexual relations from partners' emotions and feelings. Some see a substantial long-term danger that pornography tends to reduce sex to a purely physical act rather than a part of a richer human relationship.

Harmful Effects

Evaluations of harm caused by pornography generate controversy because few observers agree about what constitutes harm and how to measure it. Further, evaluators cannot always say that some harmful effects result specifically from exposure to pornography. As a result of these problems, social science research has not yet provided definitive answers to the many questions about the consequences of exposure to pornography (Fisher and Grenier 1994). Laboratory studies have tried to assess the link between exposure to pornography and subsequent acts of aggression; they have produced inconclusive but primarily negative results. The most authoritative research supports the conclusion that exposure to nonviolent pornography does not seem to lead to instances of aggression (Donnerstein, Linz, and Penrod 1987, 38–60; Smith and Hand 1987). Nevertheless, other studies report an association between exposure to "hard-core" pornography and sexual aggression. Boeringer (1994) found that exposure to violent pornography among a sample of college men shows a link to sexual coercion and aggression. Still other research suggests no causal role for pornography in the development of pedophiles (Howitt 1995).

The 1986 national pornography commission highlighted sexually violent material, and, according to the commission, this focus explains differences between its conclusions and those of the 1970 commission. The 1970 pornography commission concluded that exposure to pornography does not promote sexually aggressive behavior, either interpersonal violence or sexual crimes (Commission on Obscenity and Pornography 1970, 32). However, this commission did not conclude that such exposure produces no effects; indeed, most consumers of pornography reported feeling sexually aroused by their experience.

Materials that depict sexual violence may express sadomasochistic themes, such as the use of whips, chains, and torture devices. Some of these materials also follow a recurrent story line of a man making some sort of sexual advance to a woman, suffering rejection, and then raping the woman or in some other way forcing himself violently on her. Most of these materials, including those in magazine and motion-picture formats, depict women characters as eventually becoming sexually aroused and ecstatic by the sexual activity. Exposure to such material, the 1986 commission suggested, may lead directly to variations of this sort of behavior. Further, it also might promote attitudes that perpetuate the "rape myth" (Attorney General's Commission on Pornography 1986, 329). This rape myth holds that women say "no" but really mean "yes"; therefore, men can feel justified in acting upon the woman's refusal of sex as an indication of willingness. After all, the myth continues, even if the woman really does not want sex at the beginning, once the forced contact begins, she will change her mind and enjoy it.

The content and imagery of pornographic films confirms stereotypes of male superiority and female passivity. These films also reinforce an attitude that male sexual desires and satisfaction eclipse the importance of female needs. One study, for example, examined the content of pornographic movies made from 1979 to 1988. Over time, it noted some shift in the context of the sex—progressively fewer movies involved prostitutes and fewer took place in the workplace, while comparatively large numbers depicted sex in other settings (Brosius, Weaver, and Staab 1993). The movies continued to highlight the sexual desires and prowess of men while consistently portraying women as sexually willing and available under virtually any set of circumstances.

The 1986 commission assessed materials that portrayed highly explicit sexual acts along with violent content. "It is with respect to material of this variety," the commission concluded, "that the scientific findings and ultimate conclusions of the 1970 Commission are least reliable for today, precisely because material of this variety was largely absent from the Commission's inquiries" (Attorney General's Commission on Pornography 1986, 324). With respect to sexually violent material, the Attorney General's Commission on Pornography (1986, 324) concluded that: "In both clinical and experimental settings, exposure to sexually violent materials has indicated an increase in the likelihood of aggression," especially aggression toward women. Other research has supported this contention (Donnerstein, Linz, and Penrod 1987). However, the commission qualified its conclusions in the following manner:

> We are not saying that everyone exposed to [sexually violent] material . . . has his attitude about sexual violence changed. We are saying only that evidence supports the conclusion that substantial exposure to degrading material increases the likelihood for an individual and the incidence over a large population that these attitudinal changes will occur. And we are not saying that everyone with these attitudes will commit an act of sexual violence or sexual coercion. We are saying that such attitudes will increase the likelihood for an individual and the incidence for a population that acts of sexual violence, sexual coercion, or unwanted sexual aggression will occur. (Attorney General's Commission on Pornography 1986, 333)

The commission mentioned some less obvious but no less important effects. For one, most pornography depicts women in a "degrading" manner. It shows sexual partners, usually women, solely as tools for the sexual satisfaction of men. Other materials depict women in decidedly subordinate roles or engaged in sexual practices that many would consider humiliating. As a consequence of exposure to such materials, viewers, particularly young ones, may define both women and sexual behavior in general in a callous manner that objectifies women and removes the emotional content of sex (Weaver 1992).

Positive Effects, or Potentially Beneficial Functions of Pornography

The continuing presence of pornography in modern society suggests to some social scientists that it serves an important social and personal function. One sociologist has compared the function of pornography with that of prostitution: In a society that negatively labels impersonal, nonmarital sex, people can achieve gratification mainly in two ways, by hiring prostitutes for relations with real sex objects or by using pornography, which can lead to "masturbating, imagined intercourse with a fantasy object" (Polsky 1967, 195). If such an interpretation correctly explains these phenomena, then it might be supposed that the frequency of pornography use would decrease as recreational sex occurs more frequently and carries a lighter stigma. No evidence currently confirms this possibility.

Furthermore, numerous studies have suggested that since pornography arouses both males and females in its audience, no negative consequences follow from that condition (see the reviews in Commission on Obscenity and Pornography 1970). Exposure to pornography may even encourage healthy behavior and prevent crime. Eysenck (1972) reports that sex criminals first view pictures of intercourse at ages several years older than noncriminals. Other studies suggest that sex criminals come disproportionately frequently from sexually restrictive families; as a result, they often receive less information and exposure to sexual subjects than other people (Goldstein, Kant, and Hartman 1974). Rapists, in particular, seem to have come unusually frequently from sexually repressive environments. Other research has found that the availability of pornography, including violent pornography, is not necessarily related to aggressive criminality, such as forcible rape (Abramson and Hayashi 1984). However, other research has discovered a relationship between sales of pornographic magazines in various states and rates of reported crimes against women in these same states (Baron and Straus 1984). Data like these, as well as results from other studies, have led one observer to a rather surprising conclusion:

> Contrary to what common sense might suggest, there is a negative correlation between exposure to erotica and development of a preference for a deviant form of sexuality. The evidence even

indicates that exposure to erotica is salutary, probably providing one of the few sources in society for education in sexual matters. (Muekeking 1977, 483)

It is probably accurate to say that media portrayals of sex and violence do affect some people in ways other than sexual arousal. Social science does not currently provide a basis for accurately predicting such effects because individual and cultural differences complicate this judgment. Also, not all effects of such exposure prove negative. It will probably take some time yet to account for all of the many factors that influence the relationship between pornography and subsequent behavior. The more subtle effects of pornography—including the imagery of women, sex, and physical relationships without emotional context—may represent its most important consequences because they persist for long periods of time (Itzin 1992; Weaver 1992).

Clearly, behavioral scientists need much more information than they now have about the positive and negative effects of exposure to pornography. There may be a range of effects, depending on personal differences and specific situations. Absolutist definitions of problems and solutions from either censors or zealous libertarians probably should give way to compromises on production, sales, and distribution of pornographic materials (see also Downs 1989).

The Feminist Response to Pornography

Feminism isn't a single ideology. It is broad-based, it attacks many ideas and concepts, and it is rich in its critique. It was perhaps inevitable that feminists would be attracted to pornography because of its often violent and submissive portrayal of women. And, while the inevitable did occur, the outcome could not have easily been predicted by anyone.

The 1973 *Miller* decision had at least one additional consequence: It opened a floodgate of pornography. The industry—and its products—expanded precipitously. Among those watching these developments were feminists who had been fighting other battles. By the mid-1970s, however, a number of issues had been identified, including the exploitation and objectification of women in the pornography industry. Susan Brownmiller's (1999) excellent account of the mobilization of feminist thought and action indicated that the precipitating event was the existence of a so-called "snuff" film (a movie where a person is really killed) that was being shown in New York City. It turned out that the film was not a snuff film, but by that time feminist groups had been formed and were beginning their protest.

They were also active on the West Coast. WAVPAM (an acronym for Women Against Violence in Pornography and Media) was the first group on the scene and, like those in New York, found resources scarce. Doggedly determined, the group approached then San Francisco mayor Dianne Feinstein for assistance, who responded with $5,000 of her own money to encourage the group. Ms. Feinstein had a keen interest in cleaning up "blight" along Kearney Street, and the leaders of WAVPAM had targeted the Mitchell brothers, whose live sex theater was on Kearney Street.

Early activities in San Francisco included an antipornography conference, a "Take Back the Night" march through the pornography district, and the use of some guerrilla tactics such as pouring glue in pornographic magazines while pretending to simply browse them (Brownmiller 1999, 301). But the press ignored all of this, much to the chagrin of the organizers. Many believed the movement should be based in the media capital of the United States, New York City.

The rallies, demonstrations, and workshops in New York in the late 1970s were more powerful and drew substantial media attention. WAP (Women Against Pornography) was well organized and the energy level was high. Bent on exposing the "true" Times Square, they organized tours, newsletters, and events to proclaim their opposition to pornography.

More visible feminists were very successful in making the feminist case against pornography. Susan Griffin (1981) and Andrea Dworkin (1989) offered strong critiques. Pornography illustrates the normalization of domination over women and the tacit support given to male aggression. Dworkin argued that pornography links sex and violence by incorporating violent domination of women into sexual fantasies. Worse yet, she argued that viewing pornography incites men to sexual violence. Her remedy was to press for municipal ordinances that defined pornography as a violation of women's civil rights.

But at the same time that there was a sense of growing public opposition to pornography, there was also some sign that the antipornography movement was less monolithic than previously thought. Indeed, some feminists were put off by the movement, believing that women in the pornography industry were simply making economic choices that benefited them, much like sex workers in other areas. Others thought WAP to be too moralistic and "old fashioned." The movement was beginning to fray.

Smaller groups began to take center stage, each claiming that they were the latest oppressed group, each claming to be more militant than the previous one. Lesbians in general were not fully on board the antipornography bus, some believing that WAP was taking the sex out of lesbianism. Then there was a group of lesbian sadomasochists who were not only not upset with pornography, they valued it—or at least some parts of it as it applied to their interests.

But perhaps the strongest blow to the hegemony once enjoyed by feminist organizations was a piece of legislation in Minneapolis. Catherine MacKinnon and Andrea Dworkin (1997) were asked to consult and draft an ordinance that would deal with pornography from a civil rights perspective. The ordinance indicated that pornography was critical to the creation and maintenance of inequality and that it was a form of sex discrimination. It defined victims as those coerced to perform in pornographic scenes, those injured through assaults prompted by pornography, and those who had pornography forced on them in the home, community, or workplace.

The ordinance was passed but vetoed by the mayor, who believed the city would not be able to afford to defend the ordinance against constitutional challenges. Another version of the ordinance was drafted, passed, and vetoed seven months later. A similar ordinance was subsequently passed in Indianapolis and challenged in court the same day. Predictably, the ordinance was struck down because of its free-speech abridgments. Subsequent appeals were denied.

The ordinance was praised by some feminists and criticized by others. One supporter thought it "just brilliant the way [the ordinance] circumvented the criminal statutes and obscenity codes identified with the right wing, and took a new path through the concept of harm and civil rights discrimination" (cited in Brownmiller 1999, 319). Other feminists, however, were disheartened, especially those who viewed their role as educators, not legislators. It was one thing to pressure pornographic establishments out of business through boycotts or picketing; it was quite another to attack the problem with censorship.

The schism between the antipornography and the anti-antipornography groups grew wide and deep. In the absence of firm evidence one way or the other over the consequences of pornography, each side could make claim to any position. The antipornography groups insisted that it was bad because women were exploited for the sexual satisfaction of men and an affirmation of male dominance. The anti-antipornography groups claimed that some pornography was not only harmless but useful to those women who find explicit images of women erotic, liberating, or educational. In any case, the ordinance denied women the right to choose whether to be exposed to pornography. It is ironic that this impasse was not the result of the pornography industry but other feminists whose political agenda did not coincide with the antipornography feminists.

Susan Brownmiller (1999, 325) captured the essence of the feminist foray into pornography:

> There had been an innocent bravery to the anti-pornography campaign in the beginning, a quixotic tilting at windmills in the best radical feminist tradition. But the innocence was soon submerged in a tide of philosophical differences and name-calling. Movement women were waging a battle over who owned feminism, or who held the trademark to speak in its name, and plainly on this issue no trademark existed. Ironically, the anti-porn initiative constituted the last gasp of radical feminism. No issue of comparable passion has arisen to take its place.

Conclusion

We talked earlier in the chapter about the definition of pornography as sexually explicit materials that are intended to stimulate. There is another dimension about which we have been only implicit. In Helen Walsh's (2004) novel, *Brass,* her character Millie comes to appreciate the advantages of pornography, while at the same time acknowledging its selfishness. Millie comes to understand that pornography objectifies and makes nonhuman people who participate in the pornographic encounter. And she understands further that it is an encounter where emotions, life plans, vulnerabilities, and dreams do not figure, let alone matter. Drifting into a street culture dominated by drugs and sex, Millie's realization of the sterility of pornography appears to set her in a new direction by the end of the novel, but one wonders if she has truly grown enough to understand the difference between sex among lovers, and sex that is devoid of anything other than physical sensation. Sex is not pornographic. But if this is true, what is pornography?

Pornography cannot be identified by looking only at behavior, especially sexual behavior. People who care—even, and especially, intensely—for one another may engage in exactly the same behavior as those who do not, thereby suggesting that it is the same act. But it isn't so. An act of lovemaking between intimates is an act of sharing and respecting. One cannot determine if some act is pornographic simply by observing some behavior. Pornography involves no emotion other than lust and has regard only for self-satisfaction. And, of course, this is why some people use the term "pornography" in situations that are asexual. Justice Stewart was incorrect when he said he didn't know what pornography was but he knew it when he saw it. One would simply need more information than is commonly available.

Identifying pornography fails to address, let alone answer, moral questions regarding its nature, effects, and role in the community. Sex is so highly regulated in most societies that there are many social circumstances where at least some people will object to the act. Sex is an activity that could be immoral for some because it is the wrong time, place, partner, age, gender, orifice, or situation.

Some people have a very narrow range of conditions where sex is deemed appropriate. Some of these will find sex outside of marriage immoral, regardless of the circumstances. Others can environ sex outside of marriage but only with partners in long relationships with a particular emotional context. Still others will disapprove but not be moved to make such acts illegal. The history of the legal regulation of pornography and other forms of sexuality is one of lessened concern and less harsh penalties over time. And, in the absence of more firm evidence that pornography produces negative consequences, that history is likely to continue.

References

Abbott, Sharon A. 2000. "Motivations for Pursuing an Acting Career in Pornography." 17–34 in Ronald Weitzer, ed., *Sex for Sale: Prostitution, Pornography and the Sex Industry*. New York: Routledge.

Abramson, Paul R., and Haruo Hayashi. 1984. "Pornography in Japan: Cross-Cultural and Theoretical Considerations." 173–183 in Neil M. Malamuth and Edward Donnerstein, eds., *Pornography and Sexual Aggression*. New York: Academic Press.

Ashcroft v. ACLU. 2004. 124 S. Ct. 2783.

Attorney General's Commission on Pornography. 1986. *Final Report.* Washington, DC: Government Printing Office.

Baron, Larry, and Murray A. Straus. 1984. "Sexual Stratification, Pornography, and Rape in the United States." 186–209 in Neil M. Malamuth and Edward Donnerstein, eds., *Pornography and Sexual Aggression.* New York: Academic Press.

Boeringer, Scot B. 1994. "Pornography and Sexual Aggression: Associations of Violent and Nonviolent Depictions With Rape and Rape Proclivity." *Deviant Behavior* 15:289–304.

Brosius, Jans-Bernd, James B. Weaver III, and Joachim F. Staab. 1993. "Exploring the Social and Sexual 'Reality' of Contemporary Pornography." *The Journal for Sex Research* 30:161–170.

Brownmiller, Susan. 1999. *In Our Time.* New York: Dial Press.

Butler, Jerry. 1990. *Raw Talent: The Adult Film Industry as Seen by Its Most Popular Male Star.* Amherst, NY: Prometheus Books.

Canyon, Christi. 2003. *Lights, Camera, Sex: An Autobiography.* Los Angeles: Canyon Publishing.

Clinard, Marshall B., and Robert F. Meier. 2004. *Sociology of Deviant Behavior,* 12th ed. Belmont, CA: Wadsworth.

Commission on Obscenity and Pornography. 1970. *Final Report.* New York: Bantam Books; originally published by Government Printing Office, 1970.

Del Colliano, Jerry. 2005. "Report Says Nearly All FCC Indecency Complaints From Same Organization." *http://www.avrev.com/news/0105/6.indecency.html.*

Donnerstein, Edward, Daniel Linz, and Steven Penrod. 1987. *The Question of Pornography: Research Findings and Policy Implications.* New York: Free Press.

Downs, Donald Alexander. 1989. *The New Politics of Pornography.* Chicago: University of Chicago Press.

Dworkin, Andrea. 1989. *Pornography: Men Possessing Women*. New York: E. P. Dutton.

Eysenck, Hans J. 1972. "Obscenity—Officially Speaking." *Penthouse* 3(11):95–102.

Fisher, William A., and Guy Grenier. 1994. "Violent Pornography, Antiwoman Thoughts, and Antiwoman Acts: In Search of Reliable Effects." *Journal of Sex Research* 31:23–38.

Goldstein, Michael J., Harold S. Kant, and John J. Hartman. 1974. *Pornography and Sexual Deviance*. Berkeley: University of California Press.

Goodale, James C. 2004. "Communications and Media Law: The Strange Case of Justice Breyer." *New York Law Journal* 29:3.

Griffin, Susan. 1981. *Pornography and Silence: Culture's Revenge Against Nature*. New York: Harper and Row.

Hawkins, Gordon, and Franklin E. Zimring. 1988. *Pornography in a Free Society*. Cambridge: Cambridge University Press.

Home Office. 1979. *Report of the Committee on Obscenity and Film Censorship*. London: Her Majesty's Stationery Office.

Howitt, Dennis. 1995. "Pornography and the Paedophile: Is It Criminogenic?" *British Journal of Medical Psychology* 1:15–27.

Itzin, Catherine, ed. 1992. *Pornography: Women, Violence, and Civil Liberties*. New York: Oxford University Press.

Jacobellis v. Ohio. 1964. 378 U.S. 184, 197.

Jameson, Jenna. 2004. *How To Make Love Like a Porn Star: A Cautionary Tale*. New York: ReganBooks.

Lane, Frederick S. 2001. *Obscene Profits: Entrepreneurs of Pornography in the Cyber Age*. New York: Brunner-Routledge.

Laumann, Edward O., John H. Gagnon, Robert T. Michael, and Stuart Michaels. 1994. *The Social Organization of Sexuality: Sexual Practices in the United States*. Chicago: University of Chicago Press.

Lords, Traci Elizabeth. 2003. *Traci Lords: Underneath It All*. New York: Harper Collins.

MacKinnon, Catherine, and Andrea Dworkin, eds. 1997. *In Harm's Way: The Pornography Civil Rights Hearings*. Cambridge: Harvard University Press.

Malamuth, Neil M., and Edward Donnerstein, eds. 1984. *Pornography and Sexual Aggression*. New York: Academic Press.

McElroy, Wendy. 1995. *XXX: A Woman's Right to Pornography*. Online at: *http://www.zetetics.com/mac/xxx/index.html*.

Miller v. California. 1973. 413 U.S. 15.

Muekeking, George D. 1977. "Pornography and Society." 463–502 in Edward Sagarin and Fred Montanino, eds., *Deviants: Voluntary Actors in a Hostile World.* Morristown, NJ: General Learning Press.

Paris Adult Theatres v. Slaton. 1973. 413 U.S. 49.

Polsky, Ned. 1967. *Hustlers, Beats, and Others.* Chicago: Aldine.

Potter, Gary W. 1989. "The Retail Pornography Industry and the Organization of Vice." *Deviant Behavior* 10:233–251.

Reno v. ACLU. 1997. 521 U.S. 844.

Smith, M. Dwayne, and Carl Hand. 1987. "The Pornography/Aggression Linkage: Results From a Field Study." *Deviant Behavior* 8:389–399.

Sullivan, Laurie. 2004. "Administration Wages War on Pornography." *Baltimore Sun*, April 6, found at *http://www.baltimoresun.com/news/ bal-te.obscenity06apr06,0,3004361.story?coll=bal-home-headlines.*

van de Beer, Donald. 1992. "Pornography." *Encyclopedia of Ethics.* New York: Garland.

Walsh, Helen. 2004. *Brass.* Edinburgh, Scotland: Canongate.

Weaver, James. 1992. "The Social Science and Psychological Research Evidence: Perceptual and Behavioural Consequences of Exposure to Pornography." 284–309 in Catherine Itzin, ed., *Pornography: Women, Violence, and Civil Liberties.* New York: Oxford University Press.

Wilkins, Julia. 1997. "Protecting Our Children From Internet Smut: Moral Duty or Moral Panic?" *The Humanist* 57 (Oct/Nov):4–7.

Winick, Charles, and John T. Evans. 1994. "Is There a National Standard With Respect to Attitudes Toward Sexually Explicit Media Material?" *Archives of Sexual Behavior* 23:405–419. ✦

Chapter 7

Gambling

The absence of explicit sexual content differentiates gambling from the other moral issues we have considered so far. Sexuality plays a significant role in debates about prostitution and homosexuality: There is widespread belief that only marital heterosexual activity should be legally permissible. A considerable measure of opposition to abortion lies in the fact that it is viewed as a birth-avoidance tactic by promiscuous unmarried girls and women. The banning of certain drugs is sometimes justified on the ground that their use reduces sexual inhibitions. The nearest that gambling has been claimed to contain an element of sexuality lies in Sigmund Freud's ([1928]1945) now repudiated statement that gambling is a substitute for masturbation.

Gambling toys with and teases our cultural values, particularly those related to what has been called the Puritan ethic, a set of cultural imperatives that maintain that people should prosper and enjoy the good life only by means of their own effort (or that of their forebears from whom they have inherited wealth) and not through luck or chance. The roots of some contemporary viewpoints opposing gambling can be found in a 1674 Virginia court order which declared that only the gentry could enter horses in a race and only they could bet upon the outcome:

> James Bullocke, a Taylor, having made a race for his mare to run with a horse belonging to Mr. Matthew Slader for 2,000 pounds of tobacco and caske, it being contrary to the Law for a Laborer to make a race, being only a sport for Gentlemen, is fined for the same 100 pounds of tobacco and caske. (Chafetz 1960, 12)

Worse yet, it was learned that the Bullocke-Slader horse race had been fixed and, as a consequence, Slader was sentenced to stand in the stocks for an hour as an example to other potential wrongdoers (Robertson 1964, 8–9).

Similarly, Cotton Mather, a fire and brimstone preacher during the American colonial period, saw gambling as an attempt by mere humans to take unto themselves powers that were God's alone:

> . . . lots, being mentioned in the sacred oracles of Scripture are used only in weighty cases, and as an acknowledgment of God sitting in judgment, cannot be made the tools and parts of our common sports, without, at least, such an appearance of evil, as is forbidden in the word of God. (Chafetz 1960, 19)

This scriptural doctrine tolerates at least one major exception, the drawing of lots to determine which person in a group will be sacrificed when it is essential for the survival of those who remain. The story of the whaler *Essex*, which left Nantucket, Massachusetts, in late November of 1820, offers an example. The *Essex* sank after it was rammed by an 85-foot sperm whale, and its 20 crew members spent 93 days in three small boats sailing 5,000 nautical miles in the Pacific Ocean before the survivors—eight of the twenty—were rescued. When their supply of hardtack had run out they ate the bodies of those who had died. That source exhausted, they agreed to draw lots to determine who among them would be sacrificed to provide sustenance for the others. When the survivors were rescued and returned home there were no reprimands from their largely devout Quaker community: Divine law had to take second place to the need for the majority to preserve themselves (Philbrick 2000).

Gambling—the word is derived from the Middle English *gamen*, meaning to amuse oneself—involves taking a chance on the occurrence or nonoccurrence of some event, with a reward flowing from an accurate estimate and a loss from an inaccurate one. It can be said that all human behavior is predicated on a calculated risk that will bring about a desired result, and that everything we do entails an estimate that is based on less than all the relevant information. In this sense, our entire existence might be described as a continuous gamble. Making no choices—that is, remaining passive in a given situation—is itself a choice, and it too usually involves consequences of uncertain likelihood.

While everything we do may be a gamble, only a small subset of such activities are generally defined as "gambling." These forms of gambling typically represent an invocation of the ethos of luck that pervades American society and serves as an important cultural ingredient that provides continuing motivation for further efforts. Hard work, touched with vital portions of luck, is regarded as the key to success, and few persons of prominence—the corporate billionaires and entertainment celebrities—fail to mention luck when they tell of their achievements (Lears 2003). If luck plus work represents the key to success, then luck alone represents the major shortcut to success. This is the promise offered by gambling, a promise that also brings with it an element of anticipatory hope and excitement in what otherwise often is a drab existence. The New York Offtrack Betting program tapped into this theme with the advertisement: "Nothing Brightens the Rat Race Like a Horse Race."

Gambling can be said to serve as a ritualistic flirtation with an unknown fate. It has been called a kind of question addressed to destiny, and it has been maintained that the fascination of gambling is that it is a simulation of life; an insurance company, for instance, bets you with certain odds that your house will not burn down during the time you hold a policy with their company. "Speaking pessimistically," Clyde Davis (1956, 12) has written, "you might say that life is a one-armed bandit slot machine which, in the end, takes all your quarters."

Consideration of the moral aspects of gambling has to look at the effects on persons who gamble, scrutinized in terms of how much wagering they do, what kind of gambling they engage in, and whether they can readily, not so readily, or in no way afford the losses they are likely to sustain. Then there are others who are directly or indirectly impacted by gambling: those who run gambling operations, those who gain or suffer from a gambler's skill or luck, and the government in terms of what income it may derive and how that money is expended.

More generally and quite fundamental is the moral issue of whether gambling should be banned because it taints what might otherwise be a healthier social organism or whether there are persuasive moral reasons why gambling ought to be legally permitted. It is sometimes maintained, for instance, that the legal prospect of a magnificent improvement in one's situation by winning a multimillion-dollar lottery prize or a bet on a long-shot in a horse race discourages the more mundane routines of the workplace.

Lottery wins, however statistically unlikely for any one bettor, can bring in a great deal more money than a lifetime of labor. In 2004, Geraldine Williams, a 67-year-old cleaning woman in Braintree, Massachusetts, hit a lottery jackpot worth $294 million (or, if taken as a lump sum, $117.6 million after taxes). On the same day that Williams' windfall was announced, a Pennsylvania man won a lottery that will pay him $1,000 a week for the remainder of his life. Williams' winnings have only been exceeded in North America by those of a West Virginia man who won $314.9 million on Christmas Day in 2002.

Somewhat surprisingly (and perhaps it tells a great deal about human nature), winners of large sums in lotteries often remain at their jobs and insist that the deluge of cash made little difference in the way they intend to live. The response of a winner of a New Jersey lottery is not atypical: "You can only play so much golf or lay on so many beaches," he said, noting that he had kept his job as a telephone technician, plans no spending orgies, and intends to put his new-found wealth in safe investments. Another big winner replaced his 10-year-old car with a one-year-old one. A New York woman told reporters that she was thinking of donating her winnings for medical research. "Money never meant that much to me," she said.

Similar patterns were found among English lotto winners. David Ashcroft, a Liverpool carpenter, won £12.3 million (about $22 million) in 1997. Seven years later he was still living in a three-bedroom house with his parents and still working. He had no car. A neighbor noted: "Even in pouring rain he will walk past the taxi rank to get the bus." Similarly, the winner of £9.3 million ($16 million) was still scrubbing floors and cleaning lavatories for £4 an hour a year later. "I'm not going to go mad," she explained (Lusher 2004).

The Context of Gambling

Gambling shows an elaborate history through the annals of civilization. Stone age people tossed painted pebbles and knucklebones, but it is not certain whether their attempt was to win somebody else's axe or to invoke magic and facilitate prophecy. Records from India dating as early as 321 B.C.E. show the existence of a government department that regulated gambling, with a Superintendent of Public Games who supplied dice for a fee of 5 percent of the receipts (Durant 1954, 444).

Some form of gambling is permitted today in all American states but Hawaii and Utah. The major forms fall under six headings: (1) casino-style gambling, including the proliferation of gambling sites on Native-American reservations; (2) betting on horse and dog races, both at the track and at offtrack sites; (3) lotteries; (4) Internet gambling; (5) wagering on athletic events; and (6) betting on numbers.

Gambling offends the moral sensibilities of many persons. They regard it as sinful, frivolous, and, in some instances, highly detrimental to the well-being of the gambler and his or her family, both financially and psychologically (on family impacts see Lorenz and Shuttlesworth 1983). "Compulsive gamblers" are seen as suffering from a self-defeating complex that requires treatment to overcome. The possibility that gambling activities may be controlled by criminal syndicates is another objection. Mafia-type criminals will cheat the state on taxes, kill or maim competitors, and rig the games they operate in order to maximize profits.

Others, particularly if they can afford to lose, see gambling as an absorbing and exciting recreational activity engaged in voluntarily. To them, a wager adds drama to an event, and focuses one's attention on the proceedings. Trying to beat the odds can become an absorbing enterprise to a racetrack habitué who, before putting down a bet, studies past records of entrants, the weight each horse carries, the performance of the jockey who is riding the horse, and the condition of the track. For racetrack owners there is no gamble. Of every $1 bet, the track retains what is called a "takeout" that runs from 14 to 25 percent. Today, overseas telephonic operations, called "rebate shops," offer their customers better odds and have begun to drain funds away from domestic racetracks in the United States (Drape 2004).

Casino Gambling

As with prostitution, the state of Nevada pioneered the new surge of legal gambling in the United States. Nevada first permitted casino gambling in 1931, in large measure to generate revenue for a jurisdiction seemingly faced with little prospect of otherwise supporting itself. In its earlier days, much of Nevada gambling was under the thumb of organized crime and huge sums of money were routinely drained from Las Vegas and Reno establishments, hidden from tax investigators by a process known as "skimming," and funneled into the pockets of organized criminals who often used the money to invade legitimate businesses. Today, large gambling casinos are run by giant corporations whose shares are sold on the New York Stock Exchange. In 1978, following the Las Vegas model, Atlantic City, New Jersey, went in for large-scale casino construction. The number of casinos there— a dozen—remained stable for many years until Borgota in 2003 opened the most expensive project in the entire casino market.

However rare, gambling scandals still occasionally surface. In 2000, for instance, Edwin Edwards, the four-time governor of Louisiana, was found guilty of racketeering, money laundering, and conspiracy in connection with extortion and the awarding of casino licenses (Bridges 2001). Wiretap evidence and testimony by co-conspirators placed Edwards' take at the $1 million mark. The 75-year-old Edwards, described as a charmer, a scamp, and a honey-tongued orator, entered prison in 2001 to begin serving a ten-year sentence. Three years later, he was appealing his conviction on the grounds that the judge was taking prescription pills that made him "erratic and paranoid." Casino proponents use the Edwards case to argue that they should not be required to obtain licenses in order to operate; that the licensing procedure too easily leads to corrupt practices.

The lure of the slot machines, baccarat, blackjack, craps, roulette, and other casino games is said to be magnetic. The appeal is further fueled by various come-on devices. No casino, for instance, has a clock so that gamblers might be reminded that they are still spending money in the middle of the night, when, realistically, they should be in bed. One writer has observed of Las Vegas: "The temptations are too much for almost anyone. I've seen church bishops playing the slots. Our local Catholic charities allocates almost its entire budget to getting stranded people out of town—getting them gasoline, food baskets, and cash" (Cook 1961, 7).

It has been stated that "Las Vegas is the strangest city in America. It is the source of an infectious immorality that rides out of the desert on a golden flood of gambling wealth to spread across the nation" (Turner 1965, 113). Casino owners have made strenuous efforts in recent years to soften their image. Some featured family-friendly facilities with playgrounds and casino shows with squeaky-clean performances but found that there was little market for that product and so switched to an emphasis on "adult entertainment." Las Vegas also has become a mecca for conventions. The gambling and celebrity entertainers attract attendees who might be lukewarm to the prospect of four days in Pittsburgh or Detroit. Gambling revenues also allow hotel room and food prices to be kept lower than in most tourist sites. In addition, the fact that Nevada has no state taxes has helped to bring a large influx of retirees: Henderson, a suburb of Las Vegas, is rated as one of the most appealing places to live in the country.

Las Vegas' 793,000 population is swollen by about 250,000 daily visitors. Permanent residents, with a high proportion of Latter Day Saints (Mormons) in their midst, generally regard the Strip, where the glitz prevails, as a world apart from their own. About a third of the people living in the city report that they never gamble.

In 2004, plans were made for blockbuster corporate mergers that will change the face of casino gambling both in Las Vegas and throughout the country, creating two dominant firms—Harrah's and MGM Mirage. Harrah's has become the largest gambling company in the world with the acquisition of Caesar's Entertainment, and has an annual estimated revenue of $8.8 billion, 95,000 employees, and 54 casinos across the United States. Harrah's now controls about half the hotel rooms on the Las Vegas Strip. MGM Mirage estimates that in 2005 it will have an annual income of $6.4 billion, and 64,000 employees (Binkley 2004).

The transformation of Nevada gambling enterprises into respectability can be read from the background of the corporate executives of the dominating casino giants. Gary Loveman, Harrah's chief executive, is a former associate professor in the Harvard University School of Business Administration, while J. Terrence Lanni, who runs MGM Mirage, received an M.B.A. in business finance from the University of Southern California. Lanni is a devout Catholic and commutes from Las Vegas to his family home in Pasadena, California, each weekend (Snedeker 2001). The two companies to date have directed their appeal to differing clienteles. MGM has focused on the "whales," high-stakes players who may be flown in from around the country and remain in Nevada for a number of days. Harrah's, which started out in Reno in 1937 as a bingo parlor, caters primarily to day-trip customers.

The image that these huge enterprises now seek to project can be seen in the opening sentence of MGM's Internet statement on "Our Mission":

> MGM Mirage is a leading and respected hotel and gaming company. Our mission is to design and operate an unmatched collection of resort-casinos and provide unmatched service and amenities to our guests.

Close readers might note the use of the word "respected," a term that most nongambling corporations would not deem necessary to include; also the placement of "resort" ahead of "casinos" in the hyphenated term, and recourse to "gaming" instead of "gambling," a tactic that one commentator suggests is both "cute and evasive" (Collins 2003, 20).

Slot Machines

The greatest share of gambling casino income—about 70 percent—is derived from slot machines. Slots in earlier times were called "one-armed bandits," but today levers are superfluous; the customer typically presses a button and makes an average of six plays a minute. About 40 million Americans played a slot machine in 2003, according to industry calculations. As one gambling executive pointed out: "Slot machines never call in sick. They don't have any family problems. The only cost you have is the acquisition of the machine itself. For table games there are high labor costs." In addition, slots are a solitary indulgence; others do not intrude into your territory and observe your actions. Besides, you do not have to wait for horses to run, a dealer to deal, or a wheel to spin and settle down.

The manufacturing of slot machines is largely done by International Game Technology, a company located in Reno. A model called "The Price is Right" is one of their offerings. Slot experts dub it a "cherry dribbler," because it is designed to dispense lots of small payouts while it nibbles at your cash, rather than extracting large chunks of your money. The idea is to supply positive reinforcement to keep the player putting money into the machine. Slots on the average pay back 90 percent of what is bet, but the 10 percent they retain adds up to stunning sums. The highest earning slot is "The Wheel of Fortune," which takes in about $1 billion a year. The chance of hitting the largest jackpot is one in 46 million plays. Jackpots are often in paper receipts, but when there is a hit the machines play very loud recordings of quarters falling on a metal tray.

Slots are primarily designed to appeal to women over the age of 55, who are believed to have lots of time and disposable income (Aasved 2003, 275). In retirement communities in San Diego and Phoenix, casinos operate a fleet of vehicles that shuttle back and forth to assisted-living centers, though state laws often ban the installment of slots in nursing homes. For older people, gambling casinos provide a safe environment with omnipresent cameras and security guards and attractive shops and eating places. As a Las Vegas entrepreneur noted, casinos provide day care for the elderly. One of those elderly who lost $100,000 to the slots said that she felt "hypnotized" by the machines. "You don't think of anything else." She said that the machines' hold over her was like that of an unfaithful lover and that she would fall into a rage when one of her favorite machines paid off to another player (Rivlin 2004, 45). An employee who assists in the manufacturing of slots puts it more simply: "Slots are for losers," he says (Rivlin 2004, 81). A recommended tactic to control the financial harm suffered by losers who get transfixed in their gambling is to provide each slot machine with a "counter" which would prominently display a running total of the amount that a player has won or lost. A more in-your-face tactic suggested by a Strip comedian would be an audio that proclaimed: "Your kids don't need college anyway" (Eggert 2004, 217).

Riverboat Gambling

The re-emergence of legal riverboat gambling can be traced in part to a sense of nostalgia for the presumed romance of early America when boats traversed the major internal waterways of

America, an era brilliantly portrayed in the writings of Mark Twain. In Lake Charles, Louisiana, the riverboat vessel that hosts gamblers appears to be from the Victorian era, belying its actual youth. A huge paddle-wheel is visible behind it, a nicety required on all casino riverboats in Louisiana, even though they are powered by diesel engines and underwater propellers (Eichenwald 2000, 239).

Riverboat gambling came into being because of the need of state governments for additional revenue. The story of riverboat gambling in Missouri provides insight into the dynamics of the process by which the activity is inaugurated, fought, and redesigned. Missouri in 1992 followed Iowa's pioneering 1989 approval of riverboat gambling. Sixty-two percent of Missouri voters had endorsed a referendum favoring dockside and excursion gambling within the state on boats in the Mississippi and Missouri rivers. At first, there were limited boarding times and a $500 ceiling on the amount of money any one gambler could lose (O'Connor 2000). By creating moats with water from the rivers, operators sought to legitimate a casino located a thousand yards from the Missouri River channel, but that tactic was rejected by the state Supreme Court (*Akin v. Missouri Gaming Commission* 1997).

The enabling Missouri legislation authorized both games of skill and games of chance. Slots are games of chance. Blackjack is a game of skill, though the total results can be calibrated in terms of the number of decks of cards employed. The house has a mere 0.0001 percent advantage in casino blackjack games if only one deck is used, since experienced players can count cards fairly readily and calculate the odds of getting what they need on a draw. Two decks jump the house advantage to 0.34 percent while the use of six decks, which is now standard practice in most casinos, raises the advantage to 0.55 percent.

A lawsuit filed in the Missouri Supreme Court won the argument that games of skill were outlawed in the state constitution. Only permitted were games in which a player's expected return was not favorably increased by his or her reasoning, foresight, dexterity, sagacity, design, information, or strategy (*Harris v. Missouri Gaming Commission* 1994, 62–63). A proposed constitutional amendment to overturn the Supreme Court decision failed in a referendum vote despite the fact that gambling interests spent 60 times more than those who opposed the amendment. A second effort in the same year, however, gained 54 percent approval. Today, no gambling on sports events is allowed on riverboats in Missouri; however, most of the initial restrictions have disappeared, though a loss limit still exists but is difficult to enforce.

Native-American Casinos

Casinos run on tribal territory by Native Americans came on the scene in the 1990s and have transformed the portrait of gambling in the United States in dramatic fashion. There now are 310 such casinos run by 200 of the nation's 556 federally recognized tribes. The first major step along the path to Native-American casinos came in the federal appellate court decision in *Seminole Tribe of Florida v. Butterworth* (1981). The Seminoles were operating high-stake bingo games which the state of Florida wanted to prohibit. The court came down in favor of the tribe. Six years later, in *California v. Cabazon Band of Mission Indians* (1987), the United States Supreme Court in a 6–3 decision declared that neither state nor local laws could be used to ban gambling on the Cabazon and Morongo tribal reservations in Riverside County. The court, quoting earlier decisions, maintained that Indian tribes retain "attributes of sovereignty over their members and their territory" (*United States v. Mazurie* 1975, 557) and that "tribal sovereignty is dependent on, and subordinate to only the Federal government, not the States" (*Washington v. Confederated Tribes of the Colville Indian Reservation* 1980, 154).

The following year the Congress enacted the Indian Gaming Regulatory Act (IGRA) which legalized gambling on Native-American reservations. These are the so-called "trust lands," owned by the Indians but held "in trust" by the federal government. The IGRA law sought to promote "tribal economic development, self-sufficiency, and strong tribal government" (25 United States Code, §2202[1]). It established three classes of gambling that were permissible on reservations, with different considerations applying to each group: Class I, traditional and social gambling for minimal prizes; Class II, bingo; and Class III, casino gambling. For Class III, the state in which the reservation was located had to have legal casino gambling and the details of the reservation program had to be approved by the federal Secretary of the Interior and endorsed by a tribal ordinance (Cox 1995).

The most prominent of the Native-American gambling operations is Foxwoods Resort Casino, located in Ledyard, Connecticut, 110 miles south of Boston and 130 miles north of New York, with more than 10 percent of the American population residing within 100 miles (d'Hauteserre 1998). Foxwoods is run by the Mashantucket Pequot tribe. In 1666, the British colony of Connecticut had allocated 2,000 acres for a tribal reservation, but in 1761 this was chopped down to 989 acres, and in 1855 the state legislature authorized the sale of 800 of these acres. At the end of the second World War only two people remained on the Pequot reservation. In 1983, however, following litigation, the federal government gave the tribe, its members now scattered here and there, almost a million dollars to repurchase some of the land it earlier owned by offering the present holders more than market price. Thereafter, the re-established tribe in the case of *Mashantucket Pequot Tribe v. Connecticut* (1990) won the right to open casino gambling based on the fact that Connecticut law allowed wagering for charitable purposes. Today, the reservation is home to 300 persons who are accorded tribal membership, and Foxwoods is said to be the most lucrative gambling operation in the Western Hemisphere, with 40,000 visitors every day and 6,000 slot machines located throughout a 19-story building. It also features 350 table games and has 1,400 hotel rooms, nearly two dozen restaurants, and showcases entertainers such as Bill Cosby and the Dixie Chicks. From all of this, every member of the tribe is given at least $50,000 each year and some receive free homes, education subsidies, medical care, and retirement benefits (Rand 2002).

Foxwoods is not without its critics, however. Some have argued that those who call themselves Pequots have a conglomeration of backgrounds, that few of them are truly Native Americans (Benedict 2000; Eisler 2001; Fromson 2003). Long-time local residents complain that the arrival of Foxwoods was "like plunking Dodger Stadium in a small town and 24/7 people are going to the ball game" (Bailey 2004, B1). Traffic in the towns around Foxwoods has ballooned to four times its precasino level, tour buses are prominent, and there are five times more ambulance calls than in earlier days.

The most damaging publicity Native-American gambling arrangements have received came in a 2002 *Time* magazine feature that told the story of Maryann Martin, who, as its only member, constituted the smallest Indian tribe in the country. Martin had been raised in Los Angeles by an African-American family. At age 22 she learned that her deceased mother had been the last member of the Augustine Band of the Cahuilla Mission Indians. In 1992, she and her two younger brothers were certified as a tribe. The brothers subsequently were killed in gang fights that were said to involve drug dealing. Martin then moved a trailer onto a deserted 500-acre plot of desert land that once had been an Indian reservation. In July 2002, staked by a Las Vegas casino owner, she opened the Augustine Casino in Coachella, California, about 25 miles from Palm Springs, featuring 340 slot machines and 10 gaming tables (Bartlett and Steele 2002). Critics maintain that this was not a legitimate Native-American enterprise but rather a ruse to take advantage of the law.

States cannot tax Indian reservations, but strapped for money, many exert every pressure they can to share in the revenue from the cash-cow slot machines. In 2003, states received $759.4 million from tribal gambling, with $394.6 million of that going into Connecticut coffers (Darian-Smith 2004).

One study has found that employment in counties with Native-American tribes grew 26 percent in four years after a casino was opened, the population increased by 12 percent, and the mortality rate dropped by 2 percent. On the down side, bankruptcies, auto theft, violent crime, and larceny were up 10 percent in the same time period (Evans and Topoleski 2002).

Internet Gambling

The most controversial gambling issue today concerns the use of the Internet for placing wagers on sports events and playing games of chance on home computer terminals. "Internet gambling," one writer has observed, "is the elusive speeding car on the information superhighway, weaving through traffic and seemingly immune to efforts to slow its charge" (Friedrich 2000, 389). Fifty-four countries allow Internet wagering, but federal and state laws forbid such activity in the United States, with penalties directed against operators, not bettors, though these laws are constitutionally suspect as being in violation of free speech protections. Gambling, some argue, however, is not speech. They also insist that minors need protection from Internet gambling, but realize that this objection must overcome the barrier raised in *Reno v. ACLU* (1997), when the Supreme Court struck down the Communications Decency Act which sought to protect minors from harmful and pornographic Internet materials.

At the moment, Congress is seeking to formulate a constitutionally acceptable approach to ban or regulate Internet gambling. Reliance continues to be placed on the Wire Communications Act (18 U.S.C. 1084), passed in 1966 to deal with organized crime. The act outlaws bets made across state lines or international boundaries (*Martin v. United States* 1968; Doyle 2003; Gottfried 2004).

Internet gambling is viewed by its opponents as likely to lead to personal bankruptcies and to suicides (for opposing conclusions on gambling and suicide see Phillips, Welty, and Smith 1997; and McCleary et al. 2002). Nevada consistently has the highest suicide rate in the United States: The most recent figures put the rate at 25.8 per 100,000 population compared to 12.5 for the nation; and only about 11 percent of the Nevada suicides are of persons from out-of-state (Phillips, Welty, and Smith 1997). At Monte Carlo, the world's first major gambling casino, its owner instructed his staff to put large sums of money into the purse or wallet of customers who killed themselves on the premises or nearby in order to convey the idea that it was not gambling losses that drove them to death. Monte Carlo also forbids Monaco's residents to wager in the casino, thereby creating the best of possible fiscal scenarios: All the money taken in at the casino comes from foreign countries (Collins 2003).

The only study of completed suicides of people identified in coroner reports as having a possible gambling problem was conducted in the state of Victoria, Australia. The mean age of the victims was 40, and 84 percent were unemployed or from lower socioeconomic backgrounds. The authors point out that gambling may not have been the primary cause of the suicide, noting that the gambling could have represented an unsuccessful attempt to resolve other problems and also suggesting that gambling settings may attract persons with suicidal impulses (Blaszczynski and Farrell 1998).

Americans are the best customers of overseas Internet gambling. Costa Rica, various Caribbean countries, and the Isle of Man, which is located offshore between Britain and Ireland, are prime participants on the Internet gambling scene. A 2004 study of 100 Ohio State University students learned that 77 of them had bet online at any time and, of these, 31 did so at least once a week. Wagering on games, they said, added excitement to the sports events that they watched on television.

The advertising tactics of Internet gambling operators is illustrated by 11 identical unsolicited e-mails that arrived on our computer during the past week. All were similar except for the name of the sender. The first was dispatched by "Billy Gagnon" and the next by "Reed Bailey," and they included three other addressees. "I have a special offer available for you at our casino," the come-on began. The offer was a $20 credit. "No deposit is necessary!" All we had to do was to enter our bonus code on the website. If we were to make an initial deposit, we would receive a credit of $200. "Allow us to show you our quality operation, fast payouts, generous bonuses, and superfriendly around-the-clock customer support," the e-mails said.

It is estimated that illegal sports betting by Americans today, exclusive of the Internet, involves between $80 and $300 billion annually. If Internet gambling were permitted in the United States, much of that money presumably would be placed with Nevada casinos because of their name recognition, and the government would be able to tax revenues that are now beyond its reach.

BentonSports.com, based in Costa Rica, is one of the most prominent overseas Internet gambling facilities. It took bets in 2003 from 1.2 million Americans registered with it. But advertisers for such sites have been threatened with federal prosecution for "aiding and abetting" an illegal activity. New York buses, which advertised overseas Internet gambling, withdrew the placards, but both Google and Yahoo continue to display Internet gambling advertisements, insisting that it is their right under the constitution's free speech doctrine. In addition, the World Trade Organization, located in Geneva, Switzerland, in 2004 ruled in favor of the Caribbean island state of Antigua and Barbuda, declaring that the U.S. ban on Internet gambling was an unfair trade practice in violation of America's obligations under the General Agreement on Trade in Services (GATS) (Richtel 2004).

Lotteries

The Alabama Supreme Court in 1896 offered a simple definition of a lottery. It is, the court said, an event in which "the result of winning or losing is to be determined by the use of a contrivance or chance, in which neither choice or skill can operate to exert any effect" (*Loiseau v. State* 1896, 146). Public lotteries were common in the United States from early colonial times until the 1830s. Many institutions of higher learning, including Harvard, Princeton, Yale, and King's College (now Columbia University) were financed by lotteries; so too was the construction of roads, bridges, and public buildings (Clotfelter and Cook 1989). The early lotteries were operated by state governments or as franchises licensed by the states. They disappeared from the American scene when scandals came to light in the late 1800s, often involving political skullduggery and exorbitant profits reaped by private promoters.

Gambling on Numbers

The demise of lotteries led to the appearance of "numbers," a form of gambling particularly popular in depressed urban areas. Numbers games are also known as "policy," "bolita," "the figures," or "the digits." Their once-widespread existence can be seen from the more than 6,000 arrests made by the New York City police in 1969 for policy offenses. New York officials at the time estimated that there were half a million daily policy players in the city, and about 100,000 people employed in the numbers business in the city's five boroughs.

The appeal of playing the numbers has decreased with the availability of lotteries, though the practice still thrives in many urban neighborhoods. The odds of 600 to 1 are better than those offered by the lottery and, at least as important, no taxes need to be paid on winnings. In the summer of 2004, New York City police arrested seven persons for what they called "mutual race horse policy" or what the locals describe as "3-5-7." That label comes from the fact that the winning number is constructed from the last digit of the total bet for the first three winning horses at a selected track. The second number is the last number of the total bet on the top-finishing three horses in the first five races, while the final number is the amount bet on the first, second, and third finishing horses in the first seven races.

In a Boston slum, women would send their children to the grocery store for milk, giving them an extra nickel to put on a number (Whyte 1955, 116). Publications, so called "dream books," claimed to provide clues to likely winning numbers. "Policy is not only a business—it's a cult," two researchers noted (Drake and Cayton 1945, 474). Competition was eliminated either by mergers or by the police who were paid off regularly. Honest law enforcement officers found themselves transferred to the cemetery beat. "It's lonely out there," one observed. "Nothing ever happens" (Whyte 1955, 125).

The numbers operation that the police broke up in New York in 2004 involved a vast network of outlets, including hair salons, bodegas, coin laundries, and grocery stores. Some numbers merchants took bets in their automobiles. Tens of thousands of people are estimated to have placed bets each week. "They melted into the community," the head of the police's organized crime unit said. "No one knows about them except the people in the community" (Feuer 2004, A19).

Other illegal neighborhood gambling outlets include video poker games that are found in some cafes in southern California frequented by Vietnamese Americans. In his study, Tomson H. Nguyen (2004) noted that the tabletop machines appear to be the same as those in a legitimate video parlor, but they can be altered into a gambling mode by use of a remote control gadget, making it difficult for the police to notice them. As soon as a non-Vietnamese enters the café, a rare event, any machine being used for gambling is moved back into its innocent-looking form. The need for a high degree of secrecy—nobody is allowed to play video poker unless introduced by a regular customer—makes the recruitment of a clientele difficult. Like numbers bettors, the customers of video poker games are drifting away as casinos and other legal outlets in the area proliferate.

Lotteries Re-emerge

The lucrative and untaxed funds involved in numbers gambling, combined with chronically beleaguered budgets, in time persuaded a large number of states to get back into the lottery business. The appeal of a legal lottery lies in the relative ease with which it can be run. The possible immorality of gambling on a lottery tends to be blunted since the transaction involves buying tickets at a regular business site. The long wait between the purchase of a lottery ticket and the announcement of the drawing result rarely creates the intense emotional state that characterizes compulsive gambling.

Such considerations—with the financial windfall for the state probably paramount—coalesced to convince numerous American jurisdictions to again look favorably on state-sponsored lotteries. In 1963, 70 years after the last legal lottery in the United States, voters in New Hampshire approved a state-run lottery scheme by a margin of four to one. Proceeds were to be earmarked primarily for school districts. A sophisticated examination of lottery earnings found that they outperform voluntary giving as a means of financing public goods (Morgan 2000) and that lotteries that offer the highest payoffs are even more successful in raising funds to be used for the benefit of the public (Morgan and Sutton 2000).

The New York lottery, the second in line, had at first sought to have the best of both worlds, establishing gambling and yet cocooning it so that it became a lollipop kind of enterprise. Sales at first were restricted to banks (though this site was later declared unconstitutional), hotels, motels, and local government offices. Lottery participants had to fill out cards, provide their name and address, and the drawings for winners took place once a month.

The New York restrictions were largely abandoned when intake fell far short of estimates. New Jersey, the next state to approve a lottery, had learned its neighbor's lesson. Drawings there were scheduled weekly, tickets were sold in strips like motion picture admissions, and each ticket was decorated with a large four-leaf clover. Today, 37 states and the District of Columbia operate lotteries and typically employ high-powered advertising agents to lure customers to participate.

Off-Track Betting

Horse racing enjoys a history extending back into ancient times. The earliest reference appears in Homer's *Iliad* (1974, chapter 23), the epic Greek poem written some time prior to 700 B.C.E., which vividly portrays a chariot race staged at the funeral games in honor of the Macedonian general Patrocolus. Centuries later in Britain, horse racing became the "sport of kings," with royalty prominent in attendance at the Newmarket races where book-makers stationed themselves on the turf rather than behind cash-ier-like locations.

British racing traditions were transplanted to the United States during the colonial period. Today, placing a bet at a race-track involves transportation, parking and entrance costs, con-sumes a great deal of time, and, if it is to be done with some regularity, requires a great deal of leisure. Many bettors preferred to place wagers with bookmakers who operated illegally, primar-ily in working-class neighborhoods, before betting parlors were made legal.

The discrepancy between allowing bets to be made at a race-track and forbidding wagering on the same horse race to be done elsewhere seemed to many discriminatory. When states were hard-pressed for revenues it was almost a foregone conclusion that they would look favorably on off-track betting.

Legalized off-track betting made its debut in New York in 1971. The state-run Off-Track Betting Corporation (OTB) sought to make an exuberant affair out of its business, rather than to have it regarded as a shabby, shady kind of enterprise, to be engaged in only because of an inability to control one's more despicable im-pulses. "Start a new morning routine," an OTB advertisement proclaimed. "Coffee and doughnuts and the daily double." An-other advertisement read: "If you're in the stock market you might find this a better bet."

This last bit of waggery brought forth an unhappy response from the head of the New York Stock Exchange. Writing on behalf of "the more than 31 million shareholders who own stock in America's publicly owned corporations," Wall Street brokers pro-tested the "ill-considered" slogan. Bystanders might have antici-pated an apologetic reaction from OTB. Instead, the betting corporation counterattacked: "On behalf of the more than 48,972 horses that raced in this country last year," the OTB head an-swered, "I am sure that some of the horses feel that they have been a better investment in the past few years than some of the invest-ments on the New York Stock Exchange." A newspaper reader tried to put the matter into perspective—with a slight tilt in the direction of the horses:

> Both the stock market and offtrack betting spawn touts. Both thrive to some extent by wishful thinking. Both are susceptible to rumors, half-truths, undisciplined emotionalism and expert analysis and prophecy.
>
> There is this to be said for horse racing. When you lose—whether because of bad luck or bad judgment—you know it within minutes, whereas it might take months to discover that you've picked a loser in the market.
>
> Perhaps a balanced, diversified portfolio of racing bets and market purchases might be the best bet after all. (Gabel 1971, 27)

Among those philosophizing about the implications of off-track betting was one early writer who posed some basic questions:

> Ultimately, OTB will have to face judgment in four areas: Will it strike a blow against organized crime by draining huge sums away from bookmakers? Will it bring sudden prosperity to the hard-pressed city government? Will it eventually cripple the racing industry by drawing fans away from the tracks, or will it bring new life into racing by introducing it to millions who never thought of betting on a horse before? And, finally, how will the hundreds of projected legal betting parlors affect the quality and the pace of life in New York? (Axthelm 1971, 42)

More than three decades later, answers to these questions are far from precise. Organized crime's strength in the realm of book-making has been greatly reduced. OTB revenues have been absorbed into the city budget, which remains chronically depleted. The impact on horse racing is uncertain. Racetracks are experiencing an aging clientele, lower attendance figures, the closure of several venues, and a decrease in the number of foals registered each year (Howland 2004). In 2004, for the first time in nine years, the size of the purses paid out to winning horses declined. At the same time, revenues remain high and the best-selling book and popular movie on the famed thoroughbred Seabiscuit generated considerable public interest in horse racing, with the Kentucky Derby, the Preakness, and the Belmont Stakes getting nationwide attention focused on whether a single horse can win all three races. No one questions that the quality of life in New York City has improved considerably, but no one would argue that off-track betting has had any special role in bringing about this result.

Current plans call for the placement of slot machines at horse racetracks to bring in additional betting moneys. In Maine, slots have been located on a Bangor track, and in 2005 slot machines were installed in Pennsylvania's 61 racetracks which then were dubbed "racinos."

Conclusion

It is surprising how little emphasis there is on the moral issues in debates about gambling, despite religious taboos against such behavior (see generally MacKenzie 1899). Stephen L. Carter, a professor at Yale Law School, however, represents an exception: He places moral issues front and center in his discussion of gambling. Carter notes that voters in Alabama, one of the nation's poorest states, resoundingly defeated a referendum that would have created a state lottery. Lotteries, he points out, are a regressive tax because the poor spend a significantly higher percentage of their income on lottery tickets than the rich do, and the return is less than that from illegal numbers gambling.

It was not these considerations, however, that primarily underlaid the Alabama vote; rather it was religious conviction. Preachers had inveighed against the lottery from the pulpit. Carter's analysis takes the following path:

> When the religionists voice triumphed, supporters [of the lottery measure] retreated into sour grapes: "There were the religionists imposing their fanatical opinions on everybody else." Of course, this argument cuts both ways. Another view might be that the fanatical lottery backers were trying to impose their opinions on everybody else. It is not enough for supporters to answer that nobody is forced to play. Available choices are not simply available choices. A culture defines itself in large measure by what it chooses to make available. It is not at all fanciful for religious parents (or, for that matter, nonreligious parents) to suppose that it will be harder to raise good (disciplined, unselfish, thoughtful) children in a state that encourages its citizens to

gamble (and to make very bad bets at that) than in one that abstains from such an assault on the will. (Carter 2000, 98–99)

Today, aside from rare theological objections, seven major points consistently are raised in campaigns to ban or to at least restrict legal gambling.

The most common objection is that gambling is a dangerous vice that leads to personal problems, particularly for people who cannot afford to lose the money they wager. The power of this argument is that it is unassailable as a factual declaration: Gambling most certainly does hook some participants and for some it leads to dire consequences. The vulnerability of the argument is that the same can be said of innumerable other perfectly legal aspects of human existence, including stamp collecting, playing the stock market, or overeating.

The American Psychiatric Association defines what it labels pathological gambling as an "impulse control disorder" and indicates that it is found in about 4 percent of Americans sometime during their life. The psychological principle underlying the magnetic appeal of slots to some persons has been labeled "infrequent random reinforcement."

The American Psychiatric Association's diagnostic manual (DSM-IV) indicates that if five of the following ten items characterize a pathological gambler, he is suffering from an absence of impulse control:

1. is preoccupied with gambling
2. needs to gamble with increasing amounts of money in order to achieve the desired excitement
3. has repeated unsuccessful efforts to control, cut back, or stop gambling
4. is restless or irritable when attempting to cut down or stop gambling
5. gambles as a way of escaping from problems or of relieving a dysphoric mood (a sense of ill-being and dissatisfaction)
6. after losing money gambling often returns another day to get even
7. lies to family members, therapist, or others to conceal the extent of involvement with gambling

8. has committed illegal acts such as forgery, fraud, theft, or embezzlement to finance gambling
9. has jeopardized or lost a significant relationship, job, or educational or career opportunity because of gambling
10. relies on others to provide money to relieve a desperate financial situation caused by gambling (American Psychiatric Association 1994, 313.31; see also Lesieur 1998)

There are those who say that such an inventory is pseudo-science with no actual basis in empirical inquiry. They ask why five of the items suffice for a diagnosis rather than, say, six or four, and question the implication that each of the items is of equal weight. They also note the inclusion of lying to a therapist as an important consideration, with its implicit presumption that therapists play a key role in this issue. A rich person has a decided advantage (or disadvantage, depending on how you view it): He or she need not resort to any of the criminal behaviors listed in Item 8 to continue gambling; and a wealthy person, if living in leisure, need not jeopardize a job or other commitments noted in Item 9. Presumably, these advantages would not render the person less of a "pathological gambler."

On the other hand, few would challenge the position that gambling can seriously disrupt a person's existence and that, if possible, something ought to be done to alleviate recognized distress. But some writers insist that gambling is not the addict's problem, but rather the best solution to stresses generated by long-standing underlying difficulties (Anderson 1999). The implication—unprovable—is that if gambling had not provided an outlet, even more serious manifestations of the malaise might have occurred.

The American Psychiatric Association's focus on the personal and social characteristics of compulsive gambling has been challenged by a cadre of neuroscientists who maintain that the human brain is wired to create compulsive gamblers if sufficient stimuli come into play. Hans Breiter of Harvard University puts it this way: "Money may be abstract but to the brain it looks like cocaine, food, sex or anything a person expects is rewarding. Some persons seem to be born with vulnerable dopamine systems [brain chemicals similar to adrenaline that trigger highs] that get hijacked by social rewards" (Blakeslee 2002, E1; see also Berridge and Robinson 1998). The triggering mechanism has been labeled DRD2 (Shaffer et al. 2003, 10).

Debate centers around the question of whether a diagnosis of compulsive gambling ought to allow courts to mitigate the sentence of people who claim that their gambling was largely responsible for the criminal offense for which they were convicted, that the compulsion was so great that it overpowered the offender's will. For crimes that the Federal Bureau of Investigation denotes as Part I offenses—murder, rape, and aggravated assault, among others—courts and juries are not wont to regard a gambling compulsion as sufficient to excuse the crime or reduce the sentence (Geis 2004). The following cases, though, demonstrate the connection that can exist between gambling and very serious criminal activity (Buck, Hakim, and Spiegel 1991; Meyer and Stadler 1999).

- A woman who lost more than $30,000 at Illinois casinos was sentenced to 21 years in prison after a judge determined that she suffocated her 7-week-old child to collect insurance (Granois 2004, 146).
- A Kansas woman was sentenced to 15 years in prison for killing her husband in a parking lot. She admitted stabbing him 75 times because he would not give her gambling money. The crime occurred after the couple and a friend had left a gambling casino about midnight (Granois 2004, 146–147).

Most gambling-related crimes take the form of fraud, embezzlement, forgery, and larceny. Here the law has been somewhat more forgiving of a person ensnared by a gambling habit. In *United States v. Sadolsky* (2000), a regional manager of Sears Roebuck credited refunds on returned merchandise to himself, stealing $39,479 in order to secure money to pay off a $30,000 gambling debt and presumably to have something left over for further gambling. The trial court's grant of a downward departure from the sentencing guidelines was upheld by the federal appellate court, though Sadolsky was ordered to repay the money he had swindled from the company.

The court noted that nine years earlier it had refused to reduce the 33-month sentence of an osteopath who sold Tylenol IV, a controlled substance containing codeine, to obtain money to pay off gambling debts (*United States v. Hamilton* 1991), but it now cast aside that precedent in *Sadolsky* because the U.S. Sentencing Commission had added to its definition of "diminished capacity" the second of the two clauses in the following guideline:

> Significantly reduced mental capacity means the defendant, although convicted, has a significantly impaired ability to (A) understand the wrongfulness of the behavior comprising the offense, or to exercise the power of reason; or (B) control behavior that the defendant knows is wrongful. (USSG §5K2.13)

The possibility of reducing the sentences of people said to have committed crimes under the impulse of a gambling addiction came to an abrupt halt in 2003 when Congress enacted legislation that declared that a claim of pathological gambling no longer could be employed to mitigate the sentence stipulated in the sentencing guidelines. The measure, formulated by the Department of Justice, was swiftly endorsed by the U.S. Sentencing Commission. Previously, only alcoholism and drug addiction had been ruled unacceptable bases for reduced sentences (Geis 2004).

A commentator who takes issue with judicial leniency based on excessive gambling argues that "there is little evidence that compulsive gambling causes diminished capacity and there is no reliable way of measuring it even if it does" (Starr 2003, 386–387). Others agree: Collins (2003, 134) observes that the facts about compulsive gambling show "extreme thinness and unreliability," while Howard Shaffer (1997), a leading medical researcher, describes the state of research on compulsive gambling as chaotic.

Many of the current objections to gambling are raised in efforts to prohibit Internet wagering. It is noted that minors can freely participate, and that the state has a legitimate purpose in protecting underage persons from what might be their own folly. In addition, Internet gambling seems more likely than other forms to be susceptible to fraudulent manipulations and, if operated overseas, its earnings remain beyond the reach of American tax authorities even though Americans at present make up three-quarters of the Internet bettors.

Similarly, Internet operations, unlike brick and mortar casinos, can readily fold up and disappear, leaving customers with little recourse if they are owed money. Internet games also seem more prone to money laundering and the involvement of organized criminals.

Paul Samuelson, a Nobel Prize–winning economist, has little good to say about gambling as a permissible activity:

> There is a substantial economic case to be made against gambling. It involves simply sterile transfers of money or goods between individuals, creates no new money or goods. Although it creates no output, gambling does nevertheless absorb time and resources. When pursued beyond the limit of recreation, where the main purpose, after all, is to "kill" time, gambling subtracts from the national income. (Samuelson 1970, 402)

The progambling forces, for their part, tend to underplay any harm that the practice may produce and take the position that there are far more pressing problems that society ought to be attending to:

> But of all the foibles and weaknesses that flesh is heir to, gambling must surely be among the least harmful or risky—since nothing is lost but money. Drinking, doping, warfare, auto racing, boxing, football and politics take an immeasurably greater toll on human life, welfare, and happiness.
>
> It is as if all the primitive instincts that ordinary men expend in abusing their wives and children, making war or proclaiming their ignorance as infallible truth tend, in the gambler, to be concentrated into simple acquisitiveness. Making and losing money may not be the noblest activity known to man, but neither is it among the lowest and most vicious. And it tends to focus the attention wonderfully. (Roberts 1971, 32)

In such terms, gambling can be seen as a form of entertainment. An economist advocating this interpretation has insisted that playing a lottery is not economically irrational or uniformed but rather "creates a sense of open-ended possibility, the possibility of escaping one's current life." For him, it is a recreation, a dream production: "And all recreations—skiing, golf, sex—analyzed with sufficient wisdom, intellect, and vigor may be found wanting and misguided" (Cohen 2001, 738). Critics might sarcastically respond that opera also is entertainment, but nobody commits suicide as a result of watching an opera, except perhaps on the stage.

Nonetheless, those advocating legal gambling point out that it has no direct physical consequences, like, say, football. It may engender a philosophy that is unrealistic in terms of daily existence, but it is arguable whether such a philosophy is more detrimental than enabling. Peter Collins (2003) suggests that what a person believes public policy should dictate about gambling depends on whether that person thinks gambling is more relevantly similar to going to the movies, ingesting cocaine, watching soap operas, eating candy, playing golf, consuming pornography, smoking, having a massage, attending a ball game, visiting a brothel, riding a roller coaster, shopping, or having a drink. Collins, the executive director of the South African Responsible Gambling Program, offers the most laid-back opinion on gambling that we've encountered:

> Although I recognize that the distress caused by excessive gambling in individual cases can be as appalling as with any other addiction, I do not think this is a major social evil in comparison with, say, drugs, domestic violence, AIDS, or even reckless driving. In the great scheme of things, I think that gambling and what the government does about it are of rather limited moral and social importance. (Collins 2003, 10)

Perhaps so, perhaps not. As we have seen, there are any number of persons who take exception to Collins' viewpoint and offer strong arguments that seek to rebut it.

References

Aasved, Mikal. 2003. *The Sociology of Gambling.* Springfield, IL: Thomas.

Akin v. Missouri Gaming Commission. 1997. 956 S.W.2d 261.

American Psychiatric Association. 1994. *Diagnostic and Statistical Manual of Mental Disorders,* 4th ed. Washington, DC: The Association.

Anderson, George R. 1999. Presentation to the National Conference of State Legislatures, July 27.

Axthelm, Pete. 1971. "Howie the Horse is Ahead for the Year." *New York,* 4 (May 3):40–46.

Bailey, Eric. 2004. "Weighing Casino Cash v. Problems." *Los Angeles Times,* (July 7):B1, B7.

Bartlett, Donald L., and James B. Steele. 2002. "Look Who's Cashing in at Indian Casinos: Hint: It's Not the People Who Are Supposed to Benefit." *Time* (December 16):44–58.

Benedict, Jeff. 2000. *Without Reservation: The Making of America's Most Powerful Indian Tribe and the World's Largest Casino.* New York: HarperCollins.

Berridge, Kent C., and Terry E. Robinson. 1998. "What is the Role of Dopamine in Reward: Hedonic Impact, Reward Learning or Incentive Salience?" *Brain Research: Brain Research Review* 20:309–369.

Binkley, Christina. 2004. "Harrah's Big Deal Sets the State for Showdown of Gambling Giants." *Wall Street Journal,* (July 15):1, 2.

Blakeslee, Sandra. 2002. "Hijacking the Brain Circuits in a Nickel Slot Machine." *New York Times,* (February 19):E1.

Blaszczynski, Alex, and Einear Farrell. 1998. "A Case Series of 44 Completed Gambling-Related Suicides." *Journal of Gambling Studies* 14:109.

Bridges, Tyler. 2001. *Bad Bet on the Bayou: The Rise of Gambling in Louisiana and the Fall of Governor Edwin Edwards.* New York: Farrar, Straus, and Giroux.

Buck, Andrew J., Simon Hakim, and Uriel Spiegel. 1991. "Casinos, Crime, and Real Estate Values: Do They Relate?" *Journal of Research in Crime and Delinquency* 28:288–303.

California v. Cabazon Band of Mission Indians. 1987. 480 U.S. 202.

Carter, Stephen L. 2000. *God's Name in Vain: The Wrongs and Rights of Religion in Politics.* New York: Basic Books.

Chafetz, Henry. 1960. *A History of Gambling in the United States From 1492 to 1955.* New York: Potter.

Clotfelter, Charles T., and Philip J. Cook. 1989. *Selling Hope: State Lotteries in America.* Cambridge, MA: Harvard University Press.

Cohen, Lloyd R. 2001. "The Lure of the Lottery." *Wake Forest Law Review* 36:705–745.

Collins, Peter. 2003. *Gambling and the Public Interest.* Westport, CT: Praeger.

Cook, Fred J. 1961. *A Two-Dollar Bet Means Murder.* New York: Dial.

Cox, Michael. 1995. "The Indian Gaming Regulatory Act: An Overview." *St. Thomas Law Review* 7:769–789.

Darian-Smith, Eve. 2004. *New Capitalists: Law, Politics, and Identity Surrounding Casino Gaming on Native American Land.* Belmont, CA: Wadsworth.

Davis, Clyde Brion. 1956. *Something for Nothing.* Philadelphia: Lippincott.

d'Hauteserre, Anne-Marie. 1998. "Foxwoods Casino Resort: An Unusual Experiment in Economic Development." *Economic Geography* 74 (Extra Issue):112–121.

Doyle, Charles. 2003. *Internet Gambling: Overview of Federal Criminal Law.* New York: Novinka.

Drake, St. Clair, and Horace R. Cayton. 1945. *Black Metropolis: A Study of Negro Life in a Northern City.* New York: Harcourt, Brace.

Drape, Joe. 2004. "Horse Racing's Biggest Bettors Are Reaping Richest Rewards." *New York Times,* (April 26):D1–D2.

Durant, Will. 1954. *Our Oriental Heritage.* New York: Simon and Schuster.

Eggert, Kurt. 2004. "Truth in Gaming: Toward Consumer Protection in the Gambling Industry." *Maryland Law Review* 63:217–286.

Eichenwald, Kurt. 2000. *The Informant: A True Story.* New York: Broadway Books.

Eisler, Kim Isaac. 2001. *Revenge of the Pequots: How a Small Native American Tribe Created the World's Most Profitable Casino.* New York: Simon and Schuster.

Evans, William M., and Julie H. Topoleski. 2002. *The Social and Economic Impact of Native American Casinos.* Cambridge, MA: National Bureau of Economic Research.

Feuer, Alan. 2004. "7 Accused of Operating a Lucrative Citywide Betting Ring" *New York Times,* (July 29):A19.

Freud, Sigmund. ([1928]1945). "Dostoyevsky and Parricide." *International Journal of Psycho-Analysis* 26:1–19.

Friedrich, Thomas James. 2000. "Internet Casino Gambling: The Nightmare of Lawmaking, Jurisdiction, Enforcement and the Dangers of Prohibition." *CommLaw Conspectus* 11:369–388.

Fromson, Brett Duval. 2003. *Hitting the Jackpot: The Inside Story of the Richest Indian Tribe in History.* New York: Atlantic Monthly Press.

Gabel, Reuben. 1971. Letter to the Editor. *New York Times,* (March 15):27.

Geis, Gilbert. 2004. "Pathological Gambling and Insanity, Diminished Capacity, Dischargeability, and Downward Sentencing Departures." *Gaming Law Review* 8:347–360.

Gottfried, Jonathan. 2004. "The Federal Framework for Internet Gambling." *Richmond Journal of Law & Technology* 10:26–79.

Granois, Earl I. 2004. *Gambling: Costs and Benefits.* New York: Cambridge University Press.

Harris v. Missouri Gaming Commission. 1994. 869 S.W.2d 58.

Homer. 1974. *Iliad.* Robert Fitzgerald, trans. New York: Doubleday.

Howland, James S. 2004. "Let's Not 'Spit the Bit' in Defense of the 'Law of Horses': The Historical and Legal Development of American Thoroughbred Racing." *Marquette Sports Law Review* 14:473–507.

Lears, Jackson. 2003. *Something for Nothing: Luck in America.* New York: Viking.

Lesieur, Henry R. 1998. "Pathological Gambling Is a Psychiatric Disorder." 37–63 in Robert L. Evans and Mark Hance, eds., *Legalized Gambling: For and Against.* Chicago: Open Court.

Loiseau v. State. 1896. 22 So. 138 (Ala.).

Lorenz, Valerie C., and Duane E. Shuttlesworth. 1983. "The Impact of Pathological Gambling on the Spouse of the Gambler." *Journal of Community Psychology* 11:67–76.

Lusher, Adam. 2004. "Don't Live a Lotto: Live a Little." *Sunday Telegraph,* (London) (July 12):17.

MacKenzie, W. Douglas. 1899. *The Ethics of Gambling,* 4th ed. London: Sunday School Union.

Martin v. United States. 1968. 389 F.2d 895 (5th Cir.).

Mashantucket Pequot tribe v. Connecticut. 1990. 913 F.2d 1024 (2nd Cir.).

McCleary, Richard, Kenneth S. Y. Chew, Vincent Merrill, and Carol Napolitano. 2002. "Does Legalized Gambling Elevate the Risk of Suicide?: An Analysis of U.S. Counties and Metropolitan Areas." *Suicide and Life-Threatening Behaviors* 32:209–221.

Meyer, Gerhard, and Michael A. Stadler. 1999. "Criminal Behavior Associated With Pathological Gambling." *Journal of Gambling Studies* 15:29–43.

Morgan, John. 2000. "Financing Public Goods by Means of Lotteries." *Review of Economic Studies* 67:761–784.

Morgan, John, and Martin Sutton. 2000. "Funding Public Goods With Lotteries: Experimental Evidence." *Review of Economic Studies* 67:785–814.

Nguyen, Tomson H. 2004. "The Business of Illegal Gambling: An Examination of the Gambling Business of Vietnamese Cafés." *Deviant Behavior* 25:451–464.

O'Connor, Christopher T. 2000. "A Return to the Wild West: The Rapid Deregulation of the Riverboat Casino Gambling Industry in Missouri." *Saint Louis University Public Law Review* 19:155–175.

Philbrick, Nathaniel. 2000. *In the Heart of the Sea: The Tragedy of the Whaleship Essex.* Rockland, ME: Wheeler.

Phillips, David P., Ward R. Welty, and Marissa M. Smith. 1997. "Elevated Suicide Levels Associated With Legalized Gambling." *Suicide and Life-Threatening Behavior* 27:373–378.

Rand, Kathryn R. L. 2002. "There are No Pequots on the Plains: Assessing the Success of Indian Gaming." *Chapman Law Review* 5:47–86.

Reno v. ACLU. 1997. 521 U.S. 8.

Richtel, Mark. 2004. "Internet Gambling Feels U.S. Pressure." *New York Times,* (March 8):A1.

Rivlin, Gary. 2004. "The Chrome-Shiny, Lights-Flashing . . . Pulse-Quickening Bandit." *New York Times Magazine* (May 20):42–47, 74, 80–81.

Roberts, Myron. 1971. "Gambling in California: Why You Can Bet on It." *Los Angeles Times,* (July):30–37.

Robertson, William H. P. 1964. *The History of Thoroughbred Racing in America.* Englewood Cliffs, NJ: Prentice-Hall.

Samuelson, Paul A. 1970. *Economics,* 6th ed. New York: McGraw-Hill.

Seminole Tribe of Florida v. Butterworth. 1981. 653 F.2d 314 (54th Cir.), cert. denied 455 U.S. 1020 (1983).

Shaffer, Howard J. 1997. "The Most Important Unresolved Issues in the Addictions: Conceptual Chaos." *Substance and Misuse* 32:1573–1580.

Shaffer, Howard J., Matthew N. Hall, Joni Vander Bilt, and Lisa Vagge. 2003. "Youth and Gambling." 1–24 in Howard J. Shaffer, Matthew N. Hall, Joni Vander Bilt, and Elizabeth George, eds., *Futures at Stake: Youth, Gambling, and Society.* Reno: University of Nevada Press.

Snedeker, Lisa. 2001. "Casino Executive Puts a Face on Gambling." *Associated Press* (January 27).

Starr, Justin W. 2003. "Diminished Capacity: Departure for Compulsive Gambling." *Brigham Young University Law Review* 2003:385–418.

Turner, Wallace. 1965. "Gambler's Money: The New Force in American Life." Boston: Houghton Mifflin.

United States v. Hamilton. 1991. 949 F.2d 190 (6th Cir.).

United States v. Mazurie. 1975. 419 U.S. 544.

United States v. Sadolsky. 2000. 234 F.2d 938 (6th Cir.).

Washington v. Confederated Tribes of the Colville Indian Reservation. 1980. 447 U.S. 134.

Whyte, William F. 1955. *Street-Corner Society: The Social Structure of an Italian Slum,* 2nd ed. Chicago: University of Chicago Press. ✦

Chapter 8

Conclusion

A behavioral science approach to law explores the social antecedents and consequences of law, as reflected in both statutes and court rulings. Such a conception seeks to understand the influences that create law and the legal consequences for society of the use of the criminal sanction. This concern with causes and consequences is not the only approach to an understanding of law (cf. Sarat 2004), but it demonstrates that law and society are inextricably intertwined, and that law is only one part of the equation. It does not operate in a social vacuum. Instead, as some have argued, law is primarily a consequence of social needs and values rather than a shaper of those needs and values (Barnett 1993).

In this final chapter, we will try to identify these social and legal relationships to further explore some of the issues generated in our discussion of criminal justice and moral issues and to draw conclusions about the role and purpose of law, especially under the circumstances of dissension, that is, when there is significant disagreement.

Harm, Risk, and the Law

We began our examination of these behaviors with the observation that the idea of harm is fundamental to an understanding of why certain behaviors are defined as criminal by the law. Criminal law is often regarded as protection against harm, whether that harm is directed against persons or property, although the law is far from foolproof and does not guarantee such protection. If there are differences of opinion about laws, they often revolve around the idea of harm—how much there is, who suffers from it, and the kinds of risks against which we can reasonably expect legal protection.

Life inevitably entails a potential risk of harm. Natural processes invariably produce the risk of bodily damage or deterioration over time. To drive a car is to risk involvement in a vehicular accident. Eating certain foods may pose the risk of diseases such as cancer. But none of us can hide somewhere in a protected corner, hoping to isolate ourselves from harm. Indeed, such behavior could itself be self-destructive and lead to mental illness, suicide, or some self-directed harm. Harm and risk, therefore, are inevitable conditions of human existence.

We are constantly weighing the risks of harm against the benefits of certain behaviors. We all know, for example, that there is a risk in air travel, but the time and convenience that flying affords us is often well worth the risk. Although the consequences of a plane crash are great, the probability is small; so many—though not all—people fly. The essential question in regard to the behaviors we have discussed concerns the level of harm we are willing to tolerate in terms of other things we value, most importantly our freedom to do what we please.

We must also recognize that there are two important qualities of criminal law that temper its effectiveness: the law's ability to express moral condemnation and its ability to solve problems. The essence of criminal law is that it addresses human conduct that is so disapproved by the community that action must be taken, as opposed to civil law, which is concerned with conduct that becomes an issue only when a private citizen mobilizes the forces of law. It is the community's moral outrage that invokes—and ultimately supports—criminal law, not the personal outrage of a citizen. Although not all members of a community may feel or express such outrage, what differentiates criminal from civil law is precisely the fact that the morality violated by the crime is social, or sufficiently widespread that the community as a whole cannot ignore the conduct. In civil law, the wronged person is the only one affected, even though there may be social implications from that person's victimization.

It must also be recognized that merely outlawing problems on the basis of moral concern is not enough. Criminal law is generated and sustained by its ability to solve problems. The law, of course, cannot fruitfully address all problems, and the community must be prudent in selecting for legal attention only those matters that are deemed appropriate. It is this determination that lies at the heart of social disagreements and disappointments over law. In general, large segments of the population expect law to solve many problems for which it may in fact be inappropriate or ill-suited to solve. From the examination of the six substantive areas considered here—abortion, prostitution, homosexuality, gambling, pornography, and drugs—there also seems to be considerable disagreement about whether these are problem areas suitable for a legal solution.

To argue, for instance, that drug use is ill-suited to a legal solution is not the same as arguing that drugs are not a problem. The use of drugs, such as marijuana, heroin, and cocaine, can lead to many problems, from crime to lost productivity to destroyed interpersonal relationships. Drugs, in fact, are related to some of the greatest human tragedies in American society today. The question here is whether the law can be the sole, or at best a principle, means by which these terrible problems can be alleviated. Many observers do not believe the law can perform much of a role in controlling or reducing drug use, but others are firmly convinced that the law not only can but *must* be part of the solution (Bennett et al. 1996). The same could be said about the other behaviors we have considered in this volume.

Can the Law Create Problems?

Even in those areas where there is widespread agreement that the law must operate, we need to recognize that the use of law sometimes makes matters worse. The problems that can be created by law stem from it operating in areas where it does not enjoy a broad consensus regarding its role or limitations. Some observers have referred to these problems as the result of a "crisis of overcriminalization" (Kadish 1967). When the law is used too extensively, when it is applied to areas where the chances of success are slim, and when it does not enjoy popular support, it is apt to fail. Sometimes, the context is the failure of the police to apprehend criminals, the failure of the courts to convict guilty defendants, or the prison system's inability to reform inmates. But legal failure can also arise when the law is used inappropriately as well as when it is not invoked in those circumstances in which it should be.

Few doubt that there are many laws that have outlived their usefulness and should be eliminated from the criminal code. Many states and local jurisdictions have outdated laws that apply to life in an earlier time. It is against the law in Ames, Iowa, for example, to be drunk in public; it is also against the law, for some inexplicable reason, to *pretend* to be drunk in public (*Ames Daily Tribune* June 20, 1996). The historical origin of the law and the legislative intent behind it are obscure, though its obvious ludicrousness has not generated any action to repeal it. Prohibitions against such acts do not command much attention, largely because the behaviors reflected in outdated laws are not considered a problem these days.

Such statutes give the law an untidy veneer, but they are not important to public perceptions of either crime or law. More disturbing are those behaviors about which there is disagreement over their moral nature. For example, in the process of revising the California criminal law, a group of crimes were identified that apparently had justified criminal convictions, such offenses as "failure by a school principal to use required textbooks, failure of a teacher to carry first-aid kits on field trips, gambling on the result of an election, giving private commercial performances by a state-supported band, and allowing waste of an artesian well by the landowner" (Kadish 1967, 157–158). Although an argument can be made that such acts ought to be regulated, the question is whether criminal law is the appropriate vehicle for that control.

More serious examples of the consequences of overcriminalization include the use of unethical or questionable enforcement techniques by the police. Because by definition some crimes do not have complainants, and because the police depend on informers or citizen reports to learn about most crime, enforcing some crimes necessitates more aggressive and police-initiated action. This proactive policing is difficult to carry out within the boundaries of constitutional safeguards that are deemed so important in a free society. As a result, the police are tempted to engage in a variety of unsavory practices. These include using "sting" operations, whereby police officers impersonate criminals, develop and maintain close relationships with criminals who can inform on other offenders, and employ illegal enforcement methods, such as unauthorized wiretaps and searches. In the trial of O. J. Simpson for double murder, for instance, then-Los Angeles detective Mark Fuhrman was heard on tape discussing how he ripped off the healing scabs from the injection sites of narcotic addicts' bodies in order to prove in court that he had nabbed them in the act of using drugs (Toobin 1996, 395). Such methods are either directly illegal or morally questionable, but the police are forced to skirt the moral boundary because of the nature of crimes. Who is going to report such crimes to the police? The prostitute? The prostitute's client? The illegal drug dealer? The illegal drug buyer? Laws governing crimes without alleged victims place the police in a position of tenuous virtue.

Furthermore, the police are often stripped of the self-justifying rationale that the ends justify the means. One might be willing to excuse questionable police tactics against criminal syndicates, from whom the harm to society is both real and recognized; but the use of borderline methods against adults engaging in either a consensual homosexual (e.g., sodomy) or heterosexual (e.g., prostitution) relationship is quite another matter. These latter acts seem to generate victims without being crimes at all.

Because the law can both solve and create problems, it is essential to employ it wisely. Although the law is a necessary form of control for certain acts, in other instances it has been used to curry favor among some at the expense of others. This is especially true in regard to those crimes in which there is no agreement on the moral quality, or wrongfulness, of the act. The crimes examined here illustrate the extent to which a lack of moral consensus interferes with the operation of the law.

We believe that the meaning of these crimes must be seen in the context in which there is no consensus regarding the wrongfulness of such acts nor any consequences from them being against any criminal law. In some instances, it is clear to us that the law does more harm than good; in other cases, the law may be necessary, even if it is ineffective in changing a behavior or act. In either case, the law's role is at best uneven and uncertain in the presence of the public's moral ambiguity.

Political attention to the crimes we discuss has produced some important, far-reaching legal changes. Although the law has constricted in some areas (e.g., prostitution), it has expanded in others (e.g., drugs). Not only are there more drug laws on the books, but the penalties for their violation have increased significantly. In addition, many jurisdictions, including the federal government, have instituted mandatory minimum prison sentences for those convicted of these crimes. As of 1996, the possession of the following amounts of drugs results in a mandatory five-year prison sentence without possibility of parole in the federal criminal justice system: LSD, 1 gram; marijuana, 100 plants or 100 kilos; crack cocaine, 5 grams; powder cocaine, 500 grams; heroin, 100 grams; methamphetamine, 10 grams; and PCP, 10 grams. Ninety percent of federal judges and 75 percent of state judges disapprove of mandatory minimum sentences (Donziger 1996, 27).

The problem is not merely one of equity, although the "one size fits all" approach to drug sentencing does violate the concept of justice to many people. The real problem is that already overcrowded American prisons are housing an increasing number of inmates convicted on drug charges, and that the great majority of these are in prison for drug possession. This problem has been made greater in the past decade.

Not all negative consequences of enforcing laws against the crimes we have considered have only practical dimensions; there are moral questions as well. How does a community balance the needs of consenting adults engaged in sexual relations with the community's need to follow moral guidelines? An act of prostitution may involve willing adults, but what is the quality of the community in which prostitution occurs? Such questions are difficult to answer even in the absence of any legal controversies, and it seems unreasonable to expect the law to adjudicate a response for all concerned. Other institutions, such as religion or the family, may be better venues in which to seek settlement.

What Should We Call Them?

One issue that we have not fully addressed yet involves terminology. Crimes associated with homosexuality, prostitution, pornography, gambling, drugs, and abortion do not have any widespread consensus regarding either the degree to which each poses a problem to the community, if it is even considered a problem, or the most appropriate solution. Because of this lack of consensus, the law has been used by default. A full understanding of these behaviors requires, however, that we know not only why Americans are so optimistic about the law solving what may be nonlegal problems, but also what such crimes have in common. Why is there a lack of consensus about some crimes, but not about others? The first hurdle to overcome is the creation of a conceptual category that highlights the common features of these crimes, one that sets them apart from other crimes.

One of the first systematic statements about such crimes was made by Sanford Kadish (1967), who called our attention to a particularly serious consequence of the strain they create on the criminal justice system. Kadish used the term *the crisis of overcriminalization* to emphasize that there are crimes in which the law is inappropriate and "over-used." His argument identified a number of reasons to limit the use of law, in part because the law cannot prevent some crimes and at times can actually create more problems than it solves. Edwin Schur (1965) anticipated Kadish's concerns when he identified a group of offenses that he considered crimes without victims and that he believed should therefore be decriminalized, a theme that was amplified by Norval Morris and Gordon Hawkins (1970).

The expression *crimes without victims* drew our attention to the fact that, first, crimes are supposed to have victims, and second, there is agreement on who is and who is not a victim of a crime. At times, however, it is difficult in practice to identify a discernible victim. Who exactly is the victim of the behavior of a person drunk in public? Who is hurt except the compulsive gambler himself? Who exactly is the victim of the sexual exchange between a prostitute and his or her client? Who exactly is the victim of a drug addict who injects heroin to satisfy a physical dependency? Who is the victim if an adult views pornography? In many instances, the notion of victimization does not present itself in quite the same way as it does with other crimes, such as robbery, theft, or murder. In each of the latter crimes, identifiable people are deprived of their property or lives against their will in unlawful and often dramatic ways. In crimes without victims, the notion of victimization is more nebulous, either because the only parties involved are willing participants or, in the example of abortion, because there is disagreement on whether the fetus is a person who therefore qualifies as a victim of a crime.

One could claim, as many do, that these crimes do have tangible victims. Sometimes, the victim can be said to be a specific person, such as the robbery victim of a heroin addict who steals to support a drug habit or the victim of a drunk driver. One could argue that the victims of the compulsive gambler are his family who are deprived of money he would otherwise use for them. In other instances, the notion of victimization is more general and amorphous. One could argue that the community and its moral climate, for example, are the victims of prostitution. Although the idea of a moral climate may suggest something immaterial and too abstract to be considered "real," contemplate the following question: How many communities, even so-called "bad" neighborhoods or high-crime areas, actually *encourage* prostitution?

There is no completely satisfactory single term or expression to denote crimes that do not enjoy a widespread consensus regarding their wrongfulness (Junker 1972). Some prefer the expression "complaintless crime," but "complaintless crimes" could include the crime of bribing a public official, an offense not normally considered in this category. Others prefer the expression "public-order crime," and still others refer to these crimes as "moral offenses," a term that begs the question of whose morality and to what extent that morality is shared in a community. The expression *non-consensual crimes* may best typify these crimes, but it is not as catchy as *victimless crime,* a phrase that has generally been adopted in broad legal discussions. Yet another strategy is more conditional. Often, writers trying to convey their sense of neutrality—or perhaps uncertainty—will append words such as "so-called" before their use of the phrase "crimes without victims." Thus Schrage (1994, 83) notes of gambling and prostitution that they are "so to speak, 'victimless crimes.' "

Regardless of the term, the quality these crimes share goes beyond the unwillingness of individuals to regard themselves as victims or complainants, although this quality leads to particular enforcement practices and moral debates. In our view, these crimes reflect behavior about which there is significant disagreement concerning wrongfulness and the appropriateness of legal response. Some people, for example, strongly believe that homosexuality is not only wrong but that it should be punished severely under criminal law. Others feel just as strongly that such behavior is wrong neither in a moral nor a pragmatic sense (because it does not harm others) and thus should not be considered a crime. Likewise, some people firmly believe that using illicit drugs is wrong and should also be punished severely; others completely disagree.

Other acts, such as abortion, provide a different moral picture. Some believe that abortion under all circumstances is morally wrong. Others believe that abortion is morally undesirable but that it should be permissible under certain conditions, such as for a pregnancy resulting from rape or incest. Still others believe that abortion should not be encouraged but that it is an inappropriate matter for legal action, because the affected woman and not the law should determine whether or not there will be an abortion. Clearly, this diversity of opinion reflects fundamental differences in how this conduct is conceptualized.

Prostitution and pornography share the theme of sex for money, but since each involves consenting adults, while they can be morally condemned, many view them as simply amoral. The same could be said about gambling, although there are obvious implications for others, such as the gambler's family.

The different conceptions of crime are not always consistent with one another. A social conception might key on the normative qualities of an act; that is, whether that act should occur or not (Sellin 1938). Normative conceptions obviously go beyond law and include many acts that are not now and never will be part of the concern of a legal system. Laughter is a normative behavior at a comedy show but not at a funeral. The prevention of dental cavities is something that most people believe is necessary, but the requirement to brush one's teeth is unlikely to be incorporated into the legal system. Even conduct that is commonly disapproved of in our society, such as having offensive breath, would obviously be deemed inappropriate for legal attention. As difficult a process as it is, one of the hardest tasks of lawmaking must surely involve the ability to define unpopular behavior as inappropriate for legal response.

The Wolfenden Report

Many of the issues surrounding crimes such as those examined in this volume have been explored in public policy discussions. The Wolfenden Report, discussed earlier, was issued in England almost half a century ago with respect to the question of whether homosexuality should remain illegal. The report generated considerable public response not only in regard to homosexuality but also because the issues that surrounded homosexuality applied to other controversial behaviors, such as prostitution.

The general question that guided the Wolfenden Committee concerned the conditions under which criminal law should be used to control human behavior. In its analysis of the laws against homosexuality, the Wolfenden Report concluded that criminal law should not delve into the private lives of citizens except to preserve public order and to protect individuals from obviously dangerous and injurious action. The Committee believed that the law should also be used to protect people against exploitation and corruption, especially individuals who have some special vulnerability:

> Unless a deliberate attempt is to be made by society, acting through the agency of the law, to equate the sphere of crime with that of sin, there must remain a realm of private morality and immorality which is, in brief and crude terms, not the law's business. To say this is not to encourage private immorality. (1963, 24)

The Wolfenden Report was widely read and discussed, and many disagreed with its recommendations. Even among those who agreed in general with the conclusions, the report generated considerable conflict. Part of the problem was undoubtedly the status of the behavior at the time. Just as it is harder, for example, to expel a student than to reject the same person as an applicant, it is always harder to decriminalize conduct than to make that same conduct subject to law. Homosexuality had been against the law and it was difficult and disconcerting to think of changing that situation.

Lord Patrick Devlin claimed that criminal law, perhaps by definition, is little more than a collection of moral statements; as a result, Devlin argued, it is not surprising that there is a strong moral component to law and in fact little to separate morality and law. The legal philosopher H. L. A. Hart demurred and, following the view of John Stuart Mill, argued the law should not limit individual freedoms in the name of morality. Hart, and the Wolfenden

Committee, argued that the use of law and criminal sanction always requires compelling justification.

Devlin perceived the law not in terms of individual but of political morality: Legal norms are legal equivalents of social norms, statements of what "should" and "should not" occur; as such, they represent moral statements within a political jurisdiction. It is hardly surprising that law should generate such controversy, since people sometimes disagree on what should and should not occur. This is not a problem with the law, merely one of its characteristics. Devlin believed that the burden of proof regarding legal change (e.g., decriminalization) belongs to those who want to alter existing and longstanding legal definitions and practices.

Hart's position is not merely the result of abstract legal or philosophical reasoning. He and others cited a good deal of evidence that when the law is extended into areas where it does not belong, it can make matters worse. The law then becomes not extended, but overextended.

But Devlin was not opposed to the recommendation to decriminalize homosexuality in England. On the contrary, when the Wolfenden Committee began considering possible reforms, its chair asked two judges to provide evidence, one in favor of reform and the other against reform. Lord Devlin was the judge who testified in favor of reforming the laws against homosexuality. Devlin (1965, v) believed that these laws do more harm than good, except in those instances where it "can save youth from being led into it." In all other instances, he reasoned, the law is ineffective, although he thought that more study on the matter would be useful.

Are There Limits to Law?

To question the relevant boundaries of law is also to question the limits of criminal sanction. Criminal sanctions are powerful beyond their measure; they generate not only the direct sanction—fines, community supervision, incarceration—but social sanctions as well, often in the form of stigma and censure. Clearly, these are powerful considerations in a society that takes pride in freedom and openness. Such sanctions should not be used frivolously or without regard to their full consequences.

But if there are to be limits to law, what are they? To ask what behavior should or should not be against the law and therefore subject to criminal sanction is to ask one of the most fundamental questions about law. A number of criteria have been proposed, including individual privacy, limiting law only to those acts that are generally regarded as immoral and for which there are no reasonable alternatives (Packer), to those which cause harm in others (Mill) and those which are potentially enforceable (Schur).

Immorality

In one of the most influential books on the role of criminal law, Herbert Packer (1968, 264) proposed that "the criminal sanction should ordinarily be limited to conduct that is viewed, without significant social dissent, as immoral." Packer recognized that there are disagreements about morality, and that such disagreements can produce significant social conflicts, particularly in a diverse society such as the United States. Or as Packer put it (289), "One man's deviance is another man's pluralism."

Many people regard as immoral that which threatens them either directly (e.g., robbery) or indirectly (e.g., making false claims about a product's safety). It is difficult to conceive of a criminal law that is divorced from moral judgments, as most people's conception of crime includes the notion that it is behavior that should not occur. The reason it should not occur may vary from person to person, but a consensus exists that criminal behavior is that which should not be condoned.

Packer did not advocate making criminal all immoral acts. There are many instances of immorality that are undesirable but not of sufficient seriousness to prohibit by law. Breaking promises, forgetting a friend's birthday, and breaches of etiquette and manners are all immoral in the sense that they should not occur. But they are not by themselves good candidates for criminal law. Rather, other forms of social control are more appropriate for these acts of deviance. Those acts that generate strong, widespread condemnation are more likely to be candidates for criminalization.

No one has yet developed a mechanism to adequately measure morality or the extent of agreement in societies on moral principles. More than 70 percent of Americans find that homosexuality is immoral, but a clear majority also support equal rights for homosexuals and believe that people should not be discriminated against for being gay (Shapiro 1994). Conflicting feelings can and do exist side by side, and perhaps the only reasonable solution is to encourage conversations about morality (Feldblum 1996). Whether such conversations lead to changes in public attitudes and law does not guarantee similar changes with other moral issues.

Privacy

Some observers think that the boundary line for what should and should not be outlawed can be found in the concept of individual privacy (Alderman and Kennedy 1995). But what is and what is not private continues to be debated in the courts without any clear-cut resolution. The word "privacy" does not appear in the Constitution, although many people believe so strongly in it that they consider privacy from state intrusion a fundamental right rather than a privilege. The United States Supreme Court agreed and more than a century ago, Justice Louis Brandeis advocated the right of privacy, labeling it the "right to be let alone."

Individual privacy is more difficult to maintain in an age of computer records, video cameras, and the increasing awareness that the behavior of one person can sometimes affect many others. State and federal laws protect individuals against such invasions of privacy as unreasonable searches and seizures. There are also laws against unwanted intrusions into one's private life by the media; the First Amendment protects the press, which can be a powerful ally in privacy battles.

Although there is agreement that some acts (e.g., whether one should brush one's teeth) should remain beyond the boundary of law, there is no agreement on what criteria can be used to determine where the interests of the individual end and those of the state begin. As pointed out in chapter one, wearing a helmet while riding a motorcycle can be seen either as a risk that affects only the rider or as a matter in which the state has an interest, insofar as it affects others by triggering higher insurance or medical premium rates.

Privacy interests often must be balanced. So although an individual should be able to expect privacy at the workplace, employers have a right to run a business and try to earn a profit. As employers face increasing competition and rising costs, such as those associated with employee benefits (e.g., health care), they come to expect more information about their employees and often obtain it through new technology. Some employers obtain data from psychological and drug testing and collect information about employees' lifestyles away from work. For example, two Phoenix police officers were fired when it was discovered that they had relationships with prostitutes (Alderman and Kennedy 1995, 307–308). The officers claimed that what they did off-hours was of no concern to the police department. But a court ruled that such behavior affected their job performance as well as the internal morale of the police department, and it upheld the firing.

Alternative Controls

Many believe that criminal law should be used sparingly when other alternatives are available; the law can play a unique role only when it stands alone. This view acknowledges that law is but one means of social control and not necessarily the most effective for any given act. Other institutions, such as the family, religion, community, and the military, all have their own systems of rule making and rule enforcement. Breaches of family rules or religious expectations are often met with appropriate sanctions, such as scolding a child or requiring special penance. Most acts that are considered serious are subject to multiple social and legal controls. For example, the deliberate taking of another's life is condemned by law but also by religion and family. What keeps most people from committing murder is not the force of law but the effect of these other controls.

Harm to Others

John Stuart Mill's 1859 essay, *On Liberty,* has provided for almost 150 years an important and durable limiting condition in regard to criminal law. Mill argued that the only legitimate purpose for which state power can be exercised over citizens in a free society, against their will, is to prevent harm to others. Such a criterion recognizes that, whatever their moral quality, most crimes are dangerous. It is the physical, financial, and social costs of crime that criminal law should address. Mill did not believe that harm to the perpetrator was sufficient grounds to criminalize; nor did he think it ever proper to criminalize conduct solely because the mere thought of it offended others (see Richards 1982, 3).

Unfortunately, Mill failed to provide a concrete means by which to assess the extent or degree of harm (Feinberg 1984), although some observers have defended Mill's principle (Sartorius 1972). Harm from some acts can be both more immediate and more dangerous than from others. Similarly, Mill fails to provide a means by which to draw a meaningful distinction between those acts that have some impact and those that have substantial harm. Consider an example: A stranger yelling obscenities in a public place, to some degree will harm the sensibilities of those passing by who hear the obscene language, but that same stranger assaulting passers-by would present a more immediate and dangerous harm from which citizens have some legitimate expectation of protection. Although criminal law could be used to prohibit both acts, assault is of more personal and social importance.

All acts probably have some consequences for others, either as "victims," witnesses, or innocent bystanders. Should criminal law regulate drinking of alcoholic beverages because alcoholics can produce a substantial and negative financial impact on their families? Similarly, a public drunk may bring substantial negative social stigma on his or her family. But how are we to decide whether these consequences are sufficiently serious to use the criminal law to prohibit the manufacture, sale, and consumption of alcoholic beverages?

Are They Enforceable?

Some laws have a greater chance of controlling and preventing crime than others. When crimes are conceived as a risk of life, the law can only reduce the risk of some of those crimes. The law can do little about most drive-by shootings, random robberies, or residential burglaries. Although some gang members, robbers, and burglars will be apprehended and punished, they can return to crime later or others will take their place. In a very practical sense, the law in a democratic society is limited to responding to most crimes only after they have occurred. And although some criminals may be deterred from offending, not all are, and even those who are deterred are not deterred forever. Most drivers will be deterred enough to slow down when they spot a police car in their rear-view mirror, but they may speed up once it is gone.

Many common crimes are related to conditions over which the police have virtually no control. Poverty, systems of social and economic inequality, and subcultures that emphasize immediate gratification are all strong correlates of crime, but the police cannot control or alter those conditions. Changes in crime rates are more strongly influenced by social, historical, and political forces than by adding laws, increasing penalties, or placing more police officers on the streets.

Although laws do not change the circumstances that bring about crime in the first place, it is probably better that we have such laws. Even though the police cannot control the conditions that give rise to most murders—arguments, alcohol, and the availability of firearms—it would certainly be a mistake to decriminalize violent crime, if only because the law conveys a very powerful message about the value of life and the degree of social abhorrence toward illegitimate violence.

What Problems Are Appropriate for Law?

One practical approach to the limits of law asks whether a given act constitutes a problem that the law can solve and, if so, whether the law is effective in dealing with the problem. Problems can be divided into different categories, depending on the best solution to them. Broken arms are a problem to people who experience them, and the solution to this problem is properly sought in medicine rather than law; calculating one's income tax is not a medical but an accounting problem. The objective is to determine the nature of the problem and to apply the proper resource to solve the problem.

Criminal law has been asked, concurrently and at different times, to accomplish dissimilar and at times contradictory objectives: deterrence, rehabilitation, incapacitation, and retribution. There are other traditional objectives and different ways to define them, but these four illustrate the problem for law. Laws can be effective in extracting justice through punishment, but ineffective in changing the behavior of lawbreakers.

A pragmatic approach also requires evidence of the effectiveness of law, and such evidence is often equivocal. How do we know whether and to what extent the law deters potential criminals? How do we know whether and to what extent the law rehabilitates actual criminals? The existence of crime, of course, does not mean that the law is ineffective, except if the standard by which one measures effectiveness is complete prevention, an obviously unachievable standard. By such a standard, all laws might be ineffective because murders, rapes, robberies, and other crimes continue to exist.

Conclusion

There are many acts that are presently criminal about which there is disagreement concerning their moral status. There may be no confusion about their legal status, but there is disagreement on the extent to which people think they are wrong, or whether the law is the proper source of social control. We have discussed six such crime categories to discern the nature of the dissension and the dimensions of the behavior that lead to such disagreements.

To limit the role of law to crimes about which there is a moral consensus does not help us to generate that consensus. The debates surrounding the crimes we have looked at are serious and frequent, primarily because there is much at stake, including the morality of particular groups and the ability of the law to serve as a resource for one group or another. We can only expect that various groups and individuals will continue to explore the use of the law to solve their problems, to further their personal or collective interests, and to attempt to reduce the incidence of undesirable behavior. In this process, we can expect at various times that the law will be used inappropriately and imperfectly. As much as we would like to limit the use of the law to mutually agreeable situations and conditions, this is unlikely to occur. And until it does, we will continue to have what often is intense disagreement.

References

Alderman, Ellen, and Caroline Kennedy. 1995. *The Right to Privacy*. New York: Knopf.

Barnett, Larry D. 1993. *Legal Construct, Social Concept.* New York: Aldine de Gruyter.

Bennett, William J., John J. DiIulio Jr., and John P. Walters. 1996. *Body Count: Moral Poverty and How to Win America's War Against Crime and Drugs.* New York: Simon and Schuster.

Devlin, Patrick L. 1965. *The Enforcement of Morals.* New York: Oxford University Press.

Donziger, Steven R., ed. 1996. *The Real War on Crime: The Report of the National Criminal Justice Commission.* New York: HarperPerennial.

Feinberg, Joel. 1984. *The Moral Limits of the Criminal Law: Harm to Others.* New York: Oxford University Press.

Feldblum, Chai R. 1996. "Sexual Orientation, Morality, and the Law: Devlin Revisited." *University of Pittsburgh Law Review* 57:237–336.

Hart, Herbert L. A. 1963. *Law, Liberty and Morality.* New Haven, CT: Yale University Press.

"It's The Law." 1996. *Ames Daily Tribune,* June 20:1.

Junker, John. 1972. "Criminalization and Criminogensis." *UCLA Law Review* 19:697–714.

Kadish, Sanford. 1967. "The Crisis of Overcriminalization." *The Annals* 374:158–169.

Mill, John Stuart. [1859]1892. *On Liberty.* London: Longmans, Green.

Morris, Norval, and Gordon Hawkins. 1970. *The Honest Politician's Guide to Crime Control.* Chicago: University of Chicago Press.

Packer, Herbert A. 1968. *The Limits of the Criminal Sanction.* Stanford: Stanford University Press.

Richards, David A. J. 1982. *Sex, Drugs, Death, and the Law: An Essay on Human Rights and Overcriminalization.* Totowa, NJ: Rowman and Littlefield.

Sarat, Austin, ed. 2004. *The Social Organization of Law: Introductory Readings.* Los Angeles: Roxbury.

Sartorius, Rolf E. 1972. "The Enforcement of Morality." *Yale Law Journal* 81:891–910.

Schrage, Laurie. 1994. *Moral Dilemmas of Feminism: Prostitution, Adultery, and Abortion.* New York: Routledge.

Schur, Edwin. 1965. *Crimes Without Victims.* Englewood Cliffs, NJ: Prentice-Hall.

Sellin, Thorsten. 1938. *Culture, Conflict and Crime.* New York: Social Science Research Council.

Shapiro, Joseph H. 1994. "Straight Talk About Gays." *U.S. News and World Report,* July 5:47.

Toobin, Jeffrey. 1996. *The Run of His Life: The People v. O. J. Simpson.* New York: Random House.

Wolfenden Report. 1963. *The Wolfenden Report: Report of the Committee on Homosexual Offences and Prostitution.* London: Her Majesty's Stationery Office. ✦

Author Index

A

Aasved, Mikal, 213
Abbott, Sharon A., 180, 181
Abramson, Paul R., 195
Addams, Jane, 41
Adler, Nancy, 163
Akers, Ronald L., 113
Albert, Alexa E., 38, 44–45
Alderman, Ellen, 249, 250
Allred, Gloria, 37–38
Anderson, George R., 227
Angell, Marcia, 15
Appiah, K. Anthony, 133
Aquinas, Thomas (Saint), 30
Aristotle, 16–17
Asma, Stephen T., 144
Augustine (of Hippo), 30, 143
Axthelm, Pete, 224

B

Back, Anthony L., 15
Bader, Eleanor J., 161
Bailey, Eric, 216
Bailey, J. Michael, 112
Baird, M. Katherine, 122
Baird, Robert M., 122, 168
Baird-Windle, Patricia, 161
Banner, Stuart, 10
Barnett, Larry D., 237
Baron, Larry, 195
Barrett, Paul M., 130
Bartlett, Donald L., 217
Baum, Dan, 68, 90
Bawer, Bruce, 122, 126
Bayer, Ronald, 2, 115

Beach, Frank A., 121
Beck, Allen J., 89
Bellis, David, 44
Benedict, Jeff, 216
Bennett, William, 70, 90, 97, 239
Berridge, Kent C., 227–228
Bingham, Micloe, 38
Binkley, Christina, 211
Blakeslee, Sandra, 227
Blaszczynski, Alex, 218
Bloom, Lisa, 37–38
Boeringer, Scot B., 192
Bosanko, Deborah, 161
Boswell, John, 121
Boyer, Edward J., 37
Brandeis, Louis D., 149, 249
Brecher, Edward M., 81
Brenner, Susan W., 13
Bridges, Tyler, 210
Brind, Joel, 163
Brooks, James, 10
Brooks-Gordon, Belinda, 39, 40
Brosius, Jans-Bernd, 193
Browning, Frank, 125, 127–128
Brownmiller, Susan, 3, 147, 196–197, 198–199
Buck, Andrew J., 228
Buckley, William, 36, 101
Burgess, Ann W., 48
Butler, Jerry, 181, 183

C

Campbell, Carole, 44, 45

Canyon, Christi, 182
Carter, David, 126
Carter, Stephen L., 225–226
Cates, Jim A., 30
Cayton, Horace R., 221
Chambers, Carl D., 71, 72
Chappell, Duncan, 11
Chavetz, Henry, 205, 206
Clinard, Marshall B., 71, 188
Clotfelter, Charles T., 220
Cluse-Tolar, Terry, 51
Cohen, Lloyd R., 230
Collins, Peter, 212, 218, 229, 231
Cook, Fred J., 210
Cook, Kimberly, 162
Cook, Philip J., 220
Copeland, Peter, 111, 112
Cox, Michael, 216
Cox, Terrance, 74
Crompton, Louis, 117, 121
Cuomo, Mario, 98
Cushing, John D., 12

D

D'Alessio, Stewart J., 20
Dalla, Rochelle L., 47
Dante (Alighieri), 17
Darian-Smith, Eve, 217
Darroch, Jacqueline, 160
Davidson, Julia O'Connell, 45
Davis, Clyde, 207
Davis, Kingsley, 51–52, 106, 120
Dahl, Gordon B., 166

Subject Index